Tort Wars

Roger N. Messer, J.D.

First Edition

PAGE PUBLISHING
Conneaut Lake, PA

First originally published by Page Publishing 2023

ISBN 979-8-88793-303-0 (pbk)
ISBN 979-8-88960-279-8 (hc)
ISBN 979-8-88793-305-4 (digital)

Printed in the United States of America

This book is dedicated to Professor William McKinley "Micky" Smiley Jr. (1935–2016).

This is also dedicated to Santia Feketa and her friend, Britney Poindexter, killed by an impaired driver, February 6, 2018.

Santia Feketa

Britney Poindexter

Contents

Acknowledgment

I want to thank my paralegal of the last thirty-two years, Julie Krtausch, for her patience and perseverance in the typing and editing of some of my more disjointed thoughts. I also want to thank two other paralegals who worked for me for many years but are no longer with the living, Lana Kendall and Suzanne Larson.

Most of all, I need to thank my wife, Betsey, who's been with me through this entire journey since we were wed in 1971. She has been supportive in everything I've done in my career and in this book.

Three attorneys that I want to specifically thank for their assistance are Douglas Beam of Melbourne, Florida; Fred "Catfish" Abbott of Jacksonville, Florida; and Jack Sobel of Stuart, Florida.

Lastly, I want to thank all the nice people who were clients of mine in this journey.

BOOK 1

Mexican Death Match

Chapter 1

"Hello, Mr. Messer. This is Rafael. My brother Max is dead. Max's son, Jesus, has a broken neck and is in surgery. My other brother, Salvador, has internal injuries, and he is in surgery and may not live. There are people here at Raulerson Hospital in Okeechobee, Florida, wanting me to sign papers. Can you come here right away?"

Just how did I receive this call from a Mexican national regarding injuries to other Mexican national farm workers?

By 1981, I was a partner with Richard Sneed at our office in Fort Pierce, Florida. Richard represented several companies and individuals from the citrus industry, which was the major economic force in St. Lucie County at the time. One of his clients was a company known as Steve Harvesting Inc., which was owned by Bob Shaw. Their business consisted of picking and hauling grapefruit and oranges for various groves throughout South and Central Florida. The company provided labor and a truck for the various jobs.

Bob Shaw was an intelligent and tough businessman. He ran a tight operation and would not hesitate to litigate, if necessary, to protect his business or a profit. He was middle-aged with a young attractive wife. He had several sons from his first marriage. The boys mostly worked in their dad's business.

In February of 1984, Bob Shaw called our office with a problem. Two of his most trusted employees, Maximiano and Rafael Ayala, had been picked up by the INS in some kind of sweep, and they were being held in the federal lockup down in Broward County. At the time of arrest, they did not have their green cards with them. Bob assured us that both of them possessed green cards and that Max had worked for him for twenty-five-plus years. Rafael had worked for almost that long. The brothers each ran separate picking crews for Steve Harvesting, and Bob assured me it would be hard for his company to operate without them. I could speak some Spanish (having taken three years of the subject at FSU) and was also a member of the Bar of US District Court of the Southern District of Florida. I was drafted to go down to represent the Ayala brothers at their first appearance hearing and, hopefully, spring them and bring them back to Fort Pierce and their job.

The following morning, I got up really early and drove the two hours down to the federal courthouse in Fort Lauderdale. There were lots of cases ahead of us. The Ayala cases were reached at 11:00 a.m. Max and Rafael were brought forward by the bailiff. They both appeared to be in their forties, with Max looking like the older brother he was. They were the tallest Mexicans I had ever seen, both well over six feet tall. Both were tanned, with big barrel chests, muscular features, and wavy black hair. They had attractive features with high cheekbones, which were similar to pictures I had seen of Olmec Indians. I shook both their hands and then turned to the federal magistrate. I showed her copies of their valid green cards. The magistrate released Maximiano Ayala and Rafael Ayala to my custody without bond and indicated that she was going to dismiss the cases in the near future, but she could not do it at that time.

We started back toward Fort Pierce and stopped in West Palm Beach for some lunch. On the way, we had a very nice conversation, they in their broken English and I in my very rusty and poor Spanish. I told them I didn't think we would have much trouble clearing up their federal situation. I asked them to call me if there were any problems. After lunch, I drove the two of them to the offices of Steve

Harvesting in Fort Pierce, Florida, and I gave each of them my card with a statement if they needed anything to give me a call.

Two weeks later, on the first Friday in March, I had gotten home late after a long day in the office. By about 9:00 p.m., I had taken off my suit and donned some cutoff jeans and a T-shirt and had just popped the top on a cold beer. My home phone rang, and on the other end was a crying Mexican voice.

"Hello, Mr. Messer? This is Rafael. Max is dead. Max's son, Jesus, has a broken neck and is in surgery. My other brother, Salvador, has internal injuries, and he is in surgery and may not live. There are people here at the Raulerson Hospital in Okeechobee, Florida, wanting me to sign some papers. Can you come here right away?" I said I'd be there in forty-five minutes to an hour and told him to not sign anything.

I quickly got dressed, told Betsey the reason I was leaving, and headed out the door. About forty-five minutes later, I arrived at Raulerson Hospital in Okeechobee City. The emergency room parking lot was full. The hallways were crowded with concerned Mexican nationals. I met Rafael in the emergency waiting room, where he looked distraught and exhausted.

Someone from the hospital showed us to a small room where we could have some privacy. Rafael explained to me that Max had been driving a twelve-passenger van down US Highway 441 from a picking job near Yeehaw Junction, Florida, toward their trailer park housing in Okeechobee. There was a dirt road, known as Dark Hammock Road, that intersected with 441 in Okeechobee County. A heavy-duty pickup truck owned by Larson's Dairy was towing a large trailer loaded down with huge round bales of hay. It had run the stop sign at the intersection at a high speed. It had struck the driver side door of the van. Only the driver, Max, was killed. The ten passengers in the van, including Max's son, Jesus, and his brother, Salvador, were all injured, with the most seriously injured being Jesus and Salvador.

When I had arrived at the hospital, Jesus Ayala was still in surgery with cervical fractures, and Salvador was in surgery with a lacerated kidney. Rafael asked me if I handled Max's kind of case and if I could also handle the cases for Jesus and Salvador.

Before I could answer him, the door sprang open, and in walked a Mexican woman and her Caucasian husband. There had been no knock. She said in Spanish, "Rafael, we were so sorry to hear about Max. You should not be talking with this Gringo lawyer. He is here to steal your money. There is only one attorney in Florida authorized by the Mexican consulate to handle these cases. His name is Bulldog O'Reilly [not his real name], and we represent him."

I replied in Spanish for Rafael. I asked her what Bulldog's address and phone number was. I also asked for his Florida Bar number. I told her that what she and Mr. O'Reilly were doing was illegal and asked her for her name and the name of her husband. The two of them blanched and bolted for the door.

Rafael told me the woman and her husband were "leeches" who ran a small local store in the trailer park and made payday loans to workers and charged them high interest. They also sold groceries at three times the prices at Walmart. He said, "None of our people will go with them." He explained that all the workers from Mr. Shaw's company were legal, and the leeches held no sway over them.

True to his word, none of the ten injured workers signed up with Mr. O'Reilly.

Chapter 2

I told Rafael that I would immediately take steps to preserve evidence and would worry about signing contracts and such until a later time. I knew Rafael did not have the ability to legally bind Max's estate or his relatives to a contingency fee contract.

From the hospital pay phone, I called my part-time investigator, Tony Valicenti, and asked him to be at the accident scene first thing in the morning to take some pictures and see what he could find out. Tony was retired on disability from the NYPD and had been a detective who, at one time, had been Frank Serpico's partner. (In 1973, Al Pacino starred in the acclaimed movie *Serpico*, which portrayed the life of this famous New York cop.) But I digress. Tony had a bullet wound scar on his side to prove some of the stuff he had been through at the NYPD. Tony Valicenti worked out religiously and was in great shape. He had an attractive face with a Roman nose. He had wavy black hair with a few gray streaks peeking through. Tony was always quick with a laugh. He had a way of getting people to open up to him. He was tough, thorough, and trustworthy, and I knew he'd be there.

I stayed at the hospital until late that night (actually early the next morning) when Jesus and Salvador came out of surgery, alive. I told Rafael I would be back to talk to both of them on Monday and asked Rafael to be there. He said he would.

On the drive back to Fort Pierce in the wee hours of the morning, I was haunted by Rafael's short phone call to me that said, "Max is dead." It all seemed unreal.

I went to bed about 3:00 a.m. and dreamed about the case. Around 9:00 a.m., I was awakened by the telephone. Tony Valicenti was calling me to tell me he had been to the scene and found us a great witness. There was a Florida Power and Light lineman who was working at the location Friday afternoon and was back Saturday morning. He told Tony that he had a bird's-eye view of the crash, and it had happened pretty much as Rafael had told me. Tony said there was thick vegetation which blocked the view from Dark Hammock Road to traffic coming from the north on US 441 and likewise blocked the view of traffic on Dark Hammock Road from approaching traffic. Tony indicated he'd taken some pictures and asked if I wanted some aerial photographs taken.

He said, "If so, you should do it today or tomorrow because there's major road construction going on at the intersection that has stopped for the weekend. Everything's going to change come Monday morning."

I looked up Juan Brown's number in the phone book. I had used his services several times since the *Williams v. Gator Freightways* case in 1978 and also saw him regularly downtown. Fort Pierce was a pretty small town then. I called Juan as I was pouring my first cup of coffee. He said he could get the aerial photographs done, but it would be on tomorrow (Sunday). I said that would be great.

First thing Monday morning, my secretary, Suzanne, and I drafted two contingency fee contracts, one each for Jesus and Salvador Ayala. I reached Rafael by phone and arranged a conference call with Max's widow, Bertha Pulido de Ayala. Mrs. Ayala resided in Juiquilpan (pronounced *He-keel-paan*), Michaocan Province, Mexico, with her and Max's six minor children and Max's two parents who were both in their eighties. She had no telephone and had to arrange, in advance, to use a phone at a local market. Rafael had spoken to her the day of the tragedy and mentioned that I could probably help.

My law partner, Richard Sneed, who did lots of probate work, began preparing the necessary paperwork to have Bertha appointed as personal representative (executrix) of Max's estate so we could legally file suit in her name. We were also preparing the proposed contingency fee contract for Mrs. Ayala and the estate and were getting it translated into Spanish. Richard was also going to talk to his client, Bob Shaw, about the situation.

Before noon, we received a call from Juan Brown, who told us he got what he thought were great aerial photographs, but he wouldn't be sure until he developed them. I asked him to have the very best one blown up as big as he dared.

After lunch, I drove over to Raulerson Hospital and met with Rafael. He was trying to arrange to have Max's body shipped home to Juiquilpan for a Christian burial. Workers' compensation would not provide funds to ship bodies of deceased foreign worker's home. Also, the medical examiner wouldn't release the body until after an autopsy.

Rafael and I walked into Jesus's hospital room, and thankfully, even though it was a two-patient room, Jesus was the only one there. Jesus was tall, like his father, but was much thinner. Even though he was tied down in a hospital bed, you could tell he was wiry and muscular with almost no fat. Jesus was in a medical device known as a halo. Metal bolts were screwed into his skull (only bone-deep), and to those bolts were attached stout wires going up to the round metal halo around the head. The halo also had a strong wire frame going down to his shoulders to keep the weight of his head from resting on the spine and ruining the surgical repair. The wounds on his neck were covered with a hard Philadelphia collar, which also supplied support.

In addition, Jesus's leg was broken. It had been set and now was suspended above the bed in a sling. Jesus had adjusted the bed almost to a sitting position. I took pictures.

We asked how he was doing, and Jesus replied that the doctors had told him they thought the operation was a success, but only time would tell. A positive sign was that he could use his hands and still could wiggle his toes. He had a surprisingly good outlook on life despite having just learned of his father's death. Jesus was a nineteen-year-old and an American citizen, having been born in California. He said he would walk out of this hospital and wanted to return to Juiquilpan to help his mother and family. Jesus Ayala was now the man of his family.

Rafael had told Jesus before I got there that I was attempting to help them and hold the owners of the hay truck responsible for the horrible damage they had done. Jesus spoke fluent English, so I gave him a short explanation of just what work I did. Jesus said he understood and trusted me and signed the contract.

We next visited Salvador. He was shorter than his two brothers but had the same facial features as Max and Rafael. He was in obvious distress. Salvador had lost a kidney because of the collision and suffered other internal injuries as well. His surgery had been touch and go, but he had survived. The results obtained by the medical staff at Raulerson were really amazing, considering it was a small country hospital and not a trauma center. Salvador was suffering physically from his injuries and suffering emotionally over the death of his brother. He wanted to do something about it. I explained how our civil justice system worked, and he agreed to allow us to help him. Salvador spoke broken English, so Rafael (who spoke it better) translated some. Salvador signed my contract as well.

Chapter 3

Bob Shaw paid to have Max's body flown home to Juiquilpan. He also accompanied Rafael with the body. Rafael carried with him a briefcase containing our contingency fee contract to be signed by Bertha, as well as court documents for her to sign relating to setting up the estate. He and Bob promised to bring them back signed and notarized. Jesus and Salvador were too injured to travel home for the funeral.

On Friday of that week, I was contacted by Jose Ortega (not his real name) and asked if I would represent him as well. He was Max's best friend and had suffered a fractured orbital bone around an eye. He had other lesser injuries as well. Jose had only been in the hospital one night. He had been to visit Jesus and Salvador in the hospital, and they told him about me. Ortega had a friend drive him to our Fort Pierce offices, told us his story, and signed our contract. Jose needed follow-up surgery on his eye to clear up double vision caused by the fracture. He would eventually make a very good recovery.

Also on Friday, Juan Brown came over with the aerial photos, and they were truly outstanding. The one he had chosen to blow up showed a heavy-duty Larson's Dairy pickup truck hauling a large trailer with huge round hay bales coming down Dark Hammock

Road toward US 441. The truck and trailer were kicking up dust, as if they were moving fast. The photo also showed a car coming south on 441 approaching the intersection. The picture told almost the whole story.

Later that afternoon, I received a telephone call from Willie Gary, a noted Black personal injury attorney with offices in Stuart, Florida, and Okeechobee, Florida. Willie was known as an aggressive litigator. Mr. Gary flaunted his success and had appeared once on *Lifestyles of the Rich and Famous with Robin Leach*. He advertised heavily and was proud to have grown up in poverty over in Indiantown, a small town on the big lake just seventeen miles from Okeechobee City.

Willie asked me, "Roger, how did you get those cases from the Mexican labor van crash? You are not Latino or even Black."

I said, "Come on, Willie, cut me some slack. I only signed four cases, while I heard you got the other seven."

He said, "Yeah, but you took the cream and butter from the top of the churn and left me with the buttermilk." Willie had a way with words. He asked me if I had any good photographs of the scene that he could use, and I said I did.

By then, I had learned that Larson's Dairy was the largest dairy in Okeechobee County, a county known for its dairies. Larson's had thousands of acres, thousands of milk cows, lots of milking barns and employees and were sure to be well insured.

Chapter 4

Bob Shaw called us when he got back to Fort Pierce from Max's funeral. He had our signed contracts and other documents with him. Bob said that Max had been one of the most respected men in Juiquilpan. The Catholic Church there was full to overflowing at the funeral, and Bob sat with Bertha and Max's parents on the front pew, which was reserved for the family. He walked with them at the head of the procession to the cemetery. Bob had tears in his eyes as he told us this. Bob Shaw was a tough negotiator and successful businessman, but he had a heart when it came to Max Ayala and his family.

We filed suit as soon as the probate judge approved Bertha Pulido de Ayala as personal representative of the estate and issued her letters of administration. We also opened negotiations on the other three cases we were handling. Filing suit was delayed on those cases because none of the clients had reached their maximum medical improvement. They were all still treating medically and trying to get better. The insurance adjuster indicated a willingness to settle them amicably as soon as the total damage was known.

The discovery phase of the case proceeded much more quickly than expected. The Larson's Dairy truck driver had an excellent driving record. We learned that he claimed the brakes on the truck had failed. He was travelling faster than he should have been on Dark Hammock Road prior to the failure, and the trailer was overloaded. We discovered that not long before the crash, the subject truck had been in Larson's Dairy's garage for a brake problem, which apparently had not been fixed.

We disclosed to the defense attorneys the work history and earnings history of Maximiano Ayala, which we had obtained from Steve Harvesting. Max had worked for the same employer for twenty-five years. He supervised a work crew of from anywhere from ten to twenty workers. He was well compensated for his work. The defense team learned that Max had a green card and worked in the United States nine months a year. He lived at home in Juiquilpan the other three months. He supported his wife, Bertha, and their six minor children as well as his two elderly parents. Bertha also had a green card, but had been pretty much a stay-at-home mom down in Mexico since their son Jesus was born. When we showed the attorney for Larson's Dairy the aerial photograph, he indicated that the insurance company wanted to settle.

The negotiations took weeks and consisted of talks between the adjusters and Richard Sneed and myself. We would then telephone and relay the status of the offers to Bertha in Mexico through the use of an interpreter on her end. We always sought and obtained her approval for any counteroffer. The final numbers came out to be approximately $1.3 million, but it was a convoluted settlement. There was a large amount for the widow, Bertha; small amounts for Max's two elderly parents, who were dependent upon him for support; and separate substantial settlements for each of the kids.

Florida law requires court approval of all large settlements for minors. Judge Rupert Smith insisted that the awards for the children be a structured settlement, with the money invested in the United States and guaranteed by an A+ rated insurance company. Without Judge Smith's approval of the settlements, we had no deal.

Ultimately, we had three separate proposals, all costing the same amount. The cash for Max's elderly parents remained the same in all of them. The children's structured settlement had a couple of variations, with some providing lump sums for college and regular quarterly income thereafter.

Bertha's settlement was more troubling. She could opt for one cash payment, an idea Richard and I hated. She could opt for monthly income for life. Or she could get larger quarterly payments for life. It was too complicated to explain on the telephone, particularly through an interpreter.

The problem with a cash payment was that because it was more than $10,000 (a lot more), it would have to be exchanged into Mexican pesos before she received any money. In 1984, the Mexican economy was in shambles. The peso had been devalued. There was extremely high inflation. Many Mexican banks had failed. We feared that if she received all that cash in a lump sum, it would be wiped out in short order. Bertha didn't seem to understand this over the phone either.

It was decided to translate all three forms of the settlement agreement. Richard and I were to fly down to Michoacan Province and meet with the Ayala family to figure out the final form of the settlement.

Chapter 5

Mexico

In late September 1984, Richard and I boarded an Aero Mexico flight in Miami nonstop to Mexico City. Each of us carried a large briefcase, each packed with several copies of the three separate proposals in English and Spanish. It was anticipated we would be down in Mexico for five days. We left on a Wednesday and would fly back late Sunday. Mexico City is the largest city in North America with a population of over twenty-five million. As we were descending the Mexico City Airport to land, we could barely make out the city features because of the smog.

We had a long layover in Mexico City, so I strolled down to the National Bank on the airport concourse to exchange some dollars for pesos so I would be able to shop a little while we were there. I needed to bring back souvenirs for Betsey, as well as my two children.

At the front door of the bank, standing guard, were two uniformed Mexican soldiers with assault rifles held against their chests. It seemed weird to walk past them to the teller window. I learned the exchange rate was on that day, 261 pesos to the dollar, and picked up a large wad of paper money for $200. When we passed by the same bank five days later on our way back home, the exchange rate was 268 pesos to the dollar. A high inflation rate indeed.

After the layover, we boarded another flight to Guadalajara. At the Guadalajara airport, we rented a small car (all they had) and drove to the local Sheraton Hotel, where we spent the night. Guadalajara is Mexico's second-largest city, but it was quite different from the capital. The city itself was very beautiful, but there was something unsettling about the place. On the way to the hotel, every time we stopped for a traffic light, we were mobbed by a throng of hungry-looking beggar children. They all looked to be between six and ten years old and were in rags. We realized we were in the third world.

The Sheraton was just like any Sheraton in the US. It had hot and cold running water. We were told not to drink any of it. Fresh cold bottled water to drink was available in each room. There were telephones in the rooms, and I used mine to call Betsey and the kids back home. It was the last phone call home I was able to make until we were in the airport concourse on the way back home on Sunday afternoon. In addition, the hotel had a nice American-style restaurant. We would miss those amenities more than we could know.

We had arranged for Rafael and two of his male cousins to meet us at the Sheraton the next morning. It was late summer, and the Florida citrus picking season would start in about a month, so Rafael was spending his annual vacation at home in Mexico. The Ayala group arrived in a large Ford pickup truck which used to be white but had never seen a car wash. Rafael told us they had a shotgun under the seat "if there was trouble on the way." Rafael rode with us, and the two cousins followed close behind.

On the way out of town, we did pass a few slums, but for the most part, we were impressed with much of Guadalajara. It was green with many beautiful parks. Many of the buildings were stately and had an interesting mix of the new and the old. It was an interesting and vibrant place despite its flaws. Within thirty miles of the city or so, there were well-manicured gated communities which looked similar to those found in South Florida. Rafael explained that those were retirement communities populated, almost exclusively, by American senior citizens. It seems they had discovered that their retirement income would stretch a long way in the Mexican economy. Rafael explained that each enclave had its own security force, and entry into the walled and gated towns was limited to owners, their guests, and servants.

As we got farther from the city, the land grew arid, and settlement became scarce. In the distance, we caught sight of shimmering Lake Chalapa, a very large, miles-long, and elongated lake in the edge of the desert. Lake Chalapa was formed from mountain water runoff. The nearby mountains loomed above the horizon. We had been on the road over two hours and needed a pit stop for the usual reasons. Richard said he had forgotten to make an important phone call from the hotel and asked that I stop at the PEMEX gas station we saw up ahead. We stopped and filled up with gas and asked to use the phone. There was none. The attendant said the closest phone was in Zapotitan, a city on Lake Chalapa, just five miles up ahead and just off the main highway.

We took the detour and found ourselves in a dusty adobe city which could have come out of a Clint Eastwood spaghetti western. I stopped a man who was walking a donkey and asked where I could find the telephone. He pointed toward a storefront which had hitching posts on the street in front. Next to the door, sitting on a small barrel, was a young boy of about twelve years. The door to the store had a padlock on it. I inquired, in Spanish, as to where the proprietor was, and the kid said he would go get him.

In five minutes, he reappeared with a portly old man with the key. The door swung open, and we went inside where a ceiling fan was whirring above. Richard was able to make a long-distance call to the US Consulate in Guadalajara for 10 cents, American. I bought an ice-cold Pepsi, and it was so cheap (less than a US nickel when paid for in pesos), I bought a round for the house. I also gave the young chap an American quarter, and he was delighted.

We asked Rafael if we could find some lunch in his town, and he told us there was a much better place just up the highway. In about thirty minutes, we were pulling into a roadside establishment where they were cooking and eating outside. There was a roof, but the breeze blew through the place.

The smell from the grill was enticing. Rafael told us to eat what they ate, and we wouldn't get sick. We all ordered a cold Dos Equis to quench our thirst. To eat, we ordered carnitas (in English, "little meats") and watched as they grilled the pork and vegetables in front of us. We placed the spicy meat and cooked vegetables in a corn tortilla and feasted. We were warned to never eat fresh washed vegetables as they would make you very sick from the droplets of water. This was the best meal we had in Mexico.

Shortly after we got on the main road, we began to enter the foothills of the mountains. The land got greener, and the air smelled fresh. The road began to wind at weird angles as we got to the higher altitudes. We began to notice wrecked automobiles along the side of the road at almost every hairpin turn. Rafael explained that these cars had been left where they wrecked because no one could pay to move them. He said that sometimes, the locals would pick the carcasses of these cars for free auto parts.

Chapter 6

Juiquilpan sat in a large mountain valley with nearby forests of the largest trees we had seen in Mexico. It also had lush groves of mangoes, avocadoes, limes, and other tropical fruit which were cultivated in the area. There was a fresh smell about the place.

The little city of about forty thousand (about the size of Fort Pierce, Florida, at the time) was quite beautiful. We checked into the only hotel in town. It was so old it must have catered to Cortez when he passed through here. The rooms were large and clean but sparsely furnished. The bathroom was covered in tile and was separated from the bedroom by a six-inch-high ledge to keep the water in. There was a drain in the middle of the bathroom floor and, out of the ceiling over the drain, was the "shower." This consisted of a galvanized pipe with no showerhead. It only had ice-cold water. The toilet and sink sat in opposite corners of the bath.

After the five-hour drive, we had arrived during the afternoon siesta and would not take care of any business until later. There were no televisions in the rooms, so we went down to the lobby to see what was on. They had a small black-and-white Philco which was tuned to the Olympic games, which were ongoing at that time. The featured event on the set was "La Cantidad," the fast-walking race where, if you break into a run, you lose. The lobby was packed with screaming fans. The leader of the race was a Mexican, and he went on to win the gold medal. He barely beat another race walker, also a Mexican, who won the silver. The crowd went wild. For the three days we were there, all they had on the hotel lobby television were replays of La Cantidad.

Around 6:00 p.m., Rafael came over to guide us to la casa Ayala, Max and Bertha's home. As we drove down the cobblestone streets, I noticed that the street had a metallic glow to it and asked Rafael what caused that. He said that when we stopped, I could look down and see old Mexican coins littering all the streets in Juiquilpan. He explained that when the peso was last devalued, the Michoacanos were so disgusted, they took all their coins and threw them in the street. After all, a centavo was then worth only one one-hundredth of a peso, which was worth less than half a penny US.

The Ayala home was one of the nicest in town. It was painted stucco and was quite large, with a spacious courtyard containing a garden. We met Bertha at the door, and she escorted us to the garden. She was almost as tall as her husband and not dainty at all. She had high cheekbones and the Olmec Indian features of the Ayala men. She was dressed in black mourning clothes as befitted her station. We were invited to stay for dinner, along with Rafael. From an open courtyard window, we could hear a gentle clap, clap, clap sound. I went over and looked, and outside, two Mexican women were making the corn tortillas which were to be part of our meal. Bertha did not want to talk business this evening. She explained that she had reserved a conference room at the home of her uncle (the richest man in town). We were to begin at 9:30 a.m. tomorrow. She wanted her uncle to attend, along with two abogados (Mexican lawyers) who were cousins from the big city. Max's father and two of the older children would also attend. Rafael was told he could come if he wanted to. I got the feeling that Bertha did not totally trust Richard and me. She also did not seem that close to Rafael. It was obvious that she wanted to be sure she was doing the right thing for herself and her family.

At dinner that evening, we met the children. They were all clean, neat, and well-behaved. The children barely spoke. Bertha was obviously in charge of discipline in the household. The food was similar to what we had for lunch, except spicy chicken had been substituted for the pork, and cold Squirt grapefruit sodas had replaced the beer. No one drank anything with ice in it. The bottles were taken out of an ice bucket.

Rafael drove us back to the hotel and left us for the evening. There was no air-conditioning in the hotel. Because it was late summer and we were at altitude, it was nice and cool, so we left the windows open to the breeze. Sleep was welcomed, as I anticipated the next day's work.

At 6:00 a.m. sharp, I fell out of the bed onto the floor as I was stunned by the sound of a cannon booming. Surprised, I ran to the window, and across the city square, I saw four men dressed in bright military uniforms who had just fired a large cannon. Every morning we were there, except Sunday, the scene was repeated. That was not the only part of "quaint" that I dd not enjoy on the trip. I went into the bath and tried to shave and shower. Of course, there was nothing but ice-cold water coming out of the pipes in the shower. Shaving was also an unpleasant adventure.

Richard and I agreed to meet downstairs for breakfast at 7:30 a.m. Since I was already awake and showered, I went down early to get a newspaper. The only paper on sale at the desk was the newspaper published in Merida, the Michoacan provincial capital. The headlines took up the entire front page and yelled, "El Oro y la Plata" ("the gold and the silver"). It was the lead story of the day about two sons of Mexico winning Olympic gold and silver in La Cantidad. On the Philco, they were interviewing the two winners. There was no discussion of the other events or the medal count which we had been following in the States. This was not only the top sports story of the day; it was the top story, period. Something like the Super Bowl. After the interview, the entire race was replayed once again for everyone who might have missed it.

Chapter 7

After a breakfast of chorizo and what passed for eggs, Rafael picked us up at the hotel and drove us to the uncle's hacienda. It was almost palatial. The home was near avocado and lemon tree groves owned by the uncle and had beautiful gardens. Bertha's uncle was apparently the father of one of the abogados.

Introductions were made all around, and even though it was not his home, the place at the head of the conference table was reserved for Max's eighty-five-year-old father, who wore a small black hat and a string bolo tie. He was tall, though time had bent him over. The old man had clear eyes and seemed to understand everything going on around him.

Richard and I had arranged for a professional interpreter to be there to help us communicate. She was a pleasant enough young lady. However, when we started, I asked her to repeat everything I said exactly as I said it. She said she would. However, it soon became obvious that she was lost. My Spanish was much better than her English, and my Spanish was pretty bad. We paid her for a day and let her go.

I asked if any of the family was fluent in English, and Bertha smiled with pride and said, "Si, Mario can do it." Mario was an attractive fourteen-year-old boy who was already in the room. He was only too happy to show off his skill and be helpful.

I explained something about the Florida tort system and the wrongful death law. We explained that all settlements for the children's money had to be approved by the court. We then started the laborious task of going through each of the structured settlement documents, word for word.

Mrs. Ayala understood that the judge would only approve a settlement for the children in the form of a structure. The money would be used to purchase guaranteed annuities earning a return of about 10 percent per annum over the life of each child. Bertha was pleased with those portions of the children's structures which set out specific amounts, paid over a four-year period, to pay for a college education for each of the children. She said her kids were good students, and it was her dream for them to get an education and make something of themselves. Because the six children were of different ages, the payouts over their lifetimes were different, even though the initial cost of each of them was the same. It was a drawn-out affair. We read every page in Spanish (and showed the English translation). It became obvious that the college option was the only one Bertha would approve.

Before we could break out the pens and sign that portion of the documents, Max's father, the patrone of the family, announced in Spanish, "That's enough for now. We need a break. Mario, please bring us some cold drinks."

The old man turned around and took a large bottle of Jose Cuervo off the shelf behind him. The women fetched some glasses for everyone. He asked if Richard and I would be offended if he put mixers in our drinks, and we said, "Not at all. Mil gracias."

They poured the tumblers almost full of tequila for each of the Mexican men present. Richard's and my glass were about half full of tequila, and Bertha's had only a splash of tequila. Then the cold bottles of Squirt were opened, and it was used to fill Bertha's glass as well as Richard's and mine. The children present got straight soda pop. Everyone followed the example of the patrone and drank their libation with one quaff.

The drink gave me a warm sensation, but my head still seemed clear. We proceeded to sign and have notarized (by one of the abogados present) all the documents regarding the children. We then explained the very modest cash settlements for Max's father and mother, and they were also executed in short order. We then broke for the afternoon siesta. I did not realize the effects of the alcohol until then when I tried to stand and had rubber in my legs. I marveled at the ability of the men of the family to drink twice as much and still maintain their dignity. I, for one, needed a nap.

Later that afternoon, we reconvened for about a two-hour session. We had to explain all three settlement options for Bertha, who would get the lion's share of the settlement. This proved quite difficult.

First, we discussed the cash option. We explained that while we knew Bertha was an intelligent and frugal person, the rampant inflation in the Mexican economy and the possibility of further devaluations of the peso would probably result in a wasting away of any funds she received. We explained that the inflation rate in the United States, while not inconsequential, was tiny when compared with that of Mexico. We urged that if she chose the cash option, she come to the United States and invest it in a safe United States bank money market or brokerage house. We explained that returns at that time were running about 10 percent per annum.

The abogados (Bertha's cousins) spoke up and pointed out that the safest and largest banks in Mexico at that time were paying well over 25 percent on deposits. They noted that twenty-five was two and a half times greater than ten. We argued that while that was true, the inflation rate in Mexico was much more than two and a half times that of the United States at that time.

Bertha looked troubled, and it was late in the day. We asked her to make no quick decision on this matter and that we would discuss it again in the morning.

We broke up the meeting, and Richard and I went with Rafael to a Mexican pizza joint that he recommended for dinner. Pizza Hut has nothing to fear from that institution. We choked the food down with a cold Corona and went back to the hotel, where neither of us slept well. The next morning was a Saturday, and as expected, the men in uniform marched out on the square at 6:00 a.m. and fired off the cannon with one large *boom*! I anticipated it this time and had awakened early and was looking out the window at the ceremony. By now, I really missed the comforts of home. American newspapers, American food, color television with lots of choices, and nice soft toilet paper are all things you take for granted until you don't have them.

We reconvened our conference with Bertha and the rest of the family at 9:00 a.m. and worked all day, except for the mandatory tea break, which was followed by a short siesta. We carefully went over every structured settlement option and tried to present each of them in the best light possible. We went back over the option of taking the cash settlement and investing it in the United States and discussed the safe option of treasury bills, which were at a lower interest rate but were absolutely secure.

We failed in our task. Much to our chagrin, Bertha had listened to her cousins, the lawyers from Mexico City, after we left the evening before. She was unmovable on the issue and insisted she sign for the cash option to be wired, in pesos, to the largest bank in Mexico, where it would be deposited. We implored her to reconsider, but she refused. Ultimately, a settlement is entirely your client's decision. Attorneys have a duty to try to convince their clients to make the right decisions, but theirs is the final say. Bertha effusively thanked us for our hard work on behalf of Max's family and said she and they would always remember us. She said she had to do what she believed best for her.

We cajoled and argued late into the day, but as we had to do, we allowed her to sign the documents. She also signed our settlement agreement with her outlining our fees and all costs in the case. We returned to our hotel in a downcast mood.

The next morning, we were awakened not by cannon fire but by church bells tolling loudly beginning at 7:00 a.m. By 8:00 a.m., the street and the city square outside our hotel was filled with families with children all in their Sunday dress clothes heading to church.

Richard and I both remarked at the beauty and friendliness of all the natives of Juiquilpan we had encountered.

After breakfast, we drove out of town and made the winding trip out of the mountains and past the crashed cars beside the road. We arrived at the Guadalajara Airport in the afternoon, without incident. After a stop in Mexico City, we proceeded to Miami, where we arrived on time well after dark. A two-and-a-half-hour drive on Florida's turnpike got us home to our families around midnight.

The next morning, I was back at the office, putting the package of settlement documents together to send to opposing counsel and Larson's Dairy's insurance company. The case would be wound up, and we would be paid within a couple of weeks.

The Second Ayala Case

Chapter 8

My first morning back in my office, I received a letter from Florida Farm Bureau Insurance Company, the workers' compensation carrier for Steve's Harvesting. Steve's Harvesting had been the nominal employer of Max Ayala. The letter stated that Florida Farm Bureau had learned that we represented Bertha Pulido de Ayala and the Ayala estate. It also enclosed a check for $1,000, along with a statement that this was the entire workers' comp death benefit to which Max's survivors were entitled. While I did not routinely handle workers comp cases, I thought the letter and check were in error. I knew the death benefit was supposed to be $100,000.

I pulled Florida Statutes Annotated, chapter 440, from our library shelf and looked up the Death Benefit Section. I was shocked. The statute indicated that if a worker was a citizen of the United States or Canada and they were killed on the job, their family's death benefit would be $100,000. But if they were citizens of anywhere else, the death benefit could not exceed $1,000. I thought, *Why the difference between Canadian and Mexican citizens? Could it be because one of the groups is White and speaks mostly English or French while the other is mostly brown and speaks mostly Spanish?*

The statute just had to be unconstitutional. I quickly researched the statute and found it had never been challenged. I remembered from my law school US Constitutional Law course the case of *Yick Wo vs. Hopkins*, 118 US 356, SCt 1064; 30 LEd 220; (1886). LEXIS 1938.

In *Yick Wo*, the United States Supreme Court, back in 1886, held that the guarantee of equal protection contained in the Fourteenth Amendment to the US Constitution extended to aliens as well as citizens. Justice Matthews, writing the opinion of the court, quoted a portion of the Fourteenth Amendment:

> Nor shall any State deprive any person of life,
> Liberty, or property without due process of law;
> Nor deny to any person within its jurisdiction the
> Equal protection of the laws.

Justice Mathews then wrote:

> These provisions are universal in their application to all persons within the territorial jurisdiction, without regard to any differences of race, of color, or of nationality; and the equal protection of the laws is a pledge of the protection of equal laws.

I picked up the letter from Farm Bureau as well as the check and walked into Richard Sneed's office. I told him I thought Section 440.16(7) of the Florida statutes was unconstitutional and should be challenged. It was my opinion that we had nothing to lose by challenging the constitutionality, and our client had $100,000 to gain. In addition, she should have her attorney fees paid by the insurance company if we prevail.

Richard agreed with me. We sat and brainstormed the case for at least an hour. We had several choices to consider. We could file the case first as a workers' compensation claim. That option had several problems. First, the workers' compensation judge did not have jurisdiction to address the constitutionality of the statute. If we went that route, the first place we could bring the issue up was on appeal with the First District Court of Appeals in Tallahassee, and all workers' comp appeals were heard in the First District Court of Appeals. That was a notoriously conservative court.

The second option was filing a declaratory judgment action challenging the constitutionality before a circuit court judge. We could file such a case in various jurisdictions. We could certainly file it in Okeechobee County, where the death occurred. We could file it in St. Lucie County, where Steve's Harvesting Inc. had its headquarters. We might be able to file it in any county in Florida, including St. Lucie, where Florida Farm Bureau had an office.

St. Lucie County Circuit Court held two huge advantages to us. First, it was our home field. Second and most important, the two judges who handled all the Circuit Civil cases in St. Lucie County at that time were Rupert J. Smith and Phillip Nourse. It was fifty-fifty as to which one would be assigned the case. Judge Smith was loved and revered by all plaintiff's attorneys. While he always tried to be fair, he always seemed fairer to the side of the underdog.

Judge Nourse, on the other hand, loved the Constitution and didn't mind upsetting the Fourth District Court of Appeals. If he thought he was right, he would stick to his guns. He had a reputation of being no friend of the insurance industry. He was also a Constitutional scholar. We thought he would be awesome for this case.

The Fourth District Court of Appeals would handle the appeal that would certainly flow from any decision expected from the circuit judge. While not as conservative as the First DCA, it would be no cake walk. We felt that if we were lucky, the case would be assigned to a panel including Judge Rosemary Barkett. She had an interesting life story. She grew up an orphan raised by nuns in Mexico. After being adopted by a family in Homestead, Florida, she earned a scholarship at the University of Miami, where she also attended law school. Judge Barkett had been a trial lawyer in Broward County until she was appointed to the Circuit Court by Governor Bob Graham. Thereafter, Governor Graham had elevated her to the Fourth DCA.

She was known to be a brilliant legal scholar, and she had a reputation of being much friendlier to ordinary people than she was to insurance companies.

Because Steve's Harvesting Inc. might have to be a nominal defendant in the case, we called Bob Shaw into the office to discuss any possible conflict. Bob was furious. He was not mad at us but at his workers' compensation carrier. His very best workers were Mexican. He said he paid Farm Bureau the same ridiculous premium per worker, whether they are Black or White, Mexican or American citizen. He pointed out it cost to raise kids in Mexico the same as it does anywhere else. Bob signed a waiver of any conflict.

We mailed Farm Bureau's $1,000 check back to them and demanded the full $100,000. Florida Farm Bureau refused. I began working on the suit papers, and we filed in just a couple of days. Much to our delight, Judge Nourse was assigned the case!

After we served Florida Farm Bureau, they assigned the defense of the case to Attorneys LB "Buck" Vocelle Jr. and Thomas Koval of Vero Beach, Florida. I knew and had litigated with and against both Buck and Tom. They were both excellent attorneys, and I looked forward to mixing it up with the two of them. Buck's father, LB Vocelle Sr., was one of the finest circuit court judges I have ever appeared before in my practice. Buck was an FSU undergrad, as was I, and we were friends.

The defense filed an answer and affirmative defenses to the complaint, and Judge Nourse called both sides in for a case management conference. There, it was agreed the case would be tried on an admitted set of facts, as follows:

1. It was agreed that Maximiano Ayala had been killed while working on the job for Steve's Harvesting Inc.
2. Florida Farm Bureau was Steve's Harvesting's workers' comp carrier and had offered the $1,000 benefit called for in Florida statute 440.16(7).
3. The plaintiff had rejected the check and demanded the full $100,000 benefit given to the survivors of other workers, including Americans and Canadians.

Judge Nourse asked each side to submit briefs just as if the case were on appeal. Plaintiff would file first, followed by an answer brief by the defense. The plaintiff could then submit a reply brief. Sizes of the briefs were limited, and times were assigned for the tasks.

The brief we filed was, I thought, sufficient. I barely had to go beyond the confines of our little law library in the office. One trip to the County Courthouse Law Library was all I needed to secure enough US Supreme Court cases and other federal cases to help in the brief. We felt confident.

Two months later, we had a trial lasting about an hour. I argued the case for Mrs. Ayala while Buck Vocelle argued for Florida Farm Bureau. Judge Nourse took the case under advisement and said he would complete his opinion in a couple of weeks.

Just a few days later, we received Judge Nourse's final judgment, holding the statute unconstitutional under both the United States and Florida Constitution. It further ordered Farm Bureau to pay Mrs. Ayala the full $100,000. This was one of the last cases Judge Nourse would handle, as he retired from the bench not long after his work was complete on the Ayala case.

I got a call from Buck Vocelle. He congratulated me and told me the judgment was not unexpected by them. He also said that an appeal would be filed within the thirty days called for by the statute.

We called Mrs. Ayala and let her know what progress we were making. I also began work on our (respondent's) answer brief, which would be filed after receipt of the initial brief by Farm Bureau (petitioner). We really knew what the issues were and wanted a head start on the research.

Chapter 9

The appeal was timely filed and began to work its way through the system. Shortly after it was filed, Associated Industries of Florida Inc. filed with the Fourth DCA as Amicus Curie brief on behalf of Florida Farm Bureau. (Amicus Curie means "friend of the court.") Associated Industries is a huge conservative lobbying organization which had a reputation of approving all workers' comp law changes before the legislature takes them up. It had the reputation of being powerful. Their lobbyists write much legislation, unfortunately. Associated Industries had a political pac and donated mostly to Republic legislator's campaigns.

To counter that, we decided to contact Cesar Chavez of the United Farm Workers of America, AFL-CIO in support of our side. The Farm Workers would not file an Amicus brief but sent me an appellate lawyer, Steven Bloom, to help in the research and writing project. We had to research not only Florida law but also the law of the rest of the country. It was decided I would go over to St. Petersburg and spend a day in Stetson Law School's law library working on the federal and other forty-nine state aspects of the appeal. Steven Bloom would review the briefs from the trial and work on researching other Florida Constitutional law cases which were applicable.

We planned to get together in a week to compare notes and brainstorm with Richard Sneed with an eye to putting a great answer brief together. It was a start.

About this time, I settled the cases of Jesus Ayala, Salvador Ayala, and Jose Ortega. All settlements were substantial, and the clients were happy. By then, Jesus was walking normally. He planned to invest his money in the United States but live, for the most part, in Juiquilpan. He had a girlfriend there and thought about getting married and settling down.

Salvador said he was going to purchase some land in Michocan, plant some fruit trees, and retire with his family. Mr. Ortega didn't indicate what he was to do with his smaller settlement, but he was very happy as surgery had restored his eyesight. His bills had been paid, and he had a nice "cushion" of cash.

Tom Koval and Buck Vocelle filed their brief and sent us our copy. A focus of their brief was a challenge to the standing of Bertha Ayala and her children to bring the action in the Florida courts since they were not citizens and were not, at the time, residents of Florida. That was an interesting angle to take, and we reviewed and retooled our brief-in-progress to try to address their arguments. Under Florida law, the personal representative of a decedent (executor) of an estate could be a wife or a blood relative, so the insurance company's first argument failed. They also argued that Section 440 Florida Statutes was constitutional and had stood for sixty years.

While we were working, in earnest, on the rewrite, Steve Bloom looked thoughtful and paused. He said, "Roger, I have been an appellate attorney most of my professional life, and this is the most exciting Constitutional case I have ever seen. Most appellate lawyers in Florida would give their left arm to exchange places with you as lead counsel in the Ayala case. We are going to win this."

We completed our brief, boiled down to the maximum of twenty-five pages, and filed it on time. We asked for oral argument. The petitioner promptly filed their reply brief, and we awaited the scheduling order for the Fourth DCA. The waiting time seemed forever.

During this time, something unexpected happened. Judge Barkett was nominated to the Florida Supreme Court by Governor

Lawton Chiles, and she was now Justice Barkett. Very interesting, we thought.

The Fourth DCA assigned three conservative judges for our panel. The court finally entered an order setting oral argument. Preparation began once again in earnest.

Steve Bloom and Richard Sneed met with me in our conference room and listened to my presentation. They pretended to be judges and peppered me with interrupting questions. Two weeks out, we thought we were ready.

Just a couple of days later, I received a call from Steve Bloom's law partner, Richard Sikking. Steve Bloom had died unexpectedly, I think of a heart attack. What a shock!

I went down to West Palm Beach to the Fourth DCA Courthouse for the argument, accompanied by my partner, Richard. I had argued cases in the past before the Second, Third, and Fourth DCAs, but this time, my knees were knocking together. I was at a low point emotionally but still believed we would win.

Each side had twenty minutes to argue. The petitioners had fifteen minutes first, then we had our twenty minutes. Petitioners then had the last five minutes. I thought things did not go well. The judges barely interrupted either side, but I had bad feelings about body language and facial expressions. Richard reassured me that it had gone well.

It would be months before we would receive the court's ruling. In January 1987, almost three years after Max's death, we got the word. Back in those days, the DCA's informed counsel and the circuit judges below of their decisions by fax.

I was standing by the fax machine reading it when I realized we had lost. Citing an old 1939 Florida Supreme Court case, the unanimous three judge panel opined that:

> Where provisions of the law are not ambiguous, there is no basis for judicial construction thereof.

They noted that the statute might be unfair, but it was up to the legislature to change it.

I thought, *What do these guys mean?* Haven't they heard of *Marbury v. Madison*, cited at 5 US 137 (1803), which allows, nay, requires judicial review of legislative actions? Justice John Marshall wrote the opinion of the Supreme Court on the *Marbury* case and very importantly stated, "The constitution in the United States confirms and strengthens the principal, supposed to be essential to all written constitutions, but any law repugnant to the constitution is void, and then courts, as well as other departments, are bound by this instrument." In effect, *Marbury v. Madison* set in stone the legal theory that the acts of any legislature could be examined by a court to determine the constitutionality of those actions.

I also wondered whether the Fourth District Court of Appeals had heard of the case of *Yick Wo vs. Hopkins* (previously cited). I was boiling mad and getting ready to go in and vent with Richard when the phone rang.

It was Judge Nourse. He said, "Mr. Messer, you aren't going to let them get away with this, are you?"

I answered, "Your Honor, I am working on the Petition for Writ of Certiori as we speak."

Judge Nourse said he was sure we'd get a fair hearing of our case at the next level up.

The Florida Supreme Court only hears those civil cases it wants to hear. Besides death penalty cases, all review by the Supreme Court is on a discretionary basis. You have to petition the court for certiori ("cert" for short) to see if they will agree to hear your case. In only a small percentage of cases is certiori granted.

I met with Richard and told him I was about to start a jury trial that might take over a week. We had a very short time to research and file the Petition for Writ of Certiori to, hopefully, get the case before the Supreme Court. Richard said he would make the time and complete the cert petition himself.

De Ayala vs. Florida Farm Bureau Insurance 543 So. 2d 204 (Fla. 1989)

Supreme Court Appeal

Chapter 10

Two months or so after the filing of the Petition for Certiorari, we received an order from the Supreme Court granting certiorari by a vote of 6 to 1. We would get our day in court in Tallahassee.

By this time, other big hitters, including the Fruit and Vegetable Gardeners Association, had signed on to do amicus briefs on behalf of the insurance company. While the Farm Workers Union never filed such a brief, they did send me Attorney Richar Sikking, to help with my research and my final preparation for oral argument, if oral argument was granted by the court.

It was decided that we needed more research as we were challenging this case under the United States and the Florida Constitution. It was decided that I would go over to Stetson Law School and spend several days in the stacks at the library researching every state in the union to determine what other states have done with this question. I also did some work on the Florida Constitutional questions. I made xerox copies of the cases I thought important. Upon returning to my office, I sat down and organized my notes which ran well over a hundred pages.

Nowadays, all this research could have been accomplished sitting in my office with a computer and could have been completed in about a day. Unfortunately, effective computer research was not available until the mid-1990s.

Unfortunately, the brief could not exceed twenty-five pages. Mr. Sikking and I took a scalpel and cut out all but thirty-five pages from the fat and meat of the case. Ultimately, we took the other ten pages which included some bone, but at least I retained my knowledge of what the research had shown. We filed our brief in a timely manner.

The defense filed their reply brief, which was done well, but we thought their case was weak. We then filed a reply brief to their answer attacking a few of their points. After all briefs we filed, we filed a motion with the court to allow oral argument. It took several weeks before the Supreme Court entered its order allowing us to appear before it and argue the case. The court had the right to decide the case based on the briefs only, but we felt it was a positive sign that they had granted us the right to appear before them in person.

The court assigned a day for me, as well as defense counsel, to appear and argue our respective cases. We then began actual preparation for the oral argument. I drafted an outline of what I wanted to say and circulated it to Mr. Sikking and Richard. Sikking had argued several cases before the Supreme Court (both state and federal) while neither Richard nor I had done that.

Richard Sikking explained that the seven judges at the State Supreme Court were equals. The Chief Judgeship was simply an administrative position. He explained that the way the cases were handled within the Supreme Court is that when the court decides to take jurisdiction on the case, they meet and divide up the cases between them. If a case is particularly in the area of interest of a particular justice, he or she is assigned to be the sheppard of that case. Sikking explained that this justice will have read the transcript of the trial and all the case law cited in all the briefs and will have a tremendous understanding of what the case is about. He also explained that in the event that that person was in the majority in reaching a decision, he or she would write the opinion. Likewise, if they were not in the majority, they would write the dissent.

Mr. Sikking also explained the process of the oral argument. It was somewhat similar to the process in the Fourth District Court of Appeals. You're allowed to begin your statement, but at any time during the statement, you could be interrupted by any of the judges on the panel with questions that they might have. Sikking explained to me that the first judge who addresses me in the case would, in fact, be the sheppard of that case. He urged me to make my argument with about 90 percent of my time peering at that particular judge, but also paying deference to those other judges who in fact asked questions.

The day finally arrived for our moment of truth. The day before the argument, I had driven to my mother's home in Chattahoochee, Florida (about forty miles from Tallahassee) and spent the night there to get a good night's sleep. The next day, my mom and my sister, Ann, decided to go and listen to the argument, and I was happy to take them along. They went into the courtroom before I did and were seated on the front row on the petitioner's side. To my delight, Judge Phillip Nourse was sitting next to them and talking with them. Judge Nourse, who was by then retired, had driven up to Tallahassee the night before just to be present for this moment. I said hello to him and thanked him for coming. He said that I should "Go get 'em."

At the appointed hour, our case was called, and I approached the podium and introduced myself. I was extremely gratified when the person who asked me to proceed was Justice Rosemary Barkett.

While Mr. Sikking had indicated that I would not be able to make my entire presentation because of the incessant questions, I was, in fact, able to get through it without much difficulty at all. I was only asked three softball questions which Mr. Sikking and Mr. Sneed had gone over with me before that day, and I felt I knocked those softballs out of the park. I had reserved fifteen minutes for my opening and five minutes for my rebuttal argument. I was surprised and happy that I sat down after thirteen minutes after my first presentation.

My friend Buck Vocelle stood and approached the podium and explained that like me, this was his first case before the Supreme Court and was also the first case for Mr. Koval before the Supreme Court. He indicated they wanted to divide their time at ten minutes each between them. The judge told Mr. Vocelle to proceed. From the time he gave his name, there was a barrage of questions from all over the bench, but especially from Judge Barkett. The only semi-friendly questions were from Justice Ben Overton, who Mr. Vocelle had clerked for while he was at Florida State University's Law School. In fact, Mr. Koval never got to stand and mention his name because the court was not through with Mr. Vocelle. The court's treatment of Mr. Vocelle was a grilling.

I stood up to do my rebuttal and decided that although I had seven minutes left that less was more. I hit a couple of high points and asked for the court to be fair, and I sat down in less than three minutes.

As I walked out the front of the Supreme Court building, Mr. Vocelle was there and shook my hand and said, "Roger, I really wish I was arguing your side of the case, but you did a wonderful job." I congratulated him on the job he did as well. Judge Nourse congratulated me as well.

Months passed before we heard a decision from the Supreme Court. That opinion is found in citation *De Ayala vs. Florida Farm Bureau Insurance, 543 So. 2d 204 (Fla. 1989)*.

The vote was 6 to 1 in our favor, with Justice Barkett writing the opinion. Judge Overton was the only justice who dissented.

Justice Barkett indicated that the statute in question was violative of both the Florida Constitution as well as the United States Constitution. She indicated that it was also expensive to raise children in Mexico.

Because the judge's decision also held the statute violated Florida's Constitution, we were sure we were saved from an appeal to the US Supreme Court. The US Supreme Court is not the final arbiter of the meaning of the Florida Constitution. Florida's Supreme Court is.

Judge Barkett, in her opinion, also commented that the legislature had just, after our oral argument, amended the Florida Statute to increase the payments for non-US citizens to $50,000. Judge Barkett indicated that that change was also unconstitutional and nullified that law by the stroke of her pen. She indicated that one half is not enough, that everyone was entitled to equal protection under the laws. Thankfully, the Supreme Court also said I was entitled to seek attorney's fees in front of a lower judge. It was assigned to a workers' compensation judge in Fort Pierce, Florida, to make that decision.

I literally floated out of the office. I called my former partner, Richard, about the result. We also called our client and then called Bob Shaw to thank him for his help.

There were about a dozen Florida cases similar to ours around the state which had been placed on hold pending the Supreme Court's ruling in Ayala. Agriculture can be a dangerous job. Most of the workers there are not American citizens, but the farmers need someone to pick the fruit and vegetables.

Farm Bureau decided to fight us on the reasonableness of our attorney's fee. They hired one of the finest appellate lawyers in Palm Beach County, Florida, to argue on their behalf that my fee was not worth very much due my lack of experience handling appeals.

Richard Sneed and I sat down and thought about who we should get to be our expert on that subject.

Richard had been instrumental in the first election campaign for Circuit Judge James Alderman here in St. Lucie County. Judge Alderman had later been appointed to the Fourth District Court of Appeals and then to the Florida Supreme Court, where he was chief judge for a time. He was now retired and living on a ranch west of Fort Pierce. Justice Alderman congratulated us and agreed to be our witness, free of charge. We agreed that he would be an awesome witness. When Justice Alderman walked into the courtroom, the workers' compensation judge almost stood up and bowed.

When the decision came down from that judge, we were most pleased at the court's opinion and the fee. About that time, we received a check from Florida Farm Bureau Insurance Company payable to Mrs. Ayala for the balance of her money. I called her, and she indicated that she wanted to come to Florida to see the check and discuss things with me.

The date selected for her to be at my office was, in fact, the sixth-year anniversary of her husband's death. It took that long. When she showed up, I showed her the check, and she asked me if she could have the same deal that her sons and daughters had regarding structuring the payments. She explained that all her money had been taken by the Mexican banks within three or four years of the settlement, but the children were receiving their funds on a regular basis, and she was, all in all, happy with the result. I picked up the phone and called my good friend and stockbroker, Ronald Martin, and asked if we could do an annuity in the United States with these funds and have monthly payments sent to Ms. Ayala in American dollars for the rest of her life. He said, "Of course, we can do that. Have her sign the check and bring it here, and we'll open the account while she's here."

Mrs. Ayala and I drove her down to Mr. Martin's Stuart, Florida, office where the rest of her documents were completed, and it was a done matter. Ms. Ayala then happily returned to her native country.

Epilogue

Chapter 11

The case was effectively over when Mrs. Ayala picked up her check in early 1990. By that time, Mr. Sneed and I had parted ways, and I had opened my own office in Port St. Lucie, Florida (approximately ten miles south of Fort Pierce). Fifteen years thereafter, I had relocated my office with my new law partner, my son, Steven, to western Port St. Lucie, near where my wife and I built a home. In 2019, I was in my office tending to my work when the receptionist buzzed through to me and said, "There's a Mr. Ayala at the front window here who would like to see you."

As I only knew one Ayala family, I told her that I would meet him and asked her to bring him in. It was one of Max and Bertha's sons, grown well into a man. On behalf of the family, he thanked me, thirty-five years after his father's tragic passing. He told me Mario was now an attorney in Mexico, and one of his other brothers was a pharmacist.

Shortly after our case was decided, Bill Clinton appointed Justice Rosemary Barkett to the Federal Eleventh Circuit Appellate bench in Atlanta. Upon retiring from that office, she became a justice in the International Court of Justice at the Hague.

Book 2

Cut My Teeth

Chapter 12

How did I become a personal injury trial lawyer? I had initially gone to law school with the idea of perhaps becoming a labor lawyer, a criminal lawyer, or any kind of lawyer where I could make a decent living. I found Stetson Law School to be very challenging. Over a third of our starting class flunked out, and these were very bright students with high enough college GPA's and LSAT scores to get into law school.

There was no grade inflation at Stetson. Obtaining a grade of C in most courses was considered doing pretty good. My first year, I particularly disliked Contracts and Real Property courses. I thought both were dull and tedious.

I worked hard and found that I only earned modest grades *except* in Torts, Evidence, US Constitutional Law, Florida Constitutional Law, and Trial Practice courses. I excelled in those areas and avidly read legal articles and books about those subjects. I realized I might have a future as a tort lawyer.

While law school forces you to think like a lawyer, it certainly does not train you to practice law. When I started law school, I quit a job in the Pentagon, where I did research regarding legislation. This turned out to be excellent training for law school. There was extensive research and writing in my job with the Office of the Secretary of the Air Force.

The Pentagon is a giant government facility with over twenty-seven thousand little cogs in one huge five-sided wheel. I did not want to work in a large organization ever again. During my last year in law school, I looked at a couple of large insurance defense firms and decided that was not for me. I wanted something more personal and exciting where I could help real people, not insurance companies.

When I graduated from Stetson Law School in 1977, I had no money and had a baby on the way. I took the first job that was offered to me by a small firm. The St. Petersburg lawyer I clerked for during my last two years of law school, Dave DeSerio, gave me a job at a very low salary, handling anything that came in the door. He said he understood it would only be a temporary position until I found something better. I was a young married attorney with a new baby boy on the way and needed to start helping Betsey with the expenses. Not working was not an option. I also had student loans to pay and had no money with which to start my own practice.

David was bright, but, I thought, somewhat challenged ethically. He seemed to always have trouble in his personal and financial life. Bar complaints against him were not uncommon. I learned what *not* to do as an attorney. David earned and spent quite a bit of money. He had a heavy real estate practice as well as a general law practice. He threw everything but the real estate at me. He did not generate personal injury cases, and I had no contacts to help me get started in that field.

Four days after being sworn in as a lawyer before the Second District Court of Appeal in Lakeland, Florida, I tried my first criminal case and won. I had worked up the case as a law clerk and understood the case better than David anyway. I handled criminal, divorces, bankruptcies, contracts cases—anything and everything. I did not enjoy that work. I initially earned a lower salary than my old job as a legislative research assistant with the Office of the Secretary of the Air Force, which I'd quit to go to law school. I had a burning desire to do personal injury cases, but they did not come. Lawyers were strictly forbidden from advertising in those days. Television and radio advertising for attorneys in Florida did not exist. You could lose your license if you had more than a small listing in the phone book. There were no pictures allowed in the phone book, ever. Word of mouth was the key to a successful practice.

I let David know I was unhappy. The last straw came when I won a large contract case we had on a contingency fee basis with our client. I earned the office a $40,000 fee and was rewarded with a big "Attaboy." No bonus, no pay increase. I received nothing but a pat on the back. David took the entire fee and handed it over to the IRS to take care of a tax lien he had acquired. I told David I was leaving at my first opportunity and would try to wind down or hand off the cases I was working on.

St. Pete was a tough place to begin a law practice. I checked, and there were only about 240 people who lived there for each lawyer licensed to practice in that city. I had to find somewhere else to begin.

DeSerio had no hard feelings. In fact, he said he had just talked with an old law school classmate of his from Ft. Pierce, Florida, Richard Sneed, who was looking for an associate to do some civil trial work. I checked the Florida Bar Journal and discovered there were only about eighty lawyers in St. Lucie County for a population then of a little over sixty thousand. That worked out to about 750 souls per attorney. When you eliminated lawyers working for the state's attorney and public defender and other governmental lawyers, the numbers looked really good. I had read a Chamber of Commerce study which predicted that St. Lucie County would have 250,000 people by 2025. (In 2022, the county surpassed 500,000 people, and I managed to grow along with the county population.)

After I accepted the position, I busily tried to wind down my meager St. Petersburg practice. I drove over to Stetson Law School's campus to say goodbye to some folks who were special to me.

I met with my mentor, Professor William McKinley "Mickey" Smiley. He congratulated me on finally finding a civil trial practice job and assured me I would do well.

He had some sage advice for me:

(1) In a small town, especially, a young lawyer needs to throw himself into community activities like church, youth sports, and politics.
(2) He urged me to join the Academy of Florida Trial Lawyers (now Florida Justice Association) as soon as I could pay the initiation fee. This was the most important advice he gave me. The academy had the very best seminars for civil trial lawyers, and the relationships I have made through the academy over the years have been essential to my practice.
(3) Professor Smiley told me the smartest lawyer he had every taught was Chris Searcy. He told me Chris was to try a huge wrongful death case trial in Fort Pierce in three weeks. Mickey told me to take time and go watch it. I did manage to see much of that trial. It was a railroad intersection case. On closing argument, Chris asked for $7 million. The verdict was "only" $4 million. I took down Chris's phone number and would interact with him over the years. More than once, Chris has pointed me to the right expert for use in my cases.

I drove over to Fort Pierce with Betsey and was offered the job. I was to be paid no salary but initially was to receive 50 percent of every dollar I brought in. All expenses, including my secretary, were to be paid by Richard out of his 50 percent. I have often wished I had that deal for my entire career and not just for two years. Betsey and I and our one-year-old son, Steven, moved to St. Lucie County in May of 1978. Thankfully, Betsey got a good job as a registered nurse at Lawnwood Hospital doing intensive care work. She loved working in the ICU and had earned a National Certification in Critical Care Nursing. We greatly depended on her salary to pay living expenses before I would get some real traction.

I threw myself into the activities of the community. I joined the Fort Pierce Lions Club since it was the largest club in town (seventy members), and it had only one lawyer. He was over seventy years old.

When my young son got old enough to play T-ball, I sponsored a team and wound up being a coach. When Little League began, I volunteered as an umpire, coach, and ultimately manager in the league. I later coached Steven in American Legion Baseball. I served on the board of directors for two of the baseball leagues we were involved in.

I also got involved with the local Democratic Party and wound up being its chair in the early 1980s. I held other positions in the party (like state committeeman) until about 1990 when I got too busy in my practice to handle it. Through all these efforts, I became very well-known in the community and made many contacts.

Chapter 13

The first day I showed up for work in Fort Pierce, I brought my lunch in a brown bag, as I had no lunch money. When I got to the office, Richard said for me to put my sandwich in the office fridge and meet him in the conference room. My office furniture had not yet arrived, nor had he yet hired me a secretary. I was to start interviewing applicants later that day. Richard gave me three old mangy files (real dogs) to work up for trial and put me to work. These were small county court cases. Because his secretary was on vacation and he and the receptionist both went to lunch at the same time, he asked if I would sit at the front reception desk and answer the phone or door while I ate my lunch. There were sodas in the refrigerator—gratis.

I was just finishing my baloney sandwich when the door opened and in walked a big man in a greasy work shirt. Bobby was about six one tall and was sweaty. He was barrel chested, swarthy, and spoke with a thick New York accent. He said, "Excuse me, are you a lawyer?"

I said, "Yes, I am."

"Do you handle personal injury cases?"

Of course. I said, "Yes, I do."

Bobby then said, "Well, you probably won't like to take my case because I was hit by a big rig truck, and they have lots of money to fight us with."

I said, "PLEASE SIT DOWN."

Bobby Williams was a marine diesel mechanic who had been stopped at a red light in front of the *News Tribune* building on US Highway One in Fort Pierce when a semi-tractor and trailer owned by Gator Freight Ways had rolled up over the rear of his pickup truck. Bobby had a copy of the picture from the next day's *Tribune* showing him being removed from the wreckage on a bodyboard.

Bobby had undergone back surgery because of his injuries. He had just fired his first lawyer because the attorney tried to settle the case for only $7,500. Back in those days, lots of local lawyers dabbled in personal injury cases and really did not understand their value or, worse still, didn't care. Bobby asked me if I would go to trial with his case if the money wasn't right. I answered, "Absolutely."

Before my boss, Richard, had returned from lunch, I had signed Bobby Williams to a contingency fee contract. That afternoon, I went and interviewed Juan Brown, the photographer from the *Tribune* who had taken the picture in the paper. Juan said he heard the crash and ran outside with his camera and took quite a few shots. Juan Brown was a very talented photographer. He said he sometimes earned extra cash doing private photography jobs for lawyers and others, including aerial photographs. I purchased all his pictures he had taken of the accident scene. Juan was a witness for us at trial.

I filed the case before the end of the week. The case was not without fleas of its own. Like all cases, there were problems. The principal problem was proving lost earnings. While Bobby was in the Marine Diesel Repair business with his dad and had acquired lots of creature comforts over the years, including a nice home with no mortgage and several late model automobiles and a nice boat, he had never reported earning over $3,600 per year to the IRS. His business was mostly on a cash basis. I realized after this case that we should not always ask for lost earnings. It was a lesson well earned. With no lost wages claim, there would be no need for the defense to obtain tax records. They would be irrelevant. What a rookie mistake!

Because it was the only real case I had, I pushed it through the system with all deliberate speed. The insurance company assigned the case to Attorney Steve Hayskar from Fort Pierce. I have known and respected Steve since meeting him in this case. He is ethical and does a damn good job for his clients. He was sure to make hay out of our tax problems.

Eight months after filing suit, we were set for jury trial. Getting to trial that quickly is a record for me that I have not equaled in over forty-five years of practice. We decided to essentially try this as a pain and suffering case. I really hoped we could somehow get the case to the jury before they heard about the taxes. No progress was made toward settling the case until the morning we were set to pick the jury. The defense had offered earlier $25,000, which we rejected.

Steve Hayskar stopped me in the courthouse hall and said, "Roger, you've done a great job. We are offering you $75,000 to settle right now." I took Bobby into a conference room, and he told me he would have settled for that before, but he didn't want to take a cent less than $100,000, which was quite a sum in the late seventies. He reminded me of my promise to take the case to trial, and I said I was still happy to do so. The defense turned down our $100,000 counteroffer.

Jury voir dire, the jury selection process, went well for us. One of the venire men had actually witnessed the crash and made a helpful comment about it. Of course, the judge dismissed that juror for cause. Our final six-person jury had an eighteen-year-old student, and the rest were mostly blue-collar working men and women. One of the jurors was Black.

We made some great points in the trial and were helped by the wonderful pictures of the crash scene. My client's wife was a good before and after witness.

The defense, as always, had the truck driver there and pretended, as they always do, that the driver would have to personally pay any judgment. Of course, we had also sued Gator Freightways. We are not allowed, by Florida law, to sue the insurance company directly in these types of cases. Steve Hayskar tried the case like a tax fraud case and suggested that my client could not be believed on any subject because, according to Steve, my client had not been exactly truthful on his tax returns.

In closing argument, I asked the jury to award around $150,000, while Steve said they should give him nothing more than out of pocket medical bills, but in no wise more than $70,000. The jury deliberated for about two hours and returned a verdict of $105,000. Bobby and I were ecstatic! A *News Tribune* reporter was at the courthouse for the verdict, and any six-figure verdict made the news in those days. After the story ran in the *Tribune* the next day, I began to get new personal injury cases on a regular basis in my office.

I really worked at becoming a better trial lawyer after Bobby's case. I soon joined the Academy of Florida Trial Lawyers (now the FJA), whose educational program was awesome I had made mistakes in this case but learned from them.

Epilogue to Bobby's Case

Two weeks after the verdict, I was walking across the Indian River Community College campus, heading for the library. From across the quad, I heard someone holler my name. "Mr. Messer, Mr. Messer, hold up!" Running across the quad toward me was the eighteen-year-old juror. He asked me if I knew who he was, and I said I did. He then asked, "Do you lawyers get a third?"

I said "What?" And he repeated the question. I told him that all fees were negotiable, but in this case, a one-third fee was earned.

He said, "That's what we thought." He said the jury had decided that $70,000 was reasonable compensation for Bobby but wanted to make sure that my client got that much, so they added $35,000 on top to make sure I was paid too. I realized then and there that jurors are actually a pretty intelligent group of folks. I became a personal injury trial lawyer with the *Williams vs. Gator Freight* trial. It felt good.

Several years later, Bobby Williams was injured in another serious collision. He retained me to represent him in that case as well. By that time, he had followed my advice and taken care of his tax problem. We settled that second case for him quite satisfactorily.

Within two years of opening my practice in St. Lucie County, I was able to stop doing divorce cases. I hated divorce cases but had handled quite a few of them. The main thing that I disliked about divorce was that there were never any winners, only losers, especially the kids.

I also stopped doing criminal cases about the same time. I had a hard time trusting criminal defendants to come in my office without casing the joint. The last criminal matter I handled, I fired the client on the first day and swore I would never do another criminal case. In that case, the client was a small-time drug dealer caught by the police with scales and a very small amount of drugs. He and his wife were sitting across from my desk in two chairs, and I quoted what I thought was a large fee for the case. This scumbag indicated that it would not be a problem, but that his wife would have to work out the fee with me over a period. At that time, the wife sat back in the chair and lifted her skirt. Underneath, she was wearing nothing but a smile. I told them to leave my office, and I would not represent them. I then closed my criminal law career. I was doing a more thriving personal injury business by then and was still doing wills and the occasional business dispute.

Lawyers learn along the way what area they want to practice. There are numerous roads they can go down to obtain what they view as success. Many lawyers are not cut out to be litigators but still do very well in a huge number of legal specialties.

Book 3

Wrongful Death

Chapter 14

On a sad day in late May 1981, I had an appointment in my office in Fort Pierce, Florida, to meet two grandparents, Doris and Ken Tropf, concerning the possible adoption of their two grandchildren. I was surprised to learn the Tropfs had come to my office straight from the funeral of their daughter, Lynnette. Our office did different kinds of legal work including some family law, probate, and some civil litigation, including personal injury and wrongful death. Doris was a member of the Communication Worker's Union, and our office had a deal with the CWA for low-cost legal services for such things as wills, divorces, adoptions, and the like. I had been practicing law exactly four years and had only been doing personal injury and wrongful death work for three years.

Ken and Doris's daughter, Lynnette, had been killed in a tragic accident in Vero Beach just four days before. A young Venezuelan national, Jesus Delgado, had caused the collision. Lynnette was a young single mom, and the fathers of each of her two children were nowhere to be found.

"We don't know how we can afford to raise these kids," explained Doris. She was being laid off as an operator for Southern

Bell (replaced by machines), and Ken had just recently suffered a heart attack and was being forced to retire from the post office.

I asked how Lynnette had died. Doris explained that it was a motorcycle accident. Before I could say that folks shouldn't drive those things, she told me that the two people on the motorcycle only had broken legs. Her daughter was driving a brand-new 1981 Toyota Tercel at the time of the accident. The motorcycle driver had been drinking beer that day. The motorcycle ran a stop sign and hit the Toyota, causing it to roll over. The top of the car collapsed on Lynnette, breaking her neck. Lynnette's baby son, Jacob, was in the car with her and had a serious brachial plexus injury. He was in the hospital.

I asked about Uninsured Motorist Insurance, and Ken spoke up and said, "State Farm has been great. They already gave us a check for the full UM coverage, $25,000." Ken said that he, but not Doris, had signed a release. I was shocked, as I'd never heard of an insurance company paying Uninsured Motorist benefits before the deceased victim had been buried. I inquired as to where Lynnette resided before her death and discovered she lived with Ken and Doris, her parents. An adult brother also lived there, and *all* of them had automobiles insured with State Farm policies with Stacking UM coverage available. By my figuring, her estate and children were entitled to around $225,000 in State Farm UM benefits. Since only the personal representative of the estate could legally settle any claims, the State Farm release signed by Ken was meaningless. That was the day I started referring to the "Good Neighbor People" as SNAKE FARM.

It was decided to immediately set up an estate and name Doris as the personal representative. I then contacted Snake Farm, and in fairly short order, they threw in the towel and tendered their remaining coverage of $200,000.

Sometimes bad things happen in a fortunate way. In early 1981, I had joined the Academy of Florida Trial Lawyers. Just about two weeks before Ken and Doris Tropf came to my office, I read an article in the Academy of Florida Trial Lawyer's *Journal* about a new liability theory about *crashworthiness* of automobiles and a case that had just been won by a noted Florida attorney, John Krupnick of

Fort Lauderdale against, I believe, Honda Corporation. I then also read in *Consumer Reports* that the 1981 Toyota Tercel was the most fuel-efficient car sold in America. I also read another article indicating that the '81 Tercel was also *the most dangerous* car sold in America because they had weakened the passenger compartment strength and integrity to reduce weight.

Shortly after Ken and Doris Tropf left my office, I put in a call to John Krupnick, who I had never met. Surprisingly, I got him on the first try. I introduced myself and told him I had a case to run by him that involved a motorcycle accident. He interrupted me and said, "Motorcycles are too dangerous. I don't handle crashworthiness cases involving those."

I said, "No, you don't understand. The two people on the motorcycle are fine. The young mother in the new Toyota that they hit is dead."

He said, "I AM INTERESTED."

After about an hour's conversation, John and I had agreed to work on the case together, to share all costs evenly, and to split all fees fifty-fifty. John said, "I promise you, Toyota will be responsible for over a million dollars in this case." He put me on hold and called his accident reconstruction expert from Detroit and arranged for him to meet us at the crash scene the next afternoon. John asked me to call the highway patrolman who had worked up the crash to see if he could meet us there. He also told me to go ahead and find and purchase both the motorcycle and the automobile involved in the crash, since, without the faulty product, we would have an almost impossible time proving any defective products case. I then realized that agreeing to share all costs fifty-fifty could be a very expensive proposition.

When I spoke to the highway patrolman, Trooper Shook, later that day, he said that this accident really got to him. You could tell on the phone that he was still shaken from the experience of finding the mangled body of a young mother with her one-year-old baby, obviously badly injured, also at the scene. The job of first responders is tough. These folks are not immune to emotional injury as a result of doing their very necessary jobs. Officer Shook said he would be happy to help us and would be at the accident scene at 1:00 p.m. the next day.

When John and I and the reconstruction expert arrived the next day at 1:00 p.m. sharp, Trooper Shook had set up detours and stopped traffic at the intersection. He showed us what every orange paint mark meant. He also showed the expert every paint transfer, yaw mark in the roadway, and skid mark from the rubber on the pavement. Many photographs were taken. It had not yet rained, and the crime scene was in excellent condition. We were there with the expert for well over an hour.

I noted that the stop sign at the scene was obscured by tall grass, and the caution light. which hung over the intersection, was not operating/flashing at all. It had apparently burned out.

Doris and Ken only lived a couple of miles from the accident scene. I decided to visit with them and discuss where we were with the case. John Krupnick declined to come with me and said he'd let me be in charge of "holding hands with the clients." I really did not like that phrase as I always want to have a personal relationship with my clients so I will understand their needs and desires. I made the short drive to the Tropf home.

Ken and Doris Tropf were deeply religious people. When I met them at their home, they were surrounded by photos of their three daughters and one son and lots of grandchildren. Doris seemed to be the dominant personality present. She was mourning, she was mad, and she was determined to do something, anything, about it.

Vero Beach was a very small town where most local people know each other. One of the doctors at the hospital had spoken to Doris and indicated that Delgado was drunk when he was at the hospital. She was livid about that. Delgado's hospital record ultimately showed an illegal blood alcohol level. Ken was reserved and stoic. He was resigned to accept the horrible hand life had dealt him and his family. He had serious doubts we could do anything to help them. I was there for over an hour and admit to crying with them.

The Lawsuit

Chapter 15

We filed suit against Jesus Delgado, against Toyota Corporation, and against Indian River County, Florida, in the US District Court for the Southern District of Florida.

The suit against the county alleged that they failed to maintain the safety equipment at the dangerous intersection, where several people (believed to be seven) had been killed over the years. Speed strips to slow traffic approaching the intersection had been paved over just a month or two before Lynnette's crash. We had before and after aerial photos to prove that. When Doris read the suit papers, she was upset. She didn't want us to sue her county government. She asked if we could settle with them quickly, and we did. Not much money was obtained from the county, but it was enough to help with the cost of suit.

Jesus Delgado was a Venezuelan student at Flight Safety, a Vero Beach, Florida, school which had a reputation of specializing in training foreign rich kids to be pilots. The school would earn notoriety twenty years later when it was discovered several of the 911 terrorists had their flight training there. After the 911 horror, the trainers at the school remembered those Saudi students as not being very interested in knowing how to land the planes.

Delgado, of course, had no insurance. He also had no assets in the United States other than a crushed motorcycle. He was facing vehicular manslaughter charges in the Nineteenth Judicial Circuit. A conversation with the local prosecutor disclosed that the parents of Delgado had posted a $35,000 cash bond, which was theoretically returnable to him when he appeared for trial or a change of plea. The assistant state's attorney told us that Delgado also faced probable deportation upon completion of sentence. He assured us that Delgado would probably get some prison time. I asked for and obtained a court order to freeze his bond to assist in restitution in this case.

A few weeks later, I made an appointment and met with Lynnette's son Jacob's neurosurgeon, Dr. Romas Sakalas, in Vero Beach. He gravely explained to me that Jacob had suffered a complete severing of his brachial plexus on the left side. Even though Jacob was only one year old, he would never be able to use his left arm, never be able to do push-ups, pull-ups, or any team sports. Although the left arm would continue to grow and appear as normal as the right arm, it would be essentially useless. There was no miracle surgery or treatment to help him. Nerves do not regenerate.

Since I was already in Vero Beach that day, I went by the Tropf home and met little Jacob and his older sister, Brandi, who was a beautiful curly haired three-year-old brunette. The kids loved their grandparents and appeared to be happy. Doris, on the other hand, was in deep mourning. Ken had a distant and strained look about him and was very negative about life. I explained how the suit was progressing.

They had met John Krupnick over dinner with me and later told me they didn't particularly like him. I told them he was the best in his field, and we needed his expertise. They said, "*Okay*, but you are our lawyer."

The case against Toyota seemed to crawl along. Every discovery attempt was met with objections. No interrogatories were answered without court hearings and begrudging and convoluted explanations. They fought us throughout the discovery phase, especially when it came time to set depositions. They were demanding that we travel to Japan to take the testimony of the engineering and design experts. We wanted to take the depositions in the continental United States. We discovered documents that tended to show that Toyota had not done proper rollover tests as required by NHTSA (National Highway Traffic Safety Administration). The company had performed computer simulations which showed (falsely) that the Tercel passed.

I took the deposition of the passenger on the motorcycle. Susan was a young White female who had suffered a broken leg in the crash but was otherwise unhurt. She was still mad at the motorcycle driver. She said she met the guy at a party, and he had been drinking but appeared to her to be okay to drive. He invited her to take a short ride on his new motorcycle, and she said yes. He had no helmet for her, though he wore one. She said that once they started, the guy began driving really fast. She said she beat on his back trying to get him to stop. She was horrified when she thought he was laughing at her. She thought she was going to die as they approached the intersection. She remembered the front of the motorcycle striking the driver side door of the small red car, and then she and the motorcycle driver both flew over the car and landed in some bushes on the opposite side of the road. Delgado's helmeted head crashed into a light pole, splitting the helmet open, but amazingly, the motorcycle driver only sustained a broken leg. His helmet did its job.

Delgado's criminal case was assigned to an aging Judge Ralph Johnson (not his real name). While the case was pending, Judge Johnson's daughter was herself arrested for two counts of DUI manslaughter in St. Lucie County, Florida. It was in all the papers and was quite a scandal. Doris was concerned as to what effect that might have on the outcome of Delgado's criminal case but was assured by the assistant state's attorney that Delgado would get at least a year behind bars for his part in causing Lynnette's death.

Ultimately, after many delays, Delgado copped a plea to involuntary manslaughter and had his wrist slapped. He received no jail time but was sentenced to five years' probation. He was deported. We did manage to pinch his $35,000 bond as partial restitution. While the young man had well-off parents in Venezuela, he personally had no other assets, and his parents were not legally responsible for his actions.

Judge Johnson's daughter also got out of her legal jam with a very light sentence.

Sometimes, the criminal justice system does not result in justice While the civil justice system may help some, it also can also seem inadequate. Doris Tropf wanted to make the system better. She also wanted to make automobiles and the roads we travel on safer. She wanted to do something about drunk drivers and the carnage they cause on our roads.

Doris Tropf had joined Mothers Against Drunk Drivers, the Indian River Chapter. Shortly thereafter, she was elected chairperson of the local chapter. One of her jobs was to counsel other drunk driving victims. She worked, and still to this day, works closely with law enforcement authorities in Impact Panels, which consist of meeting with DUI offenders and showing them the effects of their so-called "victimless" crimes. She also counsels victims of drunk driving to this day.

Settlement discussions were opened between John Krupnick and the attorneys for Toyota. Meanwhile, the depositions of the design and engineering personnel of Toyota were set for a couple of months away to take place in Hawaii—a compromise location. Toyota tried unsuccessfully to make us take the depositions in Japan. Talks were at a critical stage, and John Krupnick and I were in contact with the Tropf's and Toyota's attorneys and adjusters on a more or less daily basis.

About that time, I received a call from John Krupnick. He informed me that we needed to purchase a used 1981 Toyota Tercel and hire an engineering firm he had used in the past. That firm had a crane with which to lift the car, upside down, to exactly three feet above the pavement and drop it suddenly. John said that this was the test Toyota should have but didn't run prior to putting the Tercel into the stream of commerce. John assured me that the car roof would crush flat as a pancake while we were filming it all. He said it would cost us "only" about $20,000. This test was to be set up by him to occur when we returned from Hawaii.

About two weeks before we were to leave for Hawaii, John called me late in the day and said, "Roger, I apologize. I know I promised a million dollars against Toyota, but we only got $880,000.00 But the clients are happy." John explained that the funds received by the two kids would be placed in structured settlements, which will provide tax-free income over their lifetimes which will greatly exceed a million dollars. The lawsuit was over.

Doris told me the stress of any trial would probably kill Ken, and while she wanted to make sure that Toyota made safer cars in the future, she only had ill will toward one group of individuals in the world—*drunk drivers*. She wanted to get on with raising the two grandchildren and devote her life to the cause.

Epilogue to Lynnette's Case

The next year, Doris was elected Florida's state-wide chairperson of MADD. She made numerous trips to the legislative sessions in Tallahassee over the years, lobbying for a new law lowering the legal alcohol blood limit for driving from 1.00 mg/dl to .08 mg/dl. You can look it up. She was ultimately successful. She also argued for mandatory minimum sentencing in DUI cases as well as other pro-consumer and pro-crime victim issues.

Doris urged local law enforcement to emphasize DUI enforcement—successfully. DUI task forces were set up by sheriff's departments all along the Treasure Coast area of Florida. She participated in citizen ride-along programs with the local DUI enforcement units and got me involved in the same program in St. Lucie County. It was extremely educational for me. I had never defended a drunk driver (and never will) and didn't know the drill. I came to really respect the dedicated officers who do this dangerous and essential work, usually from about 8:00 p.m. until about 4:00 a.m.

This case happened over forty years ago. Ken died in 2013 but was an invalid for about thirty-five years before that. Doris still works counseling DUI victims. She still is in mourning. Every time I talk with her, she mentions Lynnette. Time does not heal all wounds. Over the years, Mrs. Tropf has referred to me several cases, including one worth over $1 million. I have represented her son, both her surviving daughters, and ironically, her granddaughter (and adopted daughter), Brandi, in various legal matters over the years. Doris and Ken have always been invited to my Christmas parties, and I to their home any time I am in Vero Beach. I cherish the thank you notes I received from Doris.

Brandi is now a young mother of two boys who resides in Orlando, Florida. Her sons' dad was tragically killed in a motorcycle accident a couple of years ago. Jacob, Brandi's brother with the severely disabling shoulder injury, ultimately reconnected with his biological father. Jacob now has children of his own and lives with his family out in Idaho.

Doris and I regularly chat on the phone. I am so thankful that the Tropf family has been a part of my life.

BOOK 4

Good-Looking Clients, Good-Looking Verdict

Chapter 16

In late 1981, I was visited at my office in Fort Pierce by a prospective client, Linda Matthews, and her husband, Ricky Matthews (not their real names). They were a very odd couple. Linda was perhaps the most beautiful woman I had ever seen in my life. She was very tall with beautiful auburn hair and a fair but not too pale complexion. She seemed, to my eyes, perfectly proportioned. She and her husband were both, I believe, in their mid to late twenties.

It became obvious to me that the gregarious partner in this marriage was Linda. She was vivacious and had a friendly smile. Her husband, Ricky, however, was the opposite. He was big, burly, and somewhat surly. He was obviously all about working and earning a living. The couple had no children as of their visit with me.

It seems that two weeks earlier, Linda had been a victim of a rear-end crash at a red light up in Vero Beach, Florida. While sitting at the light, her small pickup truck was crashed into by a large loaded down pickup truck owned by a company known as John's Island Inc. Linda had the recently printed accident report in her hand to give to me.

She and Ricky lived in a rural part of northwestern St. Lucie County. It was almost as easy for them to get up to Vero Beach as it was to come down to the City of Fort Pierce. I'm not sure why she came to visit me, except that her husband was in the citrus business and my partner at the time, Richard Sneed, had several citrus clients. I had none.

In the accident in question, Linda had sustained what she referred to as a "serious whiplash injury." She had gone to Indian River Memorial from the accident scene and was later treated by Dr. Hooshang Hooshmand, a neurologist in Vero Beach, Florida. She also came under the care of an old chiropractor in Fort Pierce, Florida, named Dr. Gardner.

In my office, Linda's symptoms were: (a) headache, (b) sore neck, (c) restricted range of motion of the neck, and (d) occasional pain and numbness down one of her two arms. She said the injury was making it difficult for her to sleep.

From the accident report prepared by the Vero Beach Police Department, I noted that one of the witnesses to the accident listed was a highway patrolman. The accident report did not extensively discuss what this witness saw, but it did indicate that the driver of the large pickup truck was at fault in the accident based on the evidence that the police officer found, including witnesses.

I signed Mrs. Matthews and her husband up as clients. I also proceeded to order the medical records from the hospital, Dr. Hooshmand, and Dr. Gardner.

The next day, I called the local highway patrol station and was able to speak to the trooper who witnessed the accident. He recanted to me the following story:

> I was standing next to the road two lanes away from where the crash occurred. I noticed a small pick-up truck pull up to the red light and I was taken by the beauty of its driver. This red-headed lady was an absolute knockout and as I was looking at her, I heard the loud screech and saw this large pick-up truck slam into the rear of her truck. The nice lady seemed to be injured at the scene.

The highway patrolman confirmed my thoughts that we had good liability and further that my client was an amazingly beautiful woman.

We had a solid defendant with lots of coverage.

There were, however, some negatives in the case. First of all, the accident happened in Indian River County, which, even at that time, was one of the most Republican counties in the state. The county was also ethnically pure in that you rarely saw any Black faces or brown faces when you looked at a jury venire in Vero Beach. In addition, the injury was "just a whiplash." At the time of this accident, cervical flexion and extension injuries were ridiculed by numerous jokes on television. Many people did not believe that this was a real injury.

In the early eighties, a good result from a whiplash injury was in the \$15,000–\$20,0000 range. Results of zero to \$5,000 were much more common.

I went and talked to Dr. Gardner, the chiropractor, a couple of months after I signed the case up. Linda was still seeing him and getting treatment for her neck injury. She liked the fact that she did not have to take drugs and that she always felt temporarily better after leaving the chiropractor's office.

Dr. Gardner was a nice man who indicated to me that he would give Linda a 5 percent whole person impairment from the accident. He explained that she still had spasm in the neck months after the accident and was experiencing some pains down the arm, although they were getting less. He was of the opinion that there might be a pinched nerve situation going on. Amazingly, the defense never took a deposition of the chiropractor, Dr. Gardner.

Ninety days after the accident, Dr. Hooshmand had written a report and opined that Linda Matthews had a 3 percent whole person impairment. I took that report as well as all the records in the case and made a demand on the insurance company. Linda just wanted her medical bills paid and a little more. She said that she would be more than happy to accept the sum of \$15,000. I tried to settle the case for a small amount more than that but was unsuccessful. The insurance company tried to get out of the case by only paying us \$5,000. This was totally unacceptable to Linda and her husband.

I filed suit on the case and thought long and hard about possibly filing a loss of consortium claim for Ricky. A loss of consortium claim is based upon the fact that the spouse of an injured person has to go through a great deal in treating his spouse and helping them get back to normal living. A consortium claim is for "loss of services." Particularly in low back cases, there might be a tremendous drop in sexual activity. Under English common law, only the husband had the right to a loss of consortium claim. In the last one hundred years, women have gained that right as well.

I noticed from looking at other verdicts around the country that the consortium claims for husbands, if they were successful, generally resulted in a pittance. However, there had been some substantial consortium claims pursued by the wives of injured husbands. I discussed this matter with my clients, and they agreed that I would not be filing a loss of consortium claim.

Ricky told me that if necessary, he would testify on behalf of his wife regarding her condition. He said, however, that he was extremely busy as he and his brother owned a citrus servicing company which worked for numerous grove owners. They would trim the trees, clean out the brush in the groves, apply fertilizer, and assure that the proper irrigation was getting to the trees. He was busy all the time.

I took the deposition of the John's Island driver as soon as I could after filing suit. I must tell you that John's Island, at the time, was the nicest and most upscale neighborhood in the Orchard Island section of Vero Beach. Orchard Island bordered the Indian River on one side and the Atlantic Ocean on the other. It was a lush island, and all the homes on the island were expensive. John's Island Corporation was still advertising heavily but was noted to be extremely successful in their endeavors.

At the deposition of the driver, he wove a story that Linda had suddenly changed lanes in front of him and slammed on brakes. We locked that story in. Defense counsel in the case was Everett VanGasbeck, an attorney who, at that time, was an old hand at civil trial law up in Vero Beach, Florida. Everett scheduled the deposition of the highway patrolman, and he repeated the story he had told to me earlier. Everett did not look troubled by that.

The defense also took the deposition of Dr. Hooshmand. Dr. Hooshmand testified that he had given Mrs. Matthews a 3 percent whole person impairment. He said he feared that she had a herniated disc because she had intermittent pain and paresthesia down one of her arms. He said that symptom seemed to be lessening, however. Dr. Hooshmand indicated that the only way to find out whether a herniated disc was present at that time was to put the patient in the hospital and administer a very painful test called a myelogram. MRI was a very new technology which was only being researched and tested at the time. There was no MRI facility in the four county area.

In a myelogram, a radioactive dye is injected directly into the cerebral spinal fluid around the spine. Once it has been evenly dispersed, an x-ray is taken which would show any abnormalities of the disc in the spine. A myelogram was routinely given to patients in advance of surgery on the spine. Dr. Hooshmand said that he did not want to put his patients through that test unless it was absolutely necessary.

Judge Charles Smith's two-week trial docket was to start on a Monday. I attended the docket call on the prior Thursday and was one of approximately twenty cases on the docket. Before the docket call was concluded, there were only thirteen cases remaining to be tried, and Judge Smith lined them up, one after the other. He told us the first two cases had to be at the courthouse on Monday morning, with their client, ready to proceed with the trial. As my case was only number eleven at the end of the docket call, I figured the chances of us getting to trial within the next two weeks were slim to none.

Late in the day on Friday, Judge Smith called me at my office. The call was from him directly, not through his judicial assistant. He said, "Mr. Messer, you're now number two. You need to be at my courtroom in Vero Beach on Monday morning at nine o'clock with your client to proceed to trial, if necessary."

I had previously subpoenaed my witnesses, and our office contacted them and requested they be ready.

I immediately called Linda and informed her of the change. She seemed to be happy that we were actually to this point in the case. We made no progress regarding settlement in the case, although the defense understood we would accept the sum of $15,000. They were still at only $5,000. I was told by Ricky that he would not be able to attend the trial on Monday as he was backed up at work.

Around 8:30 a.m. on Monday, I pulled into the parking lot at the Vero Beach Courthouse. Following me into the parking lot was a new shiny Jaguar automobile. I was fumbling around with my paperwork when I noticed a gentleman exit the Jaguar. He was dressed to the nines. I wondered to myself, *What fancy lawyer is this guy?*

Linda was waiting for me in the courtroom as well as our court reporter. The only representative of the defendant there was Everett VanGasback. Judge Smith came on the bench and told us that our case was now number one and we should be ready to proceed. Mr. VanGasback indicated to the court that his client nor the insurance company representative were here and might not be able to make it until the afternoon. The judge informed Mr. VanGasback, "That's okay. I'm going to proceed with voir dire now."

The jury venire of about twenty-five members filed into the courtroom and took seats. The attractive and nattily dressed Jaguar driver was, to my shock, the juror in seat number one

I was also surprised to see that out of the twenty-five jurors, there was only one African American. There was also only about seven women. Almost all the White men present had at least a tie on. I thought to myself, *Boy, this is a conservative group.*

While the judge was doing his initial questions to the jury, I noticed that juror number one was staring at Linda Matthews and also had the twinkling of a smile on his face. I looked at Linda and noticed that she was aware that she was being looked at, and she seemed to be looking back. I imagined that there was a relationship going on between the two of them, although they had never met.

This trial took place in 1982, and I had not yet attended any AFTL seminars on voir dire. I'd gotten some terrible advice from a couple of non-trial lawyers, including my partner. My partner told me to "avoid jurors from the New England states." Another attorney told me to be careful to keep Jews off the jury. I thought that was strange. I decided to do my best and work without a net.

When I began questioning the jurors, I went down the line and spoke to juror number one first. I learned that he was a graduate of a prestigious though not quite Ivy League liberal arts college in New England. His accent did not disclose where in New England he was from. He was certainly not from Massachusetts or New York and probably also was not from New Jersey. I became very concerned when I learned that his occupation was a real estate developer. He was either a competitor of the defendant, John's Island, or one who might work with them occasionally. I was very careful to find out that the latter was not the case. I thought that if he were on the jury, he understood money and might give us a nice award.

I noticed throughout my questioning that the juror was not looking at me but was looking at Linda, who was sitting at counsel table.

I didn't know much yet about having a juror removed for cause, but the judge did remove one that knew Mr. VanGasback. He also eliminated one of the jurors who was hard of hearing. The Black man never got to the final cut in the jury box.

When it came time to do peremptory challenges, I got rid of the two jurors in the box who concerned me the most. One of my peremptories was to remove a White girl from the panel. This girl was, unfortunately, rather plain-looking and seemed to resent my client, but we could not nail her down to bias. She was the first person I removed from the panel. I looked at the remainder of the venire and couldn't help but notice that juror number one was still looking at my client. I thought to myself that he could be wonderful for us, or he could be death for us. I discussed this last selection with Linda, and she told me that she really liked the guy. That did it for me. I went with my gut and kept what I thought was a dangerous juror on the panel. We wound up with five White men, two of them in suits, and one elderly and attractive grandmother. The alternate was another White male.

At the time the jury was sat, the judge broke for lunch at 12:30 p.m. About 11:30 a.m., the insurance adjuster showed up and caught the last of the jury voir dire.

At the start of the break, Everett VanGasback approached me with a statement that "My insurance adjuster is here now. We've decided to pay the $15,000 your client had said she would take before the trial." I asked him whether or not the insurance adjuster believed that the jury panel was as good for us as I thought. He grudgingly said that I'd done a good job.

I spoke to Linda, and she told me to reject the offer. That we had gone this far, and she did not want to back down.

The trial itself only lasted three days. Our star witness was the highway patrolman in full uniform. He repeated the statement he made regarding noticing how beautiful Linda was as she was sitting at the red light. He said she had been sitting there a few seconds before her accident happened and that she looked to be injured in the aftermath of the accident.

We called the defendant driver to the stand, and he repeated his testimony that Linda had cut him off suddenly and slammed on her brakes. He could not be shaken from that story, even by the cross-examination of Mr. VanGasback.

Dr. Hooshmand testified to his 3 percent impairment rating and explained what it was based on. It was based upon the AMA Guides to Impairment. He explained what the AMA guides were to the jury. He said that Mrs. Matthews would continue to suffer with exacerbations of pain in her neck and periodic episodes or restricted range of motion for the rest of her life.

We placed the mortality tables into evidence which showed that Linda Matthews had remaining life expectancy of fifty-one years. It had already been almost two years since the date of the accident. One of my last witnesses was Dr. Gardner, the chiropractor. He testified to the 5 percent impairment. He explained what subtle adjustments that he would continue to make with Linda's neck. He explained that this did not result in any trauma to the neck but usually resulted in a lessening of the symptoms. He said that the relief was not permanent. He said that Mrs. Matthews would need that treatment for some time in the future. He was nonspecific about that portion of his testimony.

Mr. VanGasback decided to cross-examine the chiropractor. I had already gone over the chiropractor's educational and chiropractic experiences. Everett asked Dr. Gardner why he had given Linda a 5 percent impairment while Dr. Hooshmand had given her a 3 percent impairment using the same AMA Guides.

Dr. Gardner explained that he had not read Dr. Hooshmand's report. He also said, "I want to show you something." Dr. Gardner brought the x-ray of Linda's spine onto the screen. He had previously shown this to the jury but had been very cursory in his discussion of it. He pointed to the read and said, "You see this?" He was pointing to a slight anomaly in the alignment of the vertebrae. He said, "This is an unstable area of the spine which was caused by the accident. This does not get better. In fact, it may deteriorate. This lady is going to have pain in her neck for the rest of her life."

I decided then and there to not worry about putting a good chiropractor on the stand in an injury case.

I decided to not put Ricky Matthews on the stand at all. I wished that I had had a suitable before and after witness lined up. We learn as we go along.

The jury went into the jury room and began deliberation as soon as our short closing arguments were completed. I thought I'd only done an adequate job on closing argument and felt the case looked pretty good. The jury stayed in the jury room for just under two hours. When they came out, I was not surprised that juror number one was holding the verdict form and was the foreman of the jury. The verdict form first found that John's Island was negligent and that their negligence caused the injury to the plaintiff, Linda Matthews. Linda was found not to be negligent. The jury awarded damages for all past medical expenses and a small amount for future medical expenses in the case. For the intangible damages such as pain and suffering and loss of ability to enjoy life, the jury awarded $2,000 for the approximately two years since the date of the crash. For her future intangible damages, the jury awarded $51,000. I looked at the verdict and realized they had given her $1,000 a year for the last two years and $1,000 a year for the rest of her life. I think we got very lucky on this case, but I resolved to do better in the future and not to ignore "simple" whiplash injuries.

Epilogue

As I said before, the Matthews resided in a rural area of the county. The folks in that area were quite close-knit. Everyone out there knew everybody else. They went to the same churches, and their kids went to the same schools. They generally discussed everything. This was the first rural client that I had in my practice here in St. Lucie County, but thankfully, I've gotten approximately one such case a year for the last forty years.

Five years or so after the trial, I saw Ricky and Linda in a restaurant in Fort Pierce. They smiled at me and introduced me to one of their friends. They also had a baby sitting in a child restraint seat at the table. Linda was still strikingly beautiful.

In this case, I came up with my theory which still stands today. "Attractive clients get attractive verdicts."

BOOK 5

Motorcycle

Chapter 17

A motorcycle is an inherently dangerous form of transportation. In my forty-five-year career, I've handled literally hundreds of injury cases. Of those, only ten cases in my practice involved motorcycle accidents. A couple of those were death cases.

In all the cases I handled of all types, I've only had five cases where a crash victim suffered a loss of limb. One hundred percent of those five cases came from the motorcycle crashes I handled. People, particularly elderly people in South Florida, do not see motorcycles coming. Sometimes when they see a motorcycle coming, they panic and turn into the motorcycle.

There are cases where neither the motorcycle driver nor the driver in another automobile cause an accident which obviously occurred.

Back in 1983, my friend, Defense Attorney Mark Orr, referred me the case of Terry McIntosh (not her real name). Terry came into my office in Fort Pierce on crutches because she was missing her leg from the knee down on the right side. Terry was a very attractive twenty-five-year-old blond girl. She had a sharp mind.

Before Mark forwarded me this case, he had actually settled the case against the vehicle that hit Terry for their meager $10,000 limits.

I could not figure why the other party paid the claim, except that Terry's damages were so horrendous.

According to the accident report, the automobile involved in the crash was driven by one Pearl Harper (her real name). Ms. Harper was driving south on St. James while Terry was driving north. Suddenly, Terry's motorcycle veered into the oncoming lane. She almost made it past the car toward the ditch, but her right ankle was hit by the edge of the car, and it traumatically amputated her foot at the scene. The motorcycle was not knocked over but ended up in a large patch of briars at the side of the road. The machine was still upright. When the emergency personnel arrived, the motorcycle was still running.

I asked Terry about the history of the motorcycle. She told me she had purchased it from an ad in the newspaper for a used Kawasaki motorcycle. She said it looked pretty. She indicated that she and her boyfriend had gone over with his pickup truck and put the motorcycle in the back in the bed of the truck and brought it to their home on Fort Pierce South Beach. When they got it home after purchase, the boyfriend told Terry that he was going to test drive the motorcycle by driving it around the block to make sure it was okay for her to drive. He did that. The boyfriend came back and told Terry that he did not believe the motorcycle in question was safe. He said there was something wrong with the steering.

Terry decided to have the motorcycle repaired at the local Kawasaki dealer, JB Kawasaki, in Fort Pierce. I asked Terry if she had any of the paperwork from the purchase or repair of the motorcycle. She shocked me by telling me that she "never" threw away that kind of paperwork. I asked her to bring it in to me.

The motorcycle was supposedly repaired, and her boyfriend picked it up with his truck. The motorcycle was placed in the garage, and the next weekend, Terry went out riding with friends who were also motorcycle enthusiasts. There was a beautiful drive called St. James Boulevard which ran north and south from Port St. Lucie to Fort Pierce. In those days, it was only two lanes, and it was a winding road with beautiful trees and shrubs on either side. There were also some wild areas with native vegetation which could use some tending to.

Terry explained to me that as she was coming north on St. James, her motorcycle revved up to approximately thirty-five miles an hour. Suddenly, the front tire of the motorcycle began to wobble crazily, and before she could put on the brakes, the motorcycle suddenly veered across oncoming traffic with the horrible result we discussed.

The EMTs picked up the severed foot at the scene and transported Terry to Lawnwood Regional Medical Center. At Lawnwood, they could not save the rest of her lower leg, and it had to be amputated at the knee.

Before she left my office, I established that Terry also had an automobile that had a (minimal) $10,000 UM policy attached. I figured that if the underlying case was settled against the other driver so easily, this should be an easy matter to settle for $10,000. We would worry about the rest of the case later.

Soon, Terry came back to my office. The paperwork that Terry produced included a bill of sale from a private individual who no longer lived in town. The materials from JB Kawasaki were interesting. From that paperwork, you could see that the motorcycle was dropped off there with problems with the steering. JB Kawasaki had indicated to them that they would take care of the problem and fix anything that was wrong. They also said they would replace the ball bearings and races which they believed was the problem that caused the steering problem. There was also a signed authorization by Terry for JB Kawasaki to test drive the motorcycle before they returned it to her. They had been billed for new races and ball bearings and for labor.

I asked Terry where the motorcycle was, and she said, "On the day of the accident, my boyfriend put it in the back of his truck, and it sits in my garage under a tarp since that time." I knew that without the device, we would not be able to prove any faulty repair of the motorcycle.

I researched and came to believe that the number one motorcycle expert in the state was a man named Scott Guthrie from

Tallahassee, Florida. I hired him to assist in the case. A couple of days later, he came down from Tallahassee and wanted me to take him out to the accident scene. It had been several months since the accident happened, and I didn't know what he would find there that might help him. We drove out to the collision scene, and he asked me to help him scour the ground near where the motorcycle had obviously wound up in the briars. To my surprise, he found several small pieces of the motorcycle in the grass. While I was helping him, I had the good fortune of finding a faded ten-dollar bill. I thought to myself, this will not come close to paying the cost I'm spending on Scott Guthrie today.

Scott told me he wanted to take his trailer over to Terry's home and place the motorcycle on the back of the trailer, and he would then take the motorcycle to his research facility up in Tallahassee, Florida. He promised to videotape all the tests that he performed.

While this testing was being performed, Terry was attempting to be fitted for a prosthetic leg. That proved to be somewhat difficult. She still had the feeling of pain down into the foot that no longer existed. Sometimes, the throbbing was almost impossible to bear.

A couple of weeks later, I received a telephone call from Scott Guthrie. He told me he was putting his findings in writing, but he wanted to give me the heads-up. He said that first of all, the ball bearings and races had not been replaced. The ball bearings were quite worn, though they had been recently greased. The races involved in the bike had rust in them, which had been there a while. JB Kawasaki had charged them for new races and ball bearings they had not installed those. He also said that very likely was not the cause of the accident. He had put the motorcycle on a treadmill. He had a device that prevented it from tipping over as it was running down the treadmill. The entire test was videotaped. Shortly after the motorcycle obtained the speed of thirty-five miles an hour, the front wheel began to vibrate and gyrate on its axle, and had the motorcycle not been secured to the device, it would have veered off in one direction or another.

Scott explained that after this test was performed, he performed it a second time to make sure the same thing happened. It did.

Scott then took out some measuring devices and lined the motorcycle up. He discovered that the motorcycle had been in a previous accident. There was evidence of prior repairs. Unfortunately, when the cycle had been repaired, the front wheel and back wheel were not in alignment. They were a little less than half an inch off. Scott was of the opinion that this bike should have been trashed and not sold. He was also of the opinion that the Kawasaki dealer should have noticed this problem if they had, in fact, test driven the repair prior to returning it to Terry.

I filed suit against JB Kawasaki and alleged that they were negligent in repairing the motorcycle and that they were negligent in causing the accident. I had done a study of jury verdicts in Florida involving a single limb amputation, principally legs. Several of those were motorcycle cases. The low end of the verdict range was around $300,000 when liability was certain. The upper range was just short of $500,000. You must remember that this was the early eighties. These kinds of cases, I'm sure, result in much higher verdicts at this time.

I put together a settlement package for the insurance company, which included a copy of Scott Guthrie's film on the motorcycle as well as a copy of the documents which we had in hand. We also included my study of jury verdicts in this kind of case.

Before they let the case go to trial, the insurance company settled this case for $450,000, a settlement which was more than welcomed by Terry, as well as Mark Orr and myself.

Our attorney's fees in that case came to $150,000. Terry was able to keep $300,000, tax-free. Twenty-five percent of my fee I paid over to Mark Orr for the referral. Even today, the standard referral fee on cases such as this is 25 percent of the fee the working attorney receives.

Not many attorneys in the area referred cases to me over the years. Mark was the exception, and there were a couple of other criminal defense attorneys who referred me cases from time to time.

Epilogue

Approximately four years later, Terry came into my office in Fort Pierce, and while she was wearing slacks, I noted that she had a prosthetic leg below the knee on the right side. She was able to walk with no limping whatsoever. She said that she would be forever thankful for what we did on her behalf.

BOOK 6

Trademark Infringement

Chapter 18

In 1985, Myra DeLuca (not her real name) and Ellen Irving (not her real name) were partners in a home building business in Port St. Lucie, Florida. They had formed the corporation the year before when each of them put in an equal amount of money. They had hired an excellent contractor and had built a model home, and the business was taking off. There were yard signs placed on jobs that had quite distinctive logos. It had a picture of a home on it with a statement "Myelle Homes" and the phone number.

Myra had the office of president of the corporation while Ellen was the secretary and treasurer. Ellen was principally in charge of making sure the contractor and his people were doing their job while Myra's job was to do sales in the model home.

Things worked out fairly well between the sisters in the first year, and they both received nice bonuses at the end of the year as a share of the profit. Shortly after that occurred, Myra and her husband went on a two-week vacation. Her first day back from vacation, Myra did not notice a change in the sign in front of the business or a change in any of the yard signs which were stacked up in the office. However, a couple of days later, she looked at the signs and realized there had to have been a misprint on the signs. All the color schemes were the same, the font was all the same, but the bold letters had been changed from "MYELLE" to "MYLEE." Myra thought at first that this was a misprint and that the signs had been ordered in error.

There had been several contracts Myra was working on when she left on vacation. Ellen was to complete those. Myra pulled those contracts from the file and was shocked to see the name "Myelle Homes" had been changed in all of them to "Mylee Homes." The contracts were signed, and apparently, construction was likely underway.

Mrs. DeLuca contacted the Secretary of State's Office at the State of Florida. She inquired as to whether or not there were any corporations named Mylee Homes, and to her shock, there was. She looked at the incorporation papers, and Ellen and her husband were all over the pages, but there was no mention of Myra. They were, effectively, shutting her out of the business without a by your leave. There was not even an offer for her to be paid back the money she had brought into the business to start with.

Myra came into my office in Fort Pierce with her evidence. She had one of the old signs as well as one of the new signs. She also had copies of some of the contracts. I realized there was a major fraud that took place but thought seriously about the facts of this case and told her I would get back to her in a few days after working on it. I realized that in addition to fraud, there was very likely a violation of copyright laws, even though the name Myelle Homes had not been copyrighted.

The first year I worked as a law clerk with David DeSerrio, there was a law clerk there that was a senior at Stetson and was nearing graduation. He was a very nice guy named Ronald Greigg. Ron's father was a big-time patent lawyer in Washington, DC, and I knew that when Ron graduated, he was going to work there.

I gave Ron a call and outlined the facts of this case. I sent him pictures of the two signs. He assured me that this was an obvious violation of the common law trademark law and was further a fraud regarding the trademark in question. I asked him if he would be an expert for us in the case, and he said he would.

Not too long before my conversation with him, Ron and his wife and kids came down to Florida and spent a little bit of time with us. His wife's parents lived in the Tampa Bay area, and they had been visiting them there. They had driven down from Washington DC and decided to drive over to the east coast of Florida to speak with me and spend the night. So we were pretty close to Mr. Greigg and his family. Ron told me he would not charge me a fee as an expert witness of anything more than the defense would have to pay, but that he would do a bill. He told me he would not charge me for the transportation down here by air but would appreciate it if he would put him up in my spare bedroom once more while he was here for the trial. I was delighted with that arrangement.

I did not believe it was proper to give the perpetrator any advanced warning of what we were doing. I called my client and received permission to go ahead and proceed with the lawsuit. We filed it here in St. Lucie County in Circuit Court, and it was assigned to Judge Charles Smith, who had recently been reassigned to St. Lucie County from Indian River County.

A couple of days after I filed suit, I received a call from my reporter friend, Mary Jo Tierney, at the *News Tribune*. This was the same lady who filed a report on my first personal injury trial back in 1978. Mary Jo called me and told me that she had just read the court filing in *Myelle vs. Mylee* case. She noted that we had sued not only Mylee Homes but also Ellen Irving and her husband for their individual actions in causing this problem. She asked me to comment, and I made a brief comment to her. The next day in the *News Tribune*, there was a very nice story which quoted, word for word, many of the allegations in our complaint. There was also a statement that she had reached me for comment, and I explained the case to her. The Irvings were contacted, too, but refused to comment.

From that day forward, Mary Jo would hound me at least once every two to three weeks and ask me how the case was progressing.

After the initial hearing, Judge Smith granted an injunction preventing Mylee Homes from selling any more homes and preventing the distribution of any profit from the existing construction without further order of the court. The Irvings' lawyer was Mr. Buckman (not his real name) from a five-attorney firm in Stuart, Florida.

Unfortunately, Myra did not open a new corporation but, without discussing it with us, began to sell homes once more under the Myelle name. When the defense found out about that, they hit the roof and ultimately got an order from Judge Smith preventing Myra from doing any other business under the name of Myelle Homes.

I took depositions from some of the new home purchasers under the Mylee banner. A couple of them remembered that they had purchased these homes from Myelle Homes. One of the people referred to Myelle as "My Ellie." They said that even though they signed the contracts, they did not notice the change. The contracts also had the logo from the new Mylee signs printed on the contracts.

Trial was reached in this case in about a year from the date of filing, and we were to proceed in front of Judge Smith. Voir dire at the trial went very well for us. The voir dire started late and ran late. The judge had removed several jurors for cause, including one at my request.

I had not quite finished when we broke for the day. We were to finish voir dire early next morning. I went home exhausted. Betsey told me she didn't want to eat yet, but she asked me to take our son, Steven, out for a hamburger. We had just sat down after placing our order when a lady got up from her seat and approached us. She said, "Hi. Do you know who I am?"

I said, "Yes. You were on our jury panel today!"

She had been a lady I had removed for cause from the panel. She shocked me by saying, "We all liked you. The other lawyer just stands at the podium and looks at us over his glasses. He didn't seem friendly."

Boy, had I made a mistake bumping this juror. I decided to ask no more voir dire questions but take our chances with that group.

At the trial, Myra and her husband both testified to the truthfulness of the facts in our complaint. We called for one of the witnesses who said they had purchased homes under the Mylee name, thinking that they were purchasing from Myelle Homes. These people indicated that they had gotten recommendations for Myelle Homes by calling the homeowners who were happy with the construction of their houses.

Ron Greigg testified beautifully. He explained the nuance of English common law of trademarks which was the common law followed in the United States on this matter. He was allowed to assist the jury on the common law. There were two kinds of trademarks. One trademark where you register the trademark with the United States Patent Office. The other was a common law trademark which did not have to be registered. We had to prove that encroachment on that common law trademark occurred by competent evidence. In his qualifications, Ron described some of his companies that used his services. Those included Bic Pens from France as well as Shinley Liquor Brand, which was based in Canada. He also said that he had numerous other clients he helped with these issues. He said it was his opinion that the designs were so similar that they could be mistaken for each other. He said that was the gist of trademark infringement.

In our pleadings, we had sought both compensatory and punitive damages. Closing argument went well for us, I thought. I explained that this case screamed for punitive damages. There had been a deliberate attempt to defraud Myra and to steal the company from her. This was a cold act, whether or not the ladies were sisters. The jury was out perhaps an hour and a half and came back a plaintiff's verdict. They awarded approximately $300,000 in compensatory damages and $250,000 in punitive damages against Mr. and Mrs. Irving together. The day after the verdict, our victory was a front-page story.

As I indicated, Judge Smith was new to the bench. Unfortunately, he apparently heard about something called a motion for remittitur. The other side filed such a motion. The remittitur law in Florida was that the judge could reduce verdicts if they shocked his conscience. The judge granted a remittitur of $150,000 from the punitive damage award. He explained that we had not proved conclusively that the Irvings would be able to respond in damages without going bankrupt. This was despite the fact that during trial, we proved that they owned two Burger King franchises as well as an interest in a new home building endeavor.

Mary Jo did not write an article about the remitter, thankfully.

Under the remittitur statute, we had two choices. We could accept the judgment entered by the court, or we could reject it, in which case the court would schedule a new trial on everything. I felt that the money we were to receive was a little more than I expected anyway, and Myra did not want to go through a second trial. In addition to the amount of the judgments, we were entitled to our court costs back, including a fee for my friend, Ronald Greigg, as well as filing fees, deposition fees, etc.

Epilogue

Chapter 19

About two years later, Ellen sued her sister, Myra, and Myra's husband. She alleged that she and her husband had once loaned Myra and Mr. DeLuca funds for them to purchase an interest in a Burger King franchise. The amount of the funds in question was $150,000. There was paperwork that was obtained from DeLuca's bank which showed that about this time, there was a $150,000 deposit made. It had been almost four years that the deal allegedly took place. The statute of limitations is four years. There was no promissory note, although that is not necessary. There can be an oral promise that is enforceable. In addition, there was paperwork which showed that Mr. and Mrs. DeLuca had an ownership interest in a Burger King franchise with a down payment of $150,000.

I asked Myra about the $150,000. She explained that shortly before her mother's death, her mother had given her $150,000 so it would not go through an estate. Unfortunately, Mrs. DeLuca's mother could not testify to this as there is a "dead man statute" where you can't allege what a deceased person may have said while they were alive. Otherwise, there were also hearsay problems with that kind of testimony.

I asked Myra and her husband if there was anyone else in the world who was aware of the source of the $150,000, and they told me, "Yes." A cousin of the two girls was a bank vice president from New York City and educated. Myra explained this lady had been her and her husband's financial advisor back at the time this was taking place. The cousin gave free advice to them on all major financial moves that they were taking at that time when they resided in the State of New York. They said that she knew the source.

I was somewhat concerned I was forbidden from questioning the cousin about what her Aunt Molly did or did not do regarding $150,000.

In the trial, on direct, Mr. and Mrs. DeLuca both testified that the $150,000 was theirs and was never owned by the Irvings. Apparently, the Irvings had gotten Myra and her husband interested in purchasing a Burger King franchise, so they knew when the event took place.

On the plaintiff's side, the Irvings testified that they had, in fact, loaned the money in question with a promise to pay within four years. The statute of limitations on this type of contract at the time in Florida was four years. A written contract at that time would be five years.

We had listed the cousin as a witness, but defense counsel had not taken her deposition.

We called the cousin to enter the courtroom as a witness. We had listed her several months before on our witness list. The attorney pursuing this case on behalf of the Irvings was Willie Gary, a famous trial lawyer from Stuart, Florida. Willie always worked on behalf of plaintiffs, and for me, this was the first defense case I'd ever been on. Unfortunately for Willie, he had not bothered to go to New York and take the deposition of the cousin of both of those ladies. When we were about to break for lunch, the judge asked how many more witnesses we had and the order, and I announced the name of the cousin.

Mr. Gary spoke up and said, "Your Honor, I've not had an opportunity to take this person's deposition, and I don't know what they're going to say."

The judge told him, "Fine, you can talk with this lady over the lunch hour, but we're going to proceed at the usual time."

I went out to the hallway and saw the banker, who was appropriately dressed in a business suit. She just looked like a banker. I sat with her as Mr. Gary went over what she might know with regard to ownership of the property. She said that she was absolutely certain the money was owned by Myra and her husband.

I didn't think Willie had accomplished anything (except causing us to miss lunch) when the hour expired, and we went back into the courtroom, accompanied by the new witness.

She testified on direct to the fact that she knew who owned the money and had counseled Myra and her husband about the purchase of the Burger King franchise which this nice lady said was always an excellent investment. On cross-examination, Willie tried to shake the story of the cousin. Willie was very brusk and loud, and the jury was put off by that, I thought. He made a huge mistake, however. Willie asked a question he did not know the answer to, which you should never do on cross-examination.

Willie's question was "Isn't it true that all you know about this $150,000 is what Myra and her husband told you?"

The lady said, "No, that's not true."

He asked that question a second time with the same answer. Then he asked the bomb of a question. "How do you know it was their money?"

The banker smiled, leaned back in the chair, and said, "Because my aunt Molly told me she gave them the $150,000 when I was visiting her on her deathbed."

Willie objected to the answer. You are not allowed to object to answers, only to questions. The judge overruled the objection.

Closing argument was pretty straightforward, and the jury took the case back to the jury room for deliberation. My clients and I were sitting in the courtroom and waiting for their return as we did not know how long it was going to take, and it was getting late in the day, so we didn't want to go out to dinner. During the deliberation, on the other side of the courtroom, they were celebrating. Willie's partner at the time, JD Lewis, was there, as were a couple of members of their staff as well as the Irvings. Everyone seemed to be celebrating and having a good time.

Willie came over to my counsel table and said, "Roger, you fought the good fight. I want to invite you over to my office in Stuart, Florida, this evening for our victory celebration. The Ink Spots are in town." Willie was very much into soul music, as was I. He had booked the Ink Spots live.

I replied, "Willie, first of all, I don't like attending wakes. There will be no victory celebration at your office. I intend to have a victory party with my clients tonight." Willie closed his mouth and walked back across the courtroom.

About an hour after the deliberation started, the jury came back with a zero verdict for the Irvings. We were ecstatic. There was an appeal filed, which went absolutely nowhere. I believe it was dismissed after receipt of the briefs.

Myra had opened her own home building business and would continue in that business until her retirement. I do not believe the two sisters ever spoke again.

Three or four years later, I was attending a Workhorse Seminar with the Academy of Firodia Trial Lawyers and was standing outside the seminar room, speaking on the phone to my office. As I was about to hang up, I saw Willie Gary and another lawyer I did not know walking down the hallway. They stopped, and Willie introduced me to his friend as "one of the few guys that's ever kicked my ass."

A year later, I was watching a show on television called *Lifestyles of the Rich and Famous*. Robin Leach was the host, and he had an episode on Willie Gary and how successful his practice was. Robin Leach told everyone in the country that Willie Gary had never lost a case. I realized then the hyperbole that you can get on network television and further realized that some of the "facts" recited by them may be just made up.

Nowadays, I consider myself a friend of Willie Gary and his former partner, JD Lewis. Life is too short to make enemies.

BOOK 7

Law Enforcement

Chapter 20

How did I become involved in so many injury cases involving police officers?

I had met Bill Hardman somewhere around 1986 when I was coaching Little League with Bill's father at the Fort Pierce American Little League. Bill had a team in the adjacent Fort Pierce National Little League that he managed. We sometimes practiced together with that team. Bill got me involved as an umpire with the league, and together, we got selected for the district umpires' group and became good friends.

Not long after I met him, Bill Hardman had graduated from the Police Academy and was hired as a St. Lucie County sheriff's deputy. He soon became very prolific at arresting and ultimately prosecuting drunk drivers. The sheriff's department had a "Citizens Ride-Along" policy which allowed private citizens, like me, to accompany the officer once we had signed a complete and total release of any liability for any injuries or death we might receive as a result of being there.

I accompanied Bill, perhaps ten times, over a five-year period that he was the star of the DUI Task Force. I was impressed that Bill made the Governor's Task Force every year and, many years, finished in the top three among successful DUI arrests throughout the

State of Florida. He and I had gone up to Tallahassee for the award a couple of times. His last year in that position, he arrested (and got convictions) of over 490 drunk drivers.

Not long after Bill had become a road deputy, one of their female deputies, Jennifer Shoals (not her real name), was responding to an emergency crash well west of Fort Pierce on Highway 68, almost out to Okeechobee County. Dispatch had told her that that crash involved injured children.

Jennifer was traveling at a high rate of speed with blue lights flashing and her siren screaming. There was very little traffic on the road. Jennifer was approaching a slow-moving semi-tractor trailer on the two lane road in rural St. Lucie County. She pulled into the left lane, as there was no oncoming traffic, and just as she got even with the cab of the semi, the driver of the semi-tractor trailer suddenly, and without warning, decided to turn left into a driveway. He slammed into the police cruiser, causing it to jump off the road and down into a ditch that was perhaps twelve feet deep. The accelerator on the cruiser was stuck, and it crawled its way up the opposite side of the ditch to slam into a stone barrier. The airbag and seat belt restraints worked very well in the first crash with the semi. Unfortunately, immediately after the airbags deploy, they shrink back to normal. When the second collision occurred with the bank of the ditch, Jennifer's chest came into contact with the center of the steering column. Luckily, she was wearing a Kevlar vest, which was severely damaged in the collision. It probably saved her life.

Jennifer had several fractured ribs and a fractured sternum, but she lived.

Bill Hardman, who was her friend, referred her to my office, and we ultimately filed suit. Shortly after filing suit, the case was settled on a confidential basis.

Police officers talk a lot with each other. Over the years, Bill Hardman or Jennifer referred me numerous other cases involving either sheriff's deputies or city police officers from the two cities in our county. Two of the nastier cases involved motorcycle cops. Even these settled without a trip to court.

A very nice female road deputy, Naomi Valenzuela (not her real name), was sitting at a red light at Bayshore Boulevard and Prima Vista Boulevard in Port St. Lucie, Florida. A cable installation van rammed her vehicle at a high rate of speed. Later, the van driver testified that as he was driving along Prima Vista Boulevard, he noticed somebody he knew on a wheelchair on the sidewalk. He said he turned to stare at them as he was going past, and when he looked back, he was right on top of the rear bumper of the Valenzuela vehicle. Naomi's vehicle had then crashed into the car in front of her. Naomi had significant neck injury requiring anterior cervical discectomy and fusion surgery. She had a lesser injury to her lower back which required less serious surgery.

I believe that insurance companies are not anxious to take cases to trial when there is so much sympathy on behalf of the victim of the crash. Jurors generally respect law enforcement officers.

Naomi was a single mom with two very well-behaved children. She was strikingly attractive. She had a very sweet disposition, and she had gone through hell as a result of the momentary negligence of the driver of the cable company's truck.

I filed suit against the cable company and the driver involved in the crash. They had substantial insurance. The discovery was quite easy from our standpoint, and I could not see any negatives in the case whatsoever.

The defense did take the deposition of Naomi, and she stood up to that very well. The defense had intimated that Naomi had stopped way too close to the rear bumper of the car in front of her. They also intimated that Naomi must have stopped suddenly in front of the truck, which was absolutely not the case. Naomi calmly testified that she had been sitting behind that car for perhaps twenty seconds before the collision occurred. She testified that she was "at least six feet" behind the rear bumper of that car. On deposition, the defense lawyer asked her how she was sure that she was at least six feet, and her response was "I always stop about that far for a couple of reasons." First of all, she said she wants to be close enough, but not too close, to read the tag number on the vehicle in front of her. She, while stopped at a red light, would submit those tag numbers to the database to determine if the car in front was stolen. She did this every time she stopped behind a vehicle and had a moment to complete the task. She also explained that she was taught at the police academy to stop at a distance where she could see the back tires on the ground underneath the vehicle. She said that was so that if she was called on an emergency, she could turn on the blue light and siren and pull around that individual without striking them and proceed on the emergency call.

Naomi's testimony was solid, and the defense had nothing on her. Naomi had missed some work, especially around the time of her anterior cervical and discectomy fusion surgery from the neurosurgeon. She also missed time when her back surgery took place. We had attempted to mediate the case unsuccessfully, but shortly thereafter, the insurance company adjuster called and said the magic words. We were able to settle the case for $450,000 without going to trial.

By the time the case settled, Naomi was back on the road with the sheriff's department after a hiatus for several months.

Bill Hardman eventually made lieutenant in the sheriff's department and was given a much easier position than road deputy. He became the head of the bailiff's division at the courthouse. He supervised over fifty sheriff's deputies at both locations for the St. Lucie County Courthouse. In that position, Bill made my life much easier at court. He made sure I always had the best breakout room assigned to me. He had a key code to get in the door, and Bill gave me the code and told me he would not allow anyone else in that room during trials.

Over the years, I represented Bill Hardman in his own accident case. I also represented his wife, Zandra, in a separate accident case. I represented Zandra's brother, who had fallen in a large hole at a business, and I also represented her father in an accident case.

Deputy Hardman referred me at least six other cases of either sheriff's deputies, police officers, or the families of same. In one of those cases, the wife, mother-in-law, and sister-in-law of a deputy were hit in the rear at a high rate of speed by a drunk driver in Port St. Lucie. The drunk had gotten out of his vehicle, walked past the victims' car, and looked down and saw that they were all in distress.

He said, “Shit happens.” He decided to run from the scene on foot as his car was not operable. Of course, drunks do not run very fast, and the police, with the aid of a handy K-9, were able to apprehend this guy rather rapidly. All three of these cases ended well.

Relationships are extremely important in building a practice in a smaller town. None of these cases came to me as a result of any television or billboard advertising. Although those methods were now legal for attorneys. I do not advertise in that way. Some of those ads are okay. However, most are tasteless and create false ideas in the general public. It belittles our profession to see our services sold like dishwashing soap on television.

Chapter 21

Jason Pollack (not his real name) was a lieutenant in the Port St. Lucie Police Department, and he was in charge of the entire Traffic Enforcement Division. In 2007, Lieutenant Pollack was driving his police cruiser on St. Lucie West Boulevard, less than a mile from my office. He was stopped at the intersection of St. Lucie West Boulevard and Cashmere Boulevard. A drunk driver in a pickup truck, driving sixty miles an hour plus in a forty-mile-an-hour zone, smashed into the back of the police car. The police car was extremely damaged. The seat on the police car broke, and Lieutenant Pollack was severely injured.

When I first saw him, Lieutenant Pollack was in a great deal of pain, and his posture was like that of a ninety-year-old man with a bad back. Despite his posture, it was clear that Lieutenant Pollack was very tall, perhaps six feet, three inches, and was very trim and fit. Lieutenant Pollack's wife worked at a local Catholic elementary school, and they had a couple of children. Fairly soon after the accident occurred, Lieutenant Pollack had to have fusion surgery performed on his lower back. There was quite a time for rehabilitation from that surgery, and the lieutenant missed a lot of time from work.

Unfortunately, there was not a limitless amount of insurance coverage available to us. The drunk driver had a policy that was not big enough, only $50,000. The drunk driver also had no obvious ability to pay any excess verdict. In Florida, a person's homestead is exempt from claims of creditors so that while a driver may own his own house, you cannot take it away from him once you get a judgment. This right to a homestead exemption from attachment by creditors is enshrined in the Florida Constitution and has been so since 1868. Florida is the only state in the union that has such a provision, and it has been appealed to the highest court in Florida and has been affirmed.

Given the clear liability and damages in this case, it was relatively easy to get the uninsured motorist carrier to pay their limits, and the drunk driver's insurance company was begging us to take their limits. Jason Pollack did not think there was any future in obtaining a judgment for a large excess against the drunk driver. Any such judgment would ordinarily be discharged in bankruptcy.

We accepted the full limits in this case of $350,000 from the two insurance carriers. I then substantially reduced my fee from what was allowed by the courts in Florida. This type of reduction is routinely done by attorneys around the state who practice in this area ethically. Settlement was reached in early 2008.

Epilogue

Bill recently retired as a captain from the St. Lucie County Sheriff's Department. He was an extremely dedicated public servant. I still visit Bill at his home in Fort Pierce at least every month or two. He is a very funny individual. In later life, he became a stand-up comedian and created a country character for himself named Hank Western. He actually made some money on the circuit doing that, and I attended several of his concerts. He would tell stories in a dead-pan manner and always got lots of laughs. In his monologue, one of the jokes was that his daughter attended Penn State University, while his son was in the State Penn. Corny, but kind of funny.

Jennifer and Naomi are both still with the sheriff's department assisting the public. Lieutenant Pollack has advanced to a greater leadership role in the Port St. Lucie Police Department.

BOOK 8

Negligent Hiring and Entrustment

Chapter 22

I first met Janice DeLuca (not her real name) around 1980. Janice had called me at my office in Fort Pierce and asked me if I could travel down to Port St. Lucie to see her husband and discuss a case that they may have. She said her husband was extremely ill and could not get outside the house. I made an appointment to come down and see her and her husband that day.

Back in the early eighties, there were very few people living in Port St. Lucie, probably less than fifteen thousand. Port St. Lucie was the second-largest (by land size) city in the State of Florida. Only Jacksonville in northeast Florida boasted a larger footprint. It had been designed and built by General Development Corporation who had put in many miles of roads through the undeveloped area and installed sewer lines, etc. By the early 1980s, there was a smattering of neighborhoods at various places around this city. The homes back at that time were not of particularly high quality, and most of them were occupied by recent retirees from the northeastern United States, particularly New York.

I drove the twelve to fifteen miles from my home on surface roads. Interstate 95 was not completed in St. Lucie County at that time. The trip took thirty minutes.

I arrived at an uninteresting two-bedroom house which did not have a garage. There was a driveway, but in the driveway, there were a couple of cars, and I had to park on the street. When I got there, two of the DeLuca grown children were also present.

I entered the home, and in the living room, the family had set up a hospital bed that held Janice's husband, John. John looked really ill but still had his mind and could still talk. John explained to me that he was suffering from a cancer called mesothelioma. Mesothelioma, at that time, was an always fatal condition for which the only known cause was exposure to asbestos dust. The progression of the disease always started as asbestosis, which would often progress to mesothelioma.

I noticed in the *Journal of American Trial Lawyers Association* that there were numerous lawsuits filed around the country against a company known as John's Manville. John's Manville was the largest corporation with asbestos-based products. I had noted that John's Manville had recently lost a trial up north for one of their workers who had died from mesothelioma. From that story I read, I learned that the proof in that case showed that John's Manville knew of the carcinogenic properties of asbestos back in the 1930s. However, they did not do anything to protect their employees or the members of the public but proceeded to grow their company into a beast.

John's Manville controlled the mining of the asbestos which took place in Canada. Then that raw substance would be shipped to a few plants in the United States, including one in northern New Jersey.

John explained to me that he worked for approximately half a year for John's Manville at their New Jersey plant. I asked him what his job was. John said, "My job was unloading freight cars loaded with asbestos material." He said he worked with a shovel, along with several other guys in his crew. He indicated to me that every day, the asbestos dust was coating his coveralls when he got home. Janice verified that she would regularly wash those coveralls the night they were received and that generally, John would be wearing the same pants the next morning.

John DeLuca told me that he wanted me to handle the case because he very much wanted to take care of Janice after his passing. He explained that Janice had never worked outside the home, but she had been a great mother and housekeeper. I noted when I came in that the house was neat and clean on the inside. He said that she really didn't have any salable skills and had no experience with working for anyone else her entire life. John and Janice were both in their late fifties.

In addition to former employees of John's Manville, individuals who had been exposed to John's Manville's products and came down with mesothelioma were beginning to sue the company all over the country. There were literally thousands of lawsuits that had been filed in the last few weeks, after the verdict which I discussed above.

I told John and Janice that I would do what I could to help them. I noted that we needed to get a recorded sworn statement from John as soon as possible for use at trial as he might not be there for trial. John told me that they had given him less than one month to live. I stayed and talked with John and Janice and their son, who was present the entire time of our discussion. I had noted that the walls of their home contained pictures of Jesus Christ as well as a very large crucifix. There were pictures of the DeLuca family including John, Janice, and their two children, Angela and John Jr. There was also a large picture on the wall of John F. Kennedy. I must say that I was an avid Democrat, and the presence of that picture made me want to help John more.

I went back to my office in Fort Pierce and began to look for a videographer who could go to the DeLuca home and take a sworn statement from John. I intended to bring along my paralegal who was a notary public so she would notarize John's signature, acknowledging that he had given this statement and that it was true and correct.

The videographer I found told me they could be there on Friday of that week, which was only a couple of days away. I went ahead and scheduled that with the DeLuca family and was looking forward to seeing them sometime that Friday morning. I was told that generally, John was better in the morning.

Tragically, John DeLuca died the Thursday before he was supposed to give the statement. Janice was devastated. Janice called and asked if I could come talk to her. She was tied up until the funeral was to take place but wanted to see me the afternoon of the funeral. I told her I would attend the funeral with her and her family.

Approximately a week later, I went to St. Lucie Catholic Church in Port St. Lucie and attended my first Catholic funeral. I did not care for the service at all.

The church was huge, and John's casket was in front of the altar. The DeLuca family and I all sat in the front pew of the church. Very few other parishioners were present. Janice had told me that the church had given her a pretty hard time in scheduling things, but she had talked the local priest into officiating.

Very little of the ceremony was done in English. I understood some Latin, but not a lot. I particularly knew those Latin phrases that related to the practice of law. The funeral was long and drawn out, and no one spoke a eulogy for John DeLuca.

After the funeral, I accompanied Janice and her children back to her home in Port St. Lucie, and we sat and talked. I explained that I had almost gotten the lawsuit ready to file in the couple of days since I had seen them. I said I was going to amend that lawsuit so that it became a wrongful death action with Janice as the surviving spouse. I explained that she would be the one receiving the benefits of the case, if we were successful.

We took steps to have Janice appointed as personal representative of John's estate.

The next week, I filed suit against John Manville in federal court for the wrongful death of John DeLuca. We filed it in the US District Court of the Southern District of Florida. Less than twenty days after we filed the lawsuit and before John Manville had to file an answer to it, the corporation declared chapter 11 bankruptcy. Under the bankruptcy laws, the filing of bankruptcy petition puts an automatic stay on all pending litigation and all pending claims against the bankrupt. I could not move forward on Janice's claim as long as the bankruptcy was pending. I decided we would just sit on the file for as long as it takes and see what we could do for Janice later. We went ahead and filed a claim with the bankruptcy court.

At the time the bankruptcy was filed, there were literally tens of thousands of similar lawsuits filed around the country. Even though John's Manville supposedly had liquid assets of approximately $4 billion, it was felt that existing claims, plus all the other claims that were out there, would bankrupt them many times over.

I decided to put the DeLuca case on the back burner and would visit it again when the bankruptcy situation became clearer.

I lost track of Janice and her family, though she had given me her phone number and told me that she would let me know if that number changed.

Chapter 23

Several years later, I received a call from John DeLuca Jr. John Jr. told me that Janice was in the hospital with a severe injury which she had just suffered in an automobile crash. I asked him how Janice was doing, and he told me before this crash she was handling things better than he had expected. She had lost the family home because of lack of enough income to pay the mortgage. She had moved in with John Jr. and his family. He asked if I would go see Janice in the hospital, and I said, "Of course I will."

Later that day, I went to see Janice at St. Lucie Medical Center in Port St. Lucie, Florida. Janice had just been transferred from the ICU to the regular ward. Both legs were in casts and were elevated in a sling. Janice had tremendous trouble talking to me because in the accident she had "eaten the steering wheel" and had lost all but four of her teeth. Her jaw had also been broken. She had two broken kneecaps. She had almost died from fractured ribs. Ordinarily rib fractures aren't that significant, but in this case, one of the ribs had actually punctured her pericardium, and it was a close question as to whether or not Janice was going to live. Thankfully, the hospital staff had gotten it under control, and Janice was about to start the task of rehabilitation. John Jr. was present during my discussions with

Janice, and he explained to me his understanding of what happened to Janice in the accident. He explained that she had obtained a job as a cashier at a convenience store and that generally, she would leave for home around ten at night when the owner of the business would show up, close up, and look at the day's profits. On the evening in question, she was proceeding down Bayshore Boulevard in Port St. Lucie, heading south. A major intersection with Bayshore which was controlled by a stop sign was Carter Avenue. Carter had a stop sign which should prevent a driver from driving out onto Bayshore Boulevard, which was a busy thoroughfare. Suddenly, a commercial truck had blown through the stop sign and hit another vehicle with two women in it. Because of that collision, they had been pushed over into Janice's oncoming lane, and Janice crashed into the side of their car, head on.

I thought that if there was a commercial truck involved, we might have decent insurance. Janice did not have uninsured motorist insurance coverage. Janice signed my contract of representation.

I ordered the accident report which verified many of the facts which John Jr. had explained to me. I noted that the defendant driver was twenty years old, and he was driving a construction company small pickup truck at the time of the accident.

All three women had been injured in the crash and taken by ambulance to St. Lucie Medical Center. The at-fault driver was not hurt, nor was he checked for alcohol or drugs. His wife was allowed to drive him home.

I ordered from the State of Florida Department of Highway Safety and Motor Vehicle the complete driving record of this twenty-year-old driver. When I received it, I was shocked. This child had begun driving at age sixteen, and by the time he hit seventeen, he was incurring regular speeding tickets. Also, when he was seventeen, he was charged and convicted of driving under the influence of alcohol and had his license suspended. The license had only been reinstated seven days prior to our crash, and during those seven days, this bad boy had received another speeding ticket.

I decided to go ahead and file suit against this driver as well as the corporation he worked for. I learned that the corporation was insured by St. Paul Insurance, who only had a $300,000 single limit policy. That meant that regardless of how many people were injured, there was a maximum of $300,000 that could be collected against that insurance company.

Shortly after filing suit, I was contacted by my friend Attorney Paul Gamba from Stuart, Florida. I considered Paul to be an excellent trial lawyer. Paul explained to me that he had just filed, that day, a lawsuit on behalf of his client who was horribly injured in the accident. He also explained to me that Attorney Patrick Beatty, also of Stuart, had the other injured lady who wasn't hurt "that bad." Patrick had filed suit too. Paul explained that because the three ladies had all been injured in the same accident, there would be a requirement that the cases be tried together for judicial efficiencies. If we could have tried them separately, we would have had a much larger result. He said he understood there was only $300,000 in coverage, and he said his client was, at that time, unwilling to accept even that amount for her injuries. I assured him that Mrs. DeLuca would not accept that for her injuries either until we knew that was all there was available. We agreed to work together on liability.

Just as soon as I could legally do so, I set the deposition of the defendant driver, Johnny Ross (not his real name), to take place in my office in Fort Pierce. I notified not only the defense lawyer but also Paul Gamba and Patrick Beatty.

The deposition was extremely informative. I asked Mr. Ross about all his activities the day of the accident. His employer had just completed construction of a house. Ross said that they had finished working on the job and that the boss had a pizza and beer party afterward for all the guys who had done work. He explained that all the other workers, technically, did not work for the same company, but that the owner of the company, Mr. Romano, owned several of these corporations that he managed, and the corporations would work together to do his construction work.

I thought, *What an interesting way to limit one's liability.*

I asked him what he did after he left the pizza party. The pizza party took place in Port St. Lucie. Mr. Ross indicated that he drove up to Fort Pierce to a bar known as Dukes, and he attended Dukes's happy hour. He said, however, that he had not had anything to drink there but had gone to listen to the music. I thought, *Yeah, right!* The drinking age in Florida at that time was twenty-one years old.

I asked him what time he left there, and he said around 9:00 p.m. or 9:30 p.m. I asked, "Where did you go then?"

He answered, "I went to a friend's house located on Carter Avenue. I hung out there for a while and realized it was late and I needed to get home to my wife." He said because he was running late, he was going "a little too fast." He said he did not see the stop sign at the corner of Carter and Bayshore until the last second. He claimed to have "bailed out" before the collision occurred. I asked him to explain what "bail out" meant. He explained that in the one and a half seconds between his being at the stop sign and his striking the first car, he had turned loose the steering wheel and dove into the floorboard of the truck. Amazingly, the truck was going down Carter Avenue with no one behind the wheel at approximately fifty miles an hour in a thirty-five-mile-an-hour zone. He didn't see the cars that he hit.

Ross explained that he was not particularly injured in the accident, though he was upset that it happened. He said the police called his wife, and she came and picked him up at the scene in her car. The police officer at the scene had also called the owner of the business who this Port St. Lucie cop knew. I asked Mr. Ross about his driving record. I asked him if he ever had a speeding ticket, and he answered, "Just once." I asked him if his license had ever been suspended. He answered no. I knew that both of these were lies, but I did not disclose my knowledge to Mr. Ross at that time.

I asked Ross who actually hired him. He answered, "The owner of the business, Mr. Romano." Romano had handed the keys to Ross.

I scheduled a video deposition to take place at the Florida Highway Safety and Motor Vehicle Office in Tallahassee, Florida. I intended to take the deposition of the official who had signed the certification of Mr. Ross's driving record, Hazel Drombolis. Both Beatty and Gamba explained that they had conflicts and could not attend the deposition, but they said they were sure I would able to handle it and would share a copy of the deposition with them. Of course, they had agreed to pay their shares of the cost of the deposition (the court reporting fees).

The night before the deposition was to occur, I went to my mother's house in Chattahoochee, which was located near Tallahassee. I drove over to the Kirkman Building on Apalachee Parkway in Tallahassee and arrived about forty-five minutes before the scheduled deposition. Hazel Drombolis came out into the waiting area to see me almost immediately upon my arrival. She had on a beautiful yellow dress and was approximately fifty-five years old. She had a nice smile.

Ms. Drombolis showed me to her office. I asked her about her work for the Department of Highway Safety and Motor Vehicles. She smiled and said, "We're the only state agency that turns a profit and is not supported by taxes." She explained the accident reports which they provide to attorneys and insurance companies and employers cost $2 a piece, and there are millions of those requested per year. Also, driving records, such as the one I received on Mr. Ross, cost $5 each, and nine million of those are purchased each year by insurance companies, employers of potential drivers, and attorneys. Hazel was proud that her department carried its weight without cost to the taxpayer.

Defense counsel showed up at the scheduled time for the deposition. The videographer was already there and had set up to take the deposition. This deposition was wonderful. Hazel verified the information she gave me regarding the profit the department made from the sale of these accident reports and driving records. She explained who their customers were for those records.

I then placed upon the easel the blowup of Mr. Ross's driving record. She went through this in detail, including the numerous speeding tickets and the DUI. There was also a statement on the record that the license had been suspended after our crash because of an at-fault accent. There was no mention in the driving record of Mr. Ross driving under the influence at the time of our accident.

When I returned to Fort Pierce, we did some discovery as to how Mr. Ross's boss ran his company. We verified that his various corporations were the owners of a large number of vehicles, and all of them were insured with the same $300,000 level with St. Paul's Insurance. I also learned that Mr. Ross was married to Romano's daughter.

I had noted from the driving record that at the time Ross testified he was hired by Romano, Ross had no driver's license as it had been suspended. Mr. Ross had only reinstated his license, according to the records, seven days prior to our crash. It occurred to me that Mr. Romano either knew or should have known of Ross's driving record and his prior DUI. I had done some research and decided to file an amendment to our lawsuit to include a claim against Mr. Romano for negligently hiring Ross and negligent entrustment of the truck to Mr. Ross. I sent discovery to Mr. Romano once we had service of process. That discovery request sought, among other things, copies of all insurance policies which Mr. Romano had individually. Mr. Romano, in his reply thereto, sent me a copy of his homeowner's insurance which was issued by CNA Insurance. He also had limits of $300,000. Paul Gamba, Patrick Beatty, and myself all believed that we had a valid claim for negligent hiring and entrustment. We sent a demand for that $300,000 policy limits to CNA, in return for which we would give Mr. Romano a complete release. We received a reply in about ten days saying that there was no coverage for this accident, and their offer was zero.

I sat down in my office with Paul Gamba (Beatty wasn't there) and went over the insurance policy line by line. It had an interesting section which said, "We insure you for losses incurred as a result of negligence involving vehicles not owned." It occurred to us that Mr. Romano did not individually own the company truck which had slammed into our clients. It was owned by the corporation. We marked that section of the insurance contract with a yellow highlighter and mailed it back to CNA with a statement that we believed there was coverage. We repeated our demand. CNA repeated their offer of zero.

I took the deposition of the Port St. Lucie Police Traffic Officer. At that time, Port St. Lucie had a very small police force and, of course, did not have a very large population. Most of the police officers knew who the businessmen were in the area, and that was the case with the patrolman who handled this accident and signed the accident report. At the deposition, this patrolman indicated that he did not believe Mr. Ross had been drinking. He said that since he knew the owner of the business he saw on the truck door, he had called him to let him know about the accident. He also called, at Ross's request, Ross's wife, who, with the permission of the police, picked up her husband at the scene approximately thirty minutes later. No breathalyzer test was given to Ross. The police officer confirmed that all three of the victims of the crash had been taken to St. Lucie Medical Center. He didn't know how serious the injuries were.

I have outlined the injuries to Mrs. DeLuca. I must tell you that Paul Gamba's client was injured worse. She had a traumatically caused subluxation in her lower spine which would cause her to limp and drag her foot the rest of her life. She was in intractable pain. She had other various injures about her body as well, but that was the most significant one. We did not think that Patrick Beatty's client was that badly injured. She had an injury to her shoulder rotator cuff which had been repaired surgically. She had some continuing pain in the shoulder but was back to work without any obvious signs of distress.

Chapter 24

Mrs. DeLuca was having a rough time financially awaiting the trial date to roll around. On her behalf, I filed a claim for social security disability insurance. In those days, social security turned down every claim, initially. If you were to win your claims, it was going to be on appeal.

We filed for the appeal as soon as we got the notice of rejection. The hearing would take place before an administrative judge down in the federal courthouse in Palm Beach County, Florida.

The day of the hearing rolled around fairly quickly, and I found that Mrs. DeLuca's son had to work the day of the hearing. Therefore, I drove out to his home. John Jr., his family, and his mother lived in a small house located on Import Drive in southwest Port St. Lucie, half a mile north of Gatlin Boulevard, which was a major thoroughfare. I must say that once I turned off Gatlin onto Import, I had to drive a half mile before I saw a house which turned out to be the DeLuca abode. The house had perhaps three bedrooms and a carport and was certainly not ostentatious.

I drove Janice to the hearing. We could not go directly to Palm Beach on Interstate 95 since that section had not been completed in Martin or St. Lucie Counties at that time. There was, however, the Florida Turnpike, which had a Port St. Lucie exit. We took the turnpike, even though the turnpike dumped its traffic off far west of the downtown federal courthouse in West Palm Beach. On the way down, I had a talk with Mrs. DeLuca regarding what her family situation was, and she told me that it was not good. She was in pain every day and believed that her pain and condition were wearing on the nerves of John Jr.'s wife. She also told me that the noise of the children, whom she loved, got under her skin. Janice's teeth had not been fixed because of her lack of funds. She could barely be understood.

We arrived at the federal courthouse and parked. I placed Mrs. DeLuca in her wheelchair and went up the wheelchair access ramp to a side door on the Rogers Federal Building. I had the room number of the hearing, and it turned out it was in the middle of a very long hall in the courthouse. We went through the doors into that hall and proceeded toward the hearing location. I noticed that at about the same time we entered the hall, a very large man in a brown suit entered from the opposite direction and was walking toward us. We got to the location of the hearing at the same time, and the man explained he would open the door for us. We went inside, and he explained that he was the federal administrative law judge and that he would be going into chambers before the other side showed up and would be back. He explained where the petitioners need to sit in the well of the courtroom.

In a little while, the attorney for the social security administration showed up and sat at the other table. Shortly after that, the administrative law judge entered and sat on the bench. He was not wearing a robe.

I stood to speak to the judge and open our presentation, and the judge told me to hold it up for a minute. He looked at the social security's attorney and pointed toward him and said, "Sir, do you really believe this lady's not completely disabled?"

Under the law, a person's disability had to be one which would last in excess of a year before you qualify. It had now been almost a year since the accident, and Mrs. DeLuca was still in a wheelchair, though her knees had improved with surgery, and she was walking short distances with the help of a walker first and then a cane. Mrs. DeLuca still had not been able to get the proper dentures because she had no money to pay for them, and her face looked rather grotesque from the injuries she received. In reply to the judge, the social security attorney threw in his cards and admitted that Mrs. DeLuca had a 100 percent disability. The judge ordered social security to begin making full disability payments to Mrs. DeLuca and also backload those payments to the day we filed our petition. We had a pleasant ride on the way back, having stopped for lunch at a local restaurant in West Pam Beach. Mrs. DeLuca was thankful for the meal and explained to me that the budget at her son's house was very tight, and the meals were restricted. She said she rarely got to eat meat, although chewing was a major problem anyway.

We drove back home and began preparing for the trial, which was to start in five or six months.

Before the trial occurred, the defense sent out its usual surveillance team to follow Mrs. DeLuca around. We obtained copies of their surveillance. One section of the surveillance was Mrs. DeLuca attempting to ride her grandson's small bicycle down to a local convenience store which was over a mile away. Mrs. DeLuca was shown smoking a cigarette and was a little wobbly driving the bike. She did manage to get it most of the way there. She then got off the bike and pushed it to the store, limping noticeably. I thought that the surveillance helped us tremendously.

Chapter 25

We were approximately two weeks out from the trial when the court issued to us a copy of the jury venire for all trials that were to take place during that trial week. This included all the criminal trials and any civil trials that might be happening. There were approximately 250 names on that list. Their addresses were included. Back in those days, the court would provide you with a venire list to give you a heads-up so you could go over the list and see if there's anyone there that you knew or if you thought there was anything that you knew about any of these jurors which might disqualify them from jury duty. Nowadays, the jury list for the case you're actually trying is handed to you the morning of the trial by the clerk, and you're allowed about fifteen minutes to review it. Of course, nowadays, a skilled person with a computer can run an amazing check on anybody, and certainly, before the end of the voir dire process, you would have a pretty good idea about who you were dealing with. That was not the case in the old days. I had looked at the list myself and knew a couple of names on it, but other than that, nothing. I decided to meet with Patrick Beatty and Paul Gamba as well as my investigator, Tony Valicenti, because Tony knew lots of people. We were going to go over this list together on Friday before the trial to try to whittle it down.

The trial was to start on a Monday. On the Wednesday before the trial, Jeannie, one the workers at the Clerk of Court's office, gave me a call. Jeannie was the person who typically provided the lawyers the jury lists before trial occurred. She had other duties at the clerk's office as well. Whenever I visited the courthouse, I always went by their office and said hello to her particularly as she was extremely friendly. She liked to talk about her bowling team and the fact that she went to Las Vegas about once a year to bowl in a tournament. I had recently taken up the game of bowling with my friend, Bill Majewski, and was not very good at it, but I didn't tell her that.

Jeannie had called to tell me some important information. She said that "Judge Nourse has just released all but thirty-nine jurors from the venire. All other trials which have been scheduled for next week, except your trial, have been either settled or postponed. Would you like to have a copy of the venire with the thirty-nine people on it?"

I replied, "Absolutely."

She said it would take a little bit of time to prepare, but she should have it in thirty minutes. I explained I would be there in thirty minutes.

I picked up the venire list and thanked her and then decided it was still early enough in the day for me to go by the Supervisor of Elections Office to at least find out what the political parties each of these prospective voters belonged to. In those days, the jury was selected from registered voters. Nowadays, you only have to have a driver's license to qualify for jury duty.

I went into the supervisor's office and asked the clerk to provide me with the voter list. She gave me a huge book with all the registered voters alphabetized in the county in it. I knew it was going to be a herculean task to go over each of these jurors and put down the information that was contained in the computer printouts in the book. The jury list I had was not in alphabetical order. I just started to open the book and look for the first name when the Supervisor of Elections, Gertrude Walker, came out and said, "Roger, how are you doing?" She also wanted to know what I was doing there. I explained that I just got this jury venire list and wanted to go over it to see what the party affiliation was and any other information that was available on it. Gertrude said to me, "There's a lot more information on the cards."

I asked her what cards she was talking about. Gertrude indicated to me that her office kept index cards on all the registered voters, including information the registered voter gave them when they signed up. This had information regarding whether the person was married, whether they had children, and where they had moved from. There also might be clues in there as to the occupation of the person involved. She said that the clerk would pull me each of those cards, and I thanked her.

Gertrude Walker was a lady who I met in 1980 when I was the chairman of the local Democratic Executive Committee. Gertrude had been the chief assistant in the Supervisor of Elections Office and had, for years, run things for the supervisor, a politician named Jimmy Brooks. Jimmy was extremely popular and was a rock-ribbed Democrat, as was Gertrude. In 1980, Jimmy qualified to run for reelection. The Republicans, because they had no chance of beating Jimmy, did not put up a candidate against him. After the filing deadline passed for candidacy, Jimmy Brooks died of a heart attack.

Our local Democratic Executive Committee interviewed several individuals who wanted the job. The governor of Florida had already appointed Gertrude Walker as the interim Supervisor of Elections for the upcoming election. Our local Democratic Party had decided to add Gertrude's name to the ballot as our candidate, which the law allowed us to do.

Gertrude Walker was Black. The Republicans became upset and attempted to name their own candidate who was a popular White school board member. They filed suit when the application was denied as not being timely filed. We got involved in the litigation. The Republicans lost. Therefore, Gertrude was elected without opposition in 1980. In 1984 (before our trial), Gertrude ran and had the same popular Republican office holder run against her. Gertrude was known by then to be an extremely efficient and pleasant supervisor of elections and everyone, most Republicans included, seemed to like her. Gertrude won by 75 percent to 25 percent. Gertrude and I have been friends for quite a while.

I went through the first four index cards and had taken down the appropriate information off each one. The fifth index card I looked at was different from the other four. It had a blue inked in *L* with a circle around it on the upper righthand corner of the card. I called Gertrude out and said, "Excuse me, Gertrude, but there's something I need to know. Why is this *L* here?"

She said, "Well, whenever people sign a petition to get a constitutional amendment on the ballot, we have to verify the signature. We check every one of those signatures against the signatures we have on file. The *L* means that the petition that the voter signed was to have a limit on liability of a maximum $250,000 written into the Florida Constitution."

There had been long attempts by conservatives and the Republican Party to impose this limitation on people's rights. Some Democrats were also in favor of that. There had been a vote in 1984 on the constitutional question, and the Academy of Florida Trial Lawyers was active in their opposition thereto. The voters in the state voted that constitutional amendment down by about 51 percent to 49 percent. It took a 60 percent vote to pass.

After understanding why the person on this card had done that, I decided to give that person a zero on my one to five list of desirable jurors. It turns out there were four other *L*s in the stack of thirty-nine voters. I decided to create my own card system and, to the best of my ability, give a proposed juror a rating from 1 to 5. The five jurors who thought that $250,000 was enough regardless of the facts I gave all a 0 and was going to refuse to have them on my jury. By the way, the knowledge of this system of tracking those voters who signed petitions was the deepest darkest secret I held for many years after the DeLuca case. I did disclose it, after getting a sworn agreement to secrecy, from Paul Gamba and Patrick Beatty. I was afraid that if this information got out, the defense would learn of it.

After I had completed my cards, I called Patrick and Paul, as well as my investigator Tony Valicenti, and my paralegal, Suzanne

Larson, to meet at my conference room. We were going over all thirty-nine people, and I explained why we would give zeros to five of those folks. We went over the list, and Tony Valicenti told me, "Roger, there's a person on this list that loves you as an attorney and as a person. His name is Bob Kaste." I asked Tony if Bob was married to Barb Kaste, and he said, "Yes, he was."

Barb had been the president of the Port St. Lucie American Little League. While I was attached to the Fort Pierce American Little League as an umpire, we had a friendly relationship with the other leagues around the county. They all knew that I was an attorney, and when Port St. Lucie American Little League had a small legal problem, I, on a pro bono basis, helped them through it. In addition, on occasion, when they were having problems with umpires being out sick, I would go down to Port St. Lucie and umpire a game. Barb made sure that I had plenty of cold drinks, popcorn, etc. free of charge from the concession stand while I was there.

Tony explained to me that Mr. Kaste worked for Florida Power and Light and was a union employee and that he was one of the highest paid union employees at the St. Lucie Nuclear Plant, which was firing up at that time as a new facility out on South Hutchinson Island. He also went down the list and said, "By the way, this other guy on the list here is Bob's best friend and also works as a union employee of FP&L out at their plant." He said, "That person will do whatever Bob asks him to do."

I asked Tony how he knew this, and he told me that he played on the same softball team with both of the guys and told me that either one of them we would be a perfect juror for me. Obviously, those two gentlemen received 5s in my rating system. We had three other jurors we thought were awesome. Also, none of them knew us personally. There were about the same number of 4s on our list and a large number of 3s and a few 2s and 1s. There were many in the 3 and below groups we knew very little about.

At the meeting, Paul and Patrick both asked me to handle the vast majority of the voir dire. They said I had a real good grasp of it. We agreed to confer at the end of the voir dire process about the use of our peremptory challenges. Each of our plaintiffs had three peremptory challenges and the defense had a total of nine. We could get rid of jurors we did not like for no reason if we could not get the judge to remove them for cause. Paul and Patrick both told me they would defer to me with regard to the use of those peremptory challenges, but if they had a problem with one, they would discuss it with me.

I felt confident enough that we did not have to use a jury consultant in this case. The voir dire went famously. I only asked Bob Kaste where he worked, and he answered FP&L. I asked him how long he had worked there, and he told me. The judge asked all jurors if they personally knew any of the attorneys present. As did the others, Bob Kaste honestly answered, "No." I had never met the man. I had a similar conversation with all the other jurors and questioned the ones we did not want extensively. I did not ask them whether they had signed the stupid petition. When the time came for striking jurors for cause, the defense actually sought and obtained the disqualification of one of the jurors we had given 0 to. Judge Nourse also removed another handful of jurors from the venire but realized that out of the thirty-nine, we were getting a little low, and the eighteen peremptory challenges may reduce us to the bare minimum necessary to try the case. Interestingly, Bob Kaste was one of the jurors sitting on the first row when the jury was seated. His friend was also in the jury box. At the end of the jury selection process, amazingly, four of our six jurors we had rated at a 5 were on the main jury, and the fifth person was the alternate. The other two jurors were what we considered to be a 4. We felt like we had the upper hand from that point forward in the trial.

Chapter 26

At trial, we put on our evidence of the horrible negligence of Mr. Ross. When Ross testified that he "bailed out" before the collision and was able to escape uninjured, I asked him if they had taught him the "bail out" procedure when he was attending the mandatory defensive driving school required to get his license reinstated after his DUI conviction. He sheepishly responded, "No." I had previously shown before putting Mr. Ross on the stand the video of Hazel Drombolis's deposition. I got Mr. Ross to agree that he had been previously convicted of DUI. I also recounted what happened to him the day of the accident, including the pizza party, the trip to Dukes's happy hour, and the stop on Carter Avenue. I learned from Tony Valicenti (who was a volunteer at Port St. Lucie Police Department by that time) that the Carter Avenue address was a known den for the consumption of cannabis. Tony feared that the kid probably toked up before the accident and was probably under the influence of alcohol and drugs. There was no way we could disclose the fact about Carter Avenue except that Ross told the jury that while they were at that house, he drank nothing but Kool-Aid. In the drug-crazed period from the late sixties to the mid-eighties, it was known that marijuana smokers drank Kool-Aid to make their throats feel better when they imbibed. The jury understood that. Mr. Ross didn't remember who his friend was that had the house on Carter Avenue.

He explained that he realized he was running late and had to hurry home to his wife, which was why he was driving a little fast.

An expert witness can be anyone who could assist the jury in a relevant fact which is not known to folks generally in the population. They did not have to be even college educated, but in some technical fields, that certainly would be something that would be required. In this case, I had a friend in Fort Pierce, Florida, who was named Wayne Shaw. Wayne was an owner of River Citrus Inc., along with his brother, Jerry. They also had another brother who was somewhat involved in that type of business named Bob Shaw, who I was familiar with. I had gone hunting with Wayne Shaw, and we liked each other.

Wayne had explained to me that he hired all the drivers at River Citrus as they were haulers of citrus fruit. I asked how many drivers they had. He said at any given time in season, he had around one hundred. I asked him what procedure he followed upon hiring, and he explained that the hires would have to disclose their driving record and would have to show a commercial driver's license. He said that River Citrus did not necessarily trust driver's statements regarding their driving history. He said that they would immediately order from the State of Florida a driving record of these potential drivers. Drivers would be initially hired by River Citrus and would begin driving trucks. However, if the report came back from the state that indicated the driver was lying on his application, he was immediately fired for cause.

I used Wayne Shaw at trial as an expert witness on hiring practices for drivers. Though the defense objected, the judge allowed him to testify, and it was very effective. We had established through the testimony of Mr. Ross that he had been hired by his father-in-law, Mr. Romano, and confirmed the date of his hire. Those facts showed that at the time Mr. Ross was hired to drive this truck and work for this company, he had no license. It had been suspended for DUI. We thought we had an ironclad case of negligent hiring and entrustment.

Well, before the trial occurred, Paul Gamba, Patrick Beatty, and myself reached an agreement regarding potential settlement We had offered to take the full $600,000 from the two companies, though CNA still refused to kick in their $300,000. We had agreed that Pat Beatty's client would receive $50,000 while the balance would be equally divided between my client and Paul Gamba's client. This was even though Paul's client was slightly more injured than Mrs. DeLuca.

Once the evidence was in, the closing argument went as smoothly as you can imagine given the facts of the case. We anticipated a long deliberation since there were three cases to be decided. When the jury was sent to the jury room, I went out to the hall outside the courtroom and sat on the bench and fumbled in my briefcase for a good book.

Paul Gamba's partner was present for much of the trial, including closing argument. He sat down next to me and asked, "Roger, do you think that combined, we get $1 million?" I told him that it was a distinct possibility, but I didn't know. In the early eighties, $1 million verdicts were as rare as hen's teeth, particularly in this jurisdiction. He said, "I notice you're about to start reading a book. Do you know how to play gin rummy?"

This gentleman, Mr. Schwartz, had with him a deck of cards. I told him I did know how to play and had gambled on the game before. He and I both agreed that the Hollywood system of scoring was appropriate. I said that before we start, we need to arrive as to a reasonable stake for this game. He asked me what I thought. I told him that if the verdict came in at over $1 million, we would play for a dollar a point. If it came in for less than $1 million, we'd be playing for a penny a point. He thought that was appropriate as he could afford to pay the dollar fees if he had lost the bet regarding the $1 million. In any event, I should be able to pay the debt if the smaller verdict came in and I did not win.

Mr. Schwartz shuffled extensively. I cut the cards, and he dealt the cards. In gin, you're allowed to pick up a card and then required to discard one card faceup. The goal was to get your hand with as many sets of three or more cards, such as three kings, or your sets could be three or more runs in the same suit, such as 9, 10, jack of hearts. You would continue with the drawing procedure, alternating with the other person, and would either have to pick a card up off the top of the deck, or you could pick up the card that is discarded by your opponent, but only the top card. Any person who held all his cards in sets or in suit runs would declare, "GIN."

In addition to seeking gin, any person can knock their knuckles on the desk anytime they believe their total card count, after taking aside their established runs and sets, was lower than their opponent.

I picked up my hand, and I looked at it and moved some cards around. I discovered that I had gin dealt to me. In my life, it was the first and only time I ever saw that. I didn't even have to pick up a card from the deck to do that. I said, "You're not going to believe this, but here's gin."

He said, "We're going to kick their ass."

At the end of about an hour and a half, we reached the end of the game, and I had absolutely stomped Mr. Schwartz. I was up by over a thousand points on the three games combined. At the end of the game, we decided to not continue as Schwartz said he had had enough. I had had an amazing run of cards.

I picked up my book and began to read but was interrupted shortly thereafter by the bailiff, who announced that the jury was back. The total verdict was $900,000 with $100,000 being allocated to Patrick Beatty's client and the remaining $800,000 divided, with Mr. Gamba's client receiving $450,000 and Janice DeLuca receiving $350,000. Also, we were entitled to court costs on the case. We had not filed a proposal for settlement as that was more or less unheard of in the early eighties.

On behalf of Mr. Romano, CNA filed an appeal. St. Paul's had paid their portion of the costs together with the $300,000, which had been divided on a pro rata basis between our three clients. CNA had to put up a bond for the full amount of the judgment remaining to proceed with their appeal. We handled the appeal ourselves. The Fourth District Court ultimately affirmed Judge Nourse's judgment, per curium. In a per curium decision, the district court does not have to write an opinion unless they want to. If they think that the case is cut and dried, often, they do write, "Per curium affirmed."

After the appeal was completed, CNA paid the bond together with all interest as well as the cost of the appeal. The total amount the three clients received combined in this case, before attorney's fees, was well in excess of $1 million.

Mrs. DeLuca was very grateful for the work we had done. She came by my office three or four months later. She had new teeth and looked nice. Her medical bills were paid. She told me that her children had talked her into investing her remaining money in a restaurant venture, which they were going to jointly do with her. I explained to her that restaurants often fail miserably, regardless of how good the food is. It is a very dicey business to be involved in. I would think that would especially be the case in Port St. Lucie because there were so many other Italian restaurants and pizzerias in the area which catered to New York or New Jersey native clientele. Janice insisted that they were going to do very well and that she would supervise the kitchen but would not do the work. Her daughter was to help wait and bus tables.

I took Betsey to the restaurant for dinner. Mrs. DeLuca told me it was "on the house," but I insisted that I pay the bill. The restaurant had very few patrons seated when we were there, even though it was on a Friday night. The food was just okay. I talked to Janice and wished her the best.

Of course, the restaurant failed within a few months, and Janice lost most of the money we had won for her. It was depressing for me.

Book 9

Leap of Faith

Chapter 27

In my first ten years of practice here in St. Lucie County, I wound up in what I thought was a fifty-fifty partnership with Richard Sneed. During that period, I tried numerous cases around the State of Florida. One of the cases I tried was in Live Oak, Florida, which is hard up against the Florida Georgia border in extreme North Florida. I also had a trial in Naples, Florida. I tried a federal case in the Middle District of Florida in Tampa. I also tried cases in such places as Miami, Fort Lauderdale, West Palm Beach, Stuart, and Vero Beach, as well as my home county of St. Lucie. I had a reputation for winning.

Into my tenth year with Richard, there suddenly were problems between us. We did not see eye to eye on numerous matters, and I was hamstrung because Richard was the "managing partner" of the office.

More and more of my clients were from the city of Port St. Lucie, which, by then, had outpaced Fort Pierce in population. Port St. Lucie has always been a "magnet for population" since I came to the county. Many of my clients asked why we did not have an office in Port St. Lucie, as it was much more convenient for them to see someone down there than to come all the way up (approximately twelve miles) to see me in Fort Pierce.

I had discussed opening a branch office in Port St. Lucie with Richard, and he scotched the idea. He was more interested in perhaps practicing to the north toward Vero Beach, and although I'd had several trials in that jurisdiction, I felt that the future was Port St. Lucie.

The final straw came when Richard went on vacation, and I was able to peruse the books carefully. I came away with the feeling that some partners in our partnership were more equal than others. It seemed to be that I was bringing in more money to the partnership and was not being equally treated. Shortly before Richard had gone on vacation, another dispute arose which was between Richard and three or four of my Jewish friends. I and they felt insulted, and I was ready to bolt.

In the week that Richard was gone on vacation, I called my accountant, Chris Fogal, and told him of my decision to bolt. He was very kind and said, "You do need to get out from under Richards' shadow."

I told him I wanted him to keep me out of trouble with the IRS and to guide me through the first few years of practice financially. He said, "You can't take a salary the first year." I bit my tongue. He said, "You need to scramble and save and convert assets into cash that you may use to pay the cost of the practice."

I immediately began looking for a place to open. I settled on an office in a new bank building that was being built on US One in Port St. Lucie. It was about a month until the spaces would be completed by the builder. I was the first tenant in the building after the bank moved in.

When Richard and his wife returned from vacation, I went into his office and announced that I was putting in my two-week notice. He said, "No, you're moving out of the office this afternoon. The office lease is in my name." We had a sit-down where we divided the office furniture on a more or less equal basis. It was decided that I would receive the relatively new computer system, while Richard would retain our office library. All the wall art was also divided between us. We had already gotten most of the fees from the Ayala case and were awaiting a decision from the Supreme Court, and we agreed that when it came in, it would be equally divided. There were a few other matters like that, but I essentially left the office with very few cases.

I called a good friend of mine who was a criminal defense attorney, Mark Orr. Mark said to me, "Roger, I have a spare office in the back corner of my building with a telephone and typewriters. You and your secretary, Suzanne, are welcome to that space until your new office space becomes available."

My good wife, Betsey, was able to go back to work full time, as our daughter, Johanna, had just started kindergarten, and Betsey no longer needed a babysitter to be able to work more than part-time. It was decided that she would go back on a full-time basis at the ICU.

In addition, I had acquired a little bit of stock in a local bank, as well as a few other stock holdings which I had hoped to use as a retirement plan at a later time. I cashed all those items in and took out a loan against my life insurance policy. Some years before, Richard and I and a local veterinarian decided to purchase, as an investment, a total of four duplex apartments in Fort Pierce. I particularly did not like being a landlord, and I wanted to sell my interest in the partnership. Unfortunately, our partnership agreement relative to the duplexes indicated that if any one of the partners wanted to get out of the deal, they could sell the property, but either one of the remaining partners had the right of first refusal on any sale. I spoke with the veterinarian, and he indicated he could not swing purchasing my interest at that time. When I approached Richard about this desire to sell the property, he told me, "You got yourself in this spot. I am not going to help you get out."

Later, I was discussing this problem with a good friend of mine, Ray VanMeerten, who was a local investor who dabbled quite a bit in real estate. I knew for a fact that Ray VanMeerten and Richard Sneed hated each other. It was not just a dislike. Ray said to me, "Roger, I'll fix him." He said, "I will enter into a contract to purchase your interest in that partnership in an amount that is on the high side of reasonable. You present this contract to Richard, and there's no way that he would accept me as a partner, and therefore, he will buy out your interest for the amount in the contract."

It played out just as Ray had planned. Richard was furious, but he went ahead and paid me for my interest in the duplexes.

Chapter 28

That first solo year in practice was tough. There were weeks when on Monday, I did not know how I was going to be able to pay Suzanne her salary by Friday. But always, some small good thing happened, and I was able to meet that obligation. I had some cases ongoing, but it seemed I was having a hard time getting cases to trial, although I tried a few.

The litigation all required the use of court reporters for depositions or trials, and I was using the services of Atlantic Reporting, which was owned by my good friend, Bill Majewski. Bill knew what I was going through, and he told me that he would carry my accounts payable until I got my finances straightened out, and he said he understood I would pay him as soon as I could. I had the largest line of credit that any local bank would give me, and it was not very big. Toward the end of that year, I was at the end of my line of credit and was only paying interest thereon. Betsey and I took out a second mortgage on our home in Fort Pierce, Florida.

As soon as that year was completed, I got a call from my accountant, Chris Fogal. He said, "Congratulations, Roger, you made a profit."

I said, "I did?"

Chris said, "Yeah, you made a little over a $1,000."

I replied with an answer that was "May I take some of that money home?"

He said emphatically, "No. The congratulations were in order because over seventy-five percent of new law firms lose money the first year, and you have not lost money."

Within two weeks of that conversation, the biggest case I had in my office at that time, Kevin Petroski, settled for $1 million. I called Chris Fogal and asked him if it was okay for me to start taking a salary now. He said, "Yes, just don't make it too much." I paid off all my debts, my line of credit, and had a cushion from that point forward, so I did not have to worry about being able to pay the rent or the salary of my wonderful paralegal/secretary, Suzanne.

Within three years of my taking the leap of faith, we sold our home in Fort Pierce and built a beautiful home on the golf course which had just opened in St. Lucie West, in western Port St. Lucie, Florida. We still live in that home today. The move to Port St. Lucie turned out to be the smartest thing I could have done even though I felt that at times we had been very close to going smash.

Book 10

Death Case

Chapter 29

I had just opened my office in Port St. Lucie when I received a call from a young man named Kevin Petroski (not his real name). Kevin explained that he was at Health South Rehabilitation Facility in Vero Beach, Florida, and asked if I could come and see him. I told him I could be there in forty-five minutes. I asked him how he got my name, and he told me that Doris Tropf had told him that I was the only lawyer she liked. He asked me to discuss the case with him.

I drove up to Vero Beach and went into the rehabilitation center, where I saw Kevin lying in his bed. Both legs were elevated and in casts, and he looked the worse for wear. I found that his accident had occurred perhaps three months before he called me. He had been to numerous hospitals which seemed to dump him as soon as possible, and after his latest surgery, he had been referred to this rehab center.

I asked Kevin how his accident happened. He told me a story that caused shivers to run down my spine and caused tears to come to my eyes. Kevin told me that he and his young wife and their three-year-old daughter had come down from Connecticut to Port St. Lucie to visit his parents so that they could enjoy the grandchild. They were driving back to Connecticut and only made it to between

Jacksonville, Florida, and Savannah, Georgia. It turns out, they were on the Georgia side of the bridge straddling the state line.

They were hit head-on by a drunk driver going the wrong way on the bridge, apparently with her lights off. Kevin's wife had been killed, and she died while sitting next to him in the front seat. His young daughter in the back seat in a child restraint chair suffered a broken leg. The engine had penetrated the fire wall, and Kevin's legs were burned and broken. Kevin had, I believe, ninety-six broken bones in his body. It seemed that almost all the bones in his body, except his skull, had been broken. He was quite miserable and said he had a tremendous bout with depression.

Kevin told me that if it had not been for his daughter who needed him, he would have given up and died. He was torn up by the loss of his wife. His daughter had been treated and released a couple of days after coming to the hospital and was staying with her grandparents in Port St. Lucie. While I was there with Kevin, the grandparents showed up with the daughter, and she was a lovely little thing. She had curly brown hair and a beautiful face, and she was walking with a pair of small crutches and had her lower leg in a cast. She and her father obviously loved each other tremendously. Kevin was concerned about what the little girl had gone through seeing her mother die in front of her.

When his parents had left, Kevin told me there was something in the side table next to the bed that he wanted me to see. He reached over and opened the table and pulled out a stack of letters, perhaps twenty of them. He told me to read the first one. It was a letter from an attorney in Georgia, soliciting his case. Kevin told me all the others were similar letters, and he had received letters from attorneys in Connecticut, where he lived, in Georgia, and in Florida. He did not know what to do.

Since he was in Vero Beach and was a victim of a drunk driver, Doris Tropf was counseling him through his grief and telling him what he needed to do to get on with his life. He showed her these letters, and she told him, "I really don't like lawyers except for one." She gave Kevin my phone number. Thank you very much, Doris Tropf.

The drunk driver had survived the crash but also had been hospitalized for a short time. She now resided in jail in the State of Georgia. I feared that since she resided in Georgia and Kevin resided in Connecticut, we would have to file this in federal court. When I got the information regarding the accident, however, I noted that the drunk driver's home address was in Pensacola, Florida. I decided to file suit in Pensacola since I was licensed anywhere in the State of Florida. I learned that Kevin had uninsured motorist coverage in the amount of $1 million. The drunk driver had a minimal policy, and her family had raised some money to make her bail. It was her family's money. We ultimately settled the case for the amount of the coverage, plus the drunk driver had to kick in some cash on her own. She raised this from her family because she was in the State Penitentiary in Georgia serving a five-year sentence for DUI homicide at the time our settlement was reached.

Chapter 30

The settlement for the young girl had to be structured so that no one, including her father, could touch her money except for health, education, or welfare purposes, and those only with court approval. Kevin received his portion in cash after payment of outstanding medical bills (which our office had negotiated down to be more reasonable). The case settled so quickly that I thought it only appropriate for me to reduce my fee, which I did.

Because the mother's estate had been opened in the State of Connecticut where she had lived, I had to go to the probate court in Connecticut to get approval from the court for the settlement. I had to join the Connecticut Bar "pro hac vice." That is a procedure where you must find a competent attorney in the jurisdiction where you want to serve who will vouch for your ability and stand with you, if necessary, if you should have to go before the court. After obtaining such an attorney's recommendation, I had to send the paperwork to the court and get the court's approval for my appearance.

Finally, I flew up to Providence, Rhode Island, which was the largest airport near Kevin's home in extreme eastern Connecticut. Kevin lived in a small town known as Gale's Ferry. The county seat was in the small town of Ledyard. At the time I attended the hearing,

Ledyard was a sleepy town, and the courthouse was made of wood. This was the first wooden courthouse I had ever seen. I entered the courtroom and was somewhat surprised to see that the probate judge was a lady. Nowadays, female judges are probably about as common as male judges are on the bench. This was absolutely not the case in 1990 or before, and they were rare indeed.

I was in the courtroom with Kevin and his daughter, as well as the attorney from Connecticut. Also in the room was the daughter's maternal grandfather. I had not met him but realized he was still grieving for the loss of his daughter. When the hearing started, the grandfather loudly interrupted and told the judge the entire settlement was unfair and that I was attempting to steal his granddaughter's money.

The judge looked down from the bench at the man with a scowl on her face. She told him, "Sir, this attorney has done an awesome job with this case, and he has done it at a fee which is less than you would have paid any attorney who did this kind of work in Connecticut. You should thank your stars that Mr. Messer was involved in this case." She told him she didn't want to hear anything else from him during the hearing.

Of course, our settlement for the little girl was approved by the court. As we were walking out of the courthouse, Kevin's father-in-law was staring bullets at us.

Epilogue

Kevin was no longer able to work at the electric boat facility there in Groton, Connecticut, where they built submarines. He had to retire. He decided to move with his daughter up to Michigan and open a small arcade-type business that he thought he could handle. He was no longer in a wheelchair but had to walk with canes.

I thanked Kevin for letting me help him with this matter and thought I would not hear from him again. He thanked me in return.

A couple of years later, his brother, who lived in Okeechobee, Florida, came into my office with a nonpersonal injury problem, which I took care of. He told me that Kevin and his daughter were in Michigan and seemed happy. In about 2017, I received a call from Kevin Petroski, and we had a very long conversation. Kevin told me that he had relocated himself to Okeechobee, Florida, and was living there. He thanked me for my assistance years before. I asked him what happened with his daughter. He said that she had decided to go to college in Connecticut near where her maternal grandparents lived. She had reconnected with them and was living in that area after she graduated. He said that she calls him on a regular basis.

BOOK 11

Nunchucks

Chapter 31

In 1991, a former client of mine came into my office to discuss her brother's case. This nice young lady I had represented in a prior matter, quite successfully.

She explained that her brother, AJ Shore (not his real name), was in the hospital in Fort Pierce with a fractured skull. She said he had been injured in some sort of altercation. She asked that I go to talk to him at the hospital, and I said, of course, that I would.

When I went in to see AJ, he had bandages on his head and was obviously suffering from a significant concussion. AJ was an otherwise nice looking nineteen-year-old. He had graduated the year before from Central High School in Fort Pierce, Florida, and was taking a few courses at the local community college.

He explained that he had gone to a high school graduation party for kids in the class the year behind him, who had just graduated the week before. This party was held in rural St. Lucie County west of town at the home of one of the graduates. He explained that outside the home, there was a large crowd mulling about, perhaps fifty to seventy-five, some of whom he knew and some of whom he did not know. Everyone was drinking soda or beer and seemed to be having an excellent time. He explained that someone crept up behind him and hit him in the head with some sort of weapon, and the next thing he knew, he was waking up in the hospital.

I learned that the perpetrator of this crime was a sixteen-year-old high school dropout from Fort Pierce. When I obtained the incident report from the sheriff's department, it indicated that immediately after the attack, the other kids at the party chased the perpetrator, but he had quickly gotten in his vehicle and sped off. Several people there had taken down the perpetrator's tag number. The sheriff's department had run the tag number through its database and found out that the vehicle was registered to an individual who lived in the White City area of St. Lucie County. Immediately, a deputy drove to that location and located the automobile parked in the front yard. He noted that on the front seat of the automobile was a set of nunchucks.

Nunchucks are a rather vicious weapon which had been developed in the Far East and were being used now in martial arts demonstrations. It consists of two hard wooden dowels, joined together with a leather or chain strap fastened on one end of each stick. The wood in question was hard and heavy. A person using the nunchucks would spin them at a high rate of speed over one shoulder and then the other, and the speed of the device was what made it lethal. Apparently, this weapon was developed for use by peasants in China who had been forbidden from having swords or other metal weapons.

When the sheriff's department arrived at the White City home, the car was in the driveway, and a bloody set of nunchucks was visible on the front seat. The deputies knocked on the front door, and the mother of the perpetrator came to the door and let them in. She did not realize what her son had done. She called him into the room, and he was arrested and taken to the juvenile detention center after proper booking at the jail. The police report said that this child had told them he had purchased these nunchucks at a flea market. The child did not remember the name of the person he purchased them from or even where the flea market was located.

The parents of this bad kid were divorced, but the owner of the vehicle was the child's father. The kid's parents allowed him to use the car. Under the law, had this been an auto crash, the father would have been equally responsible for damages caused by his son. That is under the "Dangerous Instrumentality Rule" of the law. It seemed to me that the only recourse we would have would be through the homeowner's insurance on the relatively low-value home where the young man lived with his divorced mother. I decided to go ahead and sign up the case and see what I could do.

A week or so later, AJ came into my office, having lost the bandages. I told him how much we had progressed in the case and that I had reviewed the police report.

I had contacted the homeowner's insurance company for the home where the child lived and was shocked that this was the lowest coverage limit I had ever seen in a homeowner's policy for liability. This was only a $25,000 policy. When I explained the claim, the insurance company wanted to settle their case in return for a release, but I wasn't so sure. I decided to go forward and take the deposition of the young perpetrator. First, I had to file suit. We are not allowed to tell the name of the bad boy because of laws shielding juvenile defendants.

The day for the deposition rolled around, and the young man showed up in response to a subpoena. He was already out of jail, and his juvenile case had ended with a slap on the wrist and a couple of weeks in the juvenile detention center as well as probation thereafter. The insurance company provided the young man with an attorney at the deposition.

The deposition began easily enough. Early in his testimony, I asked this young man where he had obtained the nunchucks. His answer shocked me. He told me that he had bought them at the local Orange Blossom Mall in Fort Pierce from a company called Cutlery World. I called a time-out and went in the other room to call my investigator, Tony Valicenti. I asked Tony if he could go out the Orange Blossom Mall and investigate whether or not Cutlery World sold those particular types of nunchucks. I explained what the weapon looked like, having seen it at the police station. I then came back into the room and started to proceed with the deposition. An hour or so later, while the deposition was still happening, I received a call from Tony Valicenti. He established that they did, indeed, sell those nunchucks, and he had spent some of my money by purchasing an identical pair. I had him bring them by my office and had the young man testify that this was a copy of the nunchucks he had purchased. He also told me the name of the store manager that handled the transaction where he bought the nunchucks.

I asked him what sort of training he had with the nunchucks. He explained that his mother did not know that he possessed them. He said that he had had them for about three weeks, and during that time, he had gone to a remote area and practiced with them. He said he initially kept hitting himself in the shoulder, and it was quite painful and caused bruising. Unfortunately, he had not hit himself in the head.

He said he progressed to the point where he went into a watermelon patch and smashed some melons. He said that he wondered if the same result would come from hitting a human in the head. This kid had learned of the upcoming graduation celebration, to which he was not invited, and decided to invite himself. He said he got to the scene, and everyone was looking at something going on in the middle of the crowd. He came up behind AJ Shore, who he did not know, and he seemed like an easy target. The young man swung his nunchucks hard onto the head of AJ, fracturing his skull and causing a concussion. He said he ran from the scene and sped away in his car.

After the deposition, I did some legal research. I particularly researched nunchucks. There was a Florida statute on the books which made it illegal for anyone to sell nunchucks to a minor child without the express written consent of the parent. Therefore, we had violation of a statute by the store, and there was, at least, a possibility of getting punitive damages.

The insurance company for Cutlery World assigned the case to Attorney Steve Hayskar from Fort Pierce. Mr. Hayskar and I had had a few trials against each other, and I believe we respected each other. I actually liked Steve.

Shortly after the litigation began, Cutlery World filed for bankruptcy in the State of Tennessee. Under the bankruptcy laws, the filing of the bankruptcy acts as an automatic stay of any litigation pending against the bankrupt. An attorney who attempted to go forward with such a claim would find himself severely chastised by the Bar. You cannot get punitive damages against a bankrupt.

What I did was I went to Tennessee and filed a motion with the court there to allow me to go forward with the trial of the case and limit myself to the amount of the coverage, which in this case was $1 million. That motion was granted.

AJ Shore made a fairly nice recovery from his injuries. He didn't have any money to speak of but had gotten another job and was supporting himself.

At that time, the circuit civil judge in St. Lucie County required that all cases, before trial, be taken before a summary jury to see what result could be obtained. The judge believed that after summary jury trials, there was a high likelihood a case would settle, regardless of which side won the summary trial.

In the summary trial procedure, there would be no judge sitting on the bench, and the parties understood that to be effective, both sides would have to be straightforward. No voir dire is allowed. The case is tried in front of six jurors. We only had a day to do the job.

During the summary trial, Mr. Hayskar and I were very courteous to each other. I tried the case in a straightforward manner, as did Steve Hayskar. We pulled no punches. We had taken the deposition of the manager of the Cutlery World Store, and we read it to the jury. The manager admitted that they sold the subject nunchucks and that they did not have written permission to do so. She was not aware that the law required her to do that. I thought the case was pretty cut-and-dried. Before the summary trial, the highest offer from the insurance company on this case had been zero.

At the end of the summary trial, the jury of six people retired to the jury room in the courthouse just as it would have in a real trial. When they were out of the room, Steve Hayskar came over to me and shook my hand and said, "Roger, you did a very proper presentation, and I was fairly impressed with your case. Do you think that we could try this on a high-low basis and avoid a trial?"

Sometimes trials took place with an agreement between the plaintiff and the defense attorney regardless of what the verdict is.

There would be a ceiling that the award could not go beyond, and there would be a floor where it could not go below. This would result in either side not taking a total bath in case there was a strange jury verdict.

My response to Steve was "It depends on how high is the high and how low is the low." Steve wanted the ceiling set at $150,000 and the floor at $50,000. I wanted $250,000 and $100,000. We were still haggling when the knock came on the door from the jury. We had not reached agreement on a high-low. The jury had only been out perhaps forty-five minutes.

The jury came in and read their verdict, which was in favor of AJ Shore in the amount of $191,500. This was $41,500 more than the proposed high in the agreement that was being urged by the defense.

There was a representative of the insurance company (Travelers) present at the summary trial. Steve and his insurance adjuster conferred with each other, and then Steve came back and said, "Would you be upset if the insurance company paid that verdict at this time without having to go to a full-blown trial? It will save us both considerable costs." I conferred with AJ Shore, and he said he would be very happy with that result.

The verdict was promptly paid (together with our relatively modest court costs) within ten days. Approximately two months later, AJ came by my office to thank me. He told me that he was moving to Mobile, Alabama, and was opening a small business where they would sell boxer brief underwear as well as certain types of sports clothing. He had taken some of his money to begin this business.

A couple of months later, I received in the mail two pairs of boxer briefs which were beautifully decorated. I don't know why they decorate the briefs that way since they are underwear, and most people can't see them.

After the trial, I retrieved from the evidence file all physical evidence in the case. The actual pair of nunchucks that were the weapon in this case are, to this day, hanging on my office wall as a trophy.

BOOK 12

Good Hands People?

Chapter 32

I was involved in a jury trial in Fort Pierce, Florida, on behalf of Larry Hogan. Larry had been driving his pickup truck down Midway Road just south of Fort Pierce near the county park. Thankfully, Larry was not traveling that fast, about twenty-five miles an hour because of traffic. Suddenly and without warning, a drunk driver decided to turn in front of him to go into a park. The drunk driver was operating a smaller vehicle and got the worst of it from the crash. However, Larry did receive less serious injuries, the worst of which was, perhaps, a whiplash injury to his neck.

From early on in my career, I handled quite a few injury or death claims against drunk drivers. I delighted in handling those. Not only were we able to do justice, but we were also able to get awards against the drunk drivers which would be a lesson to other people. A huge advantage in suing the drunk driver in Florida was that there was an old Supreme Court case called *Ingraham vs. Pettit* which held that in a case involving a drunk driver, it was proper to seek punitive damages. In Florida, as a rule, punitive damages are difficult to get the court to allow. Drunk driving was an exception to that rule.

The trial had gone fairly well, and my client and I were sitting outside the courtroom awaiting the verdict. The jury had been in the deliberation room for approximately an hour and a half (a good sign), and Larry had gone to make a telephone call. He came back to see me and told me, "Well, it's happened again." He spoke with an extremely Southern drawl but was a good-hearted soul. I asked him what had happened again. He said, "Well, my sister-in-law, Angela, was driving home from work today and was sitting at a stop sign at the corner of Hardman Road and Orange Avenue in Fort Pierce, Florida, and was waiting to turn left. Suddenly, a large van veered off Orange Avenue and slammed into the driver's side door of Angela's car. The drunk driver, a very large Mexican migrant worker, got out of his van at the scene and tried to run from the scene. Thankfully, several local good ole boys saw the crash and ran the perpetrator down and tackled him and held him until the police arrived."

I later learned that the police had excellent film of the defendant, Pedro Garcia, failing the field sobriety test. The police always do this test with their cameras on so it creates evidence for the jury in the criminal case. We also had film of Mr. Garcia at the crash scene. He was obviously drunk.

Angela, unfortunately, got the worst of this accident. She had a neck injury, but the most painful thing that she had was a severe TMJ injury. TMJ stands for temporo-mandibular joint syndrome, which is an injury that can take place to the jaw of an individual. It makes it very difficult to open and close your mouth to eat. The pain can be quite intolerable. The pain and impairment can be permanent.

Larry told me that his sister-in-law and his brother had just left Lawnwood Regional Medical Center's Emergency Room and were heading home. He told me they requested that I drive by their home and discuss their rights with them as soon as our trial was over.

Larry's case was concluded after a little less than two hours when the jury came back with a nice verdict for us, which was considerably more than the last offer from the defense.

Chapter 33

I was in an excellent frame of mind as I drove the approximate ten miles from the Fort Pierce courthouse into the country west of town. The countryside out there is a far cry from the developments, subdivisions, and golf courses along the coast. The people in that area are rural. There were large groves of orange and grapefruit trees. There were a couple of large cattle ranches, including the massive Adams Ranch, which stretched over two or three counties. Interspersed between those large agricultural holdings were small farms with shade trees in the yards of the residences. Many of them had a fishpond on the property to provide food for the families and relaxation through fishing. I followed Larry's instructions and finally turned onto the dirt road leading up to the home of Angela and Kenny Hogan. It was a fairly large and nice wood-framed home. The yard sported lots of flowers. The first people I was saw were two small boys playing in the front yard with a dog. I parked the car and was walking up to the stairs when the door opened, and it was Kenny Hogan. I had met Kenny once before when I visited the welding shop owned by the two brothers. He and Larry were both accomplished welders and had a successful welding business just west of Fort Pierce rebuilding propellors and, principally, manufacturing and servicing large pumps which were used in the citrus industry for irrigation purposes.

Kenny invited me into their home, which was very neat and clean. His wife, Angela, was sitting on a comfortable chair, wearing a bath robe. Her face was swollen and beat up, but you could not help but notice that she was an attractive woman. Angela told me how the accident happened and was happy the perpetrator had been hauled off to jail. However, she was in a great deal of pain. She told me she was scheduled to see her dentist because of the pain in her mouth. She said, "My teeth weren't broken, but my jaw hurts like the dickens."

During our discussions, the two young boys came into the house, and they were introduced to me by their parents. The children were then excused, and they exited the room quietly and went back to their rooms. I thought they were tremendously well-behaved.

I discovered that Angela was a secretary for Tom Deal, the vice president of Indian River State College. Tom was a close old friend of mine. He occasionally played in a floating card game that I sometimes participated in. The following week after my visit at the home, I called and talked to Tom Deal about Angela. He had nothing but rave reviews about her work ethic and what a wonderful person she was. He knew she had sustained an injury and hoped for the very best. Tom agreed if it was necessary, he would come to court and testify as to the way Angela was before the accident happened. Before and after witnesses are important in every injury case.

On my first visit with the Hogans, I had no idea whether or not the at-fault driver had any insurance. I asked Kenny and Angela if they had uninsured motorist insurance, and they assured me that they did. They showed me the declarations page of their insurance policy. Unfortunately, the amount of coverage under that policy was only $25,000. These funds were available in the event that Angela got an excess verdict beyond the ability of the at-fault party's insurance to pay.

I had not had time to go back to my office and prepare a proposed contract and a complete package. However, I did have a copy of a Statement of Client's Rights that the Florida Bar and the Florida

Supreme Court require all lawyers in these kinds of cases to show their clients their rights and have them sign off on the document. I explained my fee schedule and told them I would bring back a contract in a day or two and explained that we would do the best we could to help her. Under Florida law, a contract for representation in a personal injury case can be canceled by the client within three days of signing the contract.

The next day, Angela went in to see her dentist, Dr. Fox, who was very knowledgeable about temporomandibular joint syndrome and had treated TMJ patients in the past. He diagnosed the TMJ condition and explained to Angela that she would have to wear a splint for many months. This splint was on one side of her jaw and was designed to keep the jaw from opening too far. It also served to reduce the urge to clench. It was uncomfortable to wear, but if you followed the therapy, oftentimes it was successful in giving some relief to the patient. The option other than the splint was surgery to the temporomandibular joint (the jaw). In either event, she would wind up with a permanent impairment.

Angela was also scheduled to see a local orthopedic surgeon regarding her neck injury.

Once I obtained the signed contract from my client, I obtained a copy of the accident report. I learned that the at-fault party had a $10,000 policy with State Farm. I also learned that Mr. Garcia had a blood alcohol level of over 3.00 BAC. The legal limit in Florida is only 0.80. My belief was that the case was worth more than that $10,000, plus the $25,000 in uninsured motorist coverage.

Chapter 34

On Monday, after signing the contract the previous Thursday, Kenny and Angela called me at my office. They told me that they wanted to cancel the contract. I had assured them that obtaining the $10,000 from the at-fault party was not a problem, but I urged them not to settle with that person before obtaining a settlement with their uninsured motorist carrier, which was Allstate. They told me they had been customers with Allstate "ever since we were married." They knew their local agent and felt that Allstate would treat them fairly. I told them that I had no hard feelings, but if they had problems with Allstate, I would be happy to represent them. I put the file away for a couple of weeks.

If we were to settle with an at-fault party first, the uninsured motorist insurance company got a credit that did not apply if the first settlement was with the uninsured motorist carrier.

Two weeks later, Kenny gave me a call at my office and was hopping mad. He said, "Those assholes have only offered us $5,000 to settle the claim. We want you to go forward and sue them. We also want you to hold the drunk driver responsible and our insurance company responsible."

The insurance company for the drunk driver, State Farm, was begging us to accept their $10,000 and give them a release, but we refused.

I wrote Allstate a letter advising them of my representation and demanding the meager policy limits in this case. I forwarded them the medical records I had already received from Dr Fox's office and the orthopedic surgeon, together with the accident report.

After receipt of that letter from me, Allstate wrote me a letter and offered to settle the claim for $15,000. That offer was promptly turned down by Angela and Kenny.

I filed suit fairly rapidly and got service of process upon the drunk driver, personally, and upon Allstate through the state insurance commissioner's office. We had filed a Civil Remedy Notice upon Allstate. Under the bad faith law in Florida, if your own insurance company fails to settle the case when it should have and could have, you are allowed to seek additional damages in excess of their policy limits in the event you get an excess jury verdict. Under the law, after the Civil Remedy Notice is received, the insurance company has sixty days to do the right thing (pay the limits), or the offer to settle is off the table, and you can proceed with your lawsuit. Within that time, Allstate filed a response stating, "This is not bad faith. It is an honest disagreement with our insured as to the value of the case."

As we always did in these drunk driving cases, we sought both compensatory and punitive damages. When you have a substantial defendant (one with assets at risk), a punitive damage claim is quite handy as you are allowed to discover the financial condition of the at-fault party. The reason you can discover that is that the purpose of punitive damages is to punish the individual but not bankrupt them. The main reason that I file for punitive damages in these cases, however, is that it makes it very unlikely that the defense will admit liability and ask for a trial on damages only. When that occurs, there can be no discussion of the acts of negligence that caused the injury. You cannot discuss the financial condition of the defendant. The entire case becomes about your client only. A skillful defense lawyer will turn your case into a believability duel with your client. He or she will obtain all the social media posts that your client has made, particularly discussions about the injuries the client received in the accident and any comments the client has made about the case to other individuals. The defense will also obtain past medical records on you for the last ten years. In addition, the defense almost always has surveillance film of your client doing their daily activities. Once all those are in hand, they will take the deposition of your client and hope that she will forget about some of the medical treatment that she has received. If there is a slipup in the deposition, they will typically accuse your client of not being straightforward or truthful.

While those matters are still a subject of concern, we don't worry about it that much. Usually, drunk driving cases hinge on the character and actions of the drunk driver.

In 1995, MRIs were still relatively new. The MRI of Angela's neck showed a herniated disc, but it did not touch the spinal cord, and it was deemed not to need surgery. It was real and caused some pain, however. It also might get worse. The TMJ pain was rather intractable and was a continuing issue with days of remission and days of aggravation.

As expected, State Farm was again begging us to accept their $10,000, which we refused to do since we would have to give the defendant, Pedro Garcia (not his real name), a complete release.

Allstate was represented by local attorney Bradley Pierce (not his real name). Bradley was a member of a law firm in Fort Pierce, Florida, who, at that time, represented most all the insurance companies. Bradley and I had a history. We had tried many cases against each other. He had a reputation of not settling many cases. He seemed to be in trial once or twice a month. He was a serious and skilled adversary.

Bradley scheduled Angela for a compulsory medical examination with a TMJ specialist, Dr. Engebretsen, from Port St. Lucie. Dr. Engebretsen had impeccable credentials, and I had never seen him in court before. Almost never will defense counsel send a patient to a compulsory examination when they did not know what the examiner was going to say. They usually use "safe" doctors who would bend over backward to reduce the result for your client.

When I received the copy of Dr. Engebretsen's report, I was pleasantly shocked. Dr. Engebretsen indicated that Angela did, in fact, have a very severe case of temporomandibular joint syndrome. He agreed with the treatments that Dr. Fox was performing and agreed that there may be surgery in Angela's future. I added Dr. Engebretsen to my list of witnesses and would later call him to trial by subpoena. I was certain the defense would never again use Dr. Engebretsen as an expert because he was honest.

We early on offered to take the $25,000 policy limits from Allstate, and their response was that they would give us $15,000. After thirty days, I promptly withdrew our offer to settle the case. The case moved on to trial in fairly rapid order.

The defense, as they often do, hired a surveillance team to secretly follow Angela around and take video of her. As I stated earlier, Angela was a beautiful woman. She was also very nice and courteous. I took the deposition of the defense investigator who took the video, and I obtained copies of the videos. In the first video, the videographer had hidden in the bushes across the road from the Hogan home, and with the very powerful lens on his camera, he was able to take pictures of Angela doing nothing in the front yard except watching her children play. The next film was of Angela and her husband and children going fishing. They were boating over to the back side of a barrier island off the coast of Fort Pierce. It was an extremely calm day, and there was no chop on the water. Angela was dressed in a bathing suit in which she was absolutely gorgeous. The only thing that was not gorgeous about her was the pained look on her face when she had to move. Angela got down in the small boat after her children were in, and from that point on, she stared away from the dock without moving her head. The water was calm. Kenny got into the back of the boat and started the engine and putt-putted across the Indian River to the barrier island. They went around to the other side of the island, where they docked and spent the day surf fishing while the children played in the Atlantic waters. The videographer could not see what was going on on the other side of the island.

We took the deposition of Mr. Garcia at the county jail and learned that he had been drinking the day of the accident since about two in the afternoon. The crash happened around 5:00 p.m. He had been consuming tequila and beer. Garcia didn't know how much he had taken in. He was at least truthful to us regarding that.

Chapter 35

We were at trial sooner than I expected. The voir dire in the case seemed to go very well for us. Since there were two defendants in the case, the defendants each had three peremptory challenges, and the plaintiff (Angela Hogan) had six. I had not spent the money necessary for a jury consultant given the relatively small coverage in the case, but I was extremely prepared for the voir dire. We got a few negative jurors off for cause. The venire was a pretty good group, and not many cause challenges were necessary. The defendants used all their peremptory challenges while I still had two bullets in the gun when we decided to accept the jury.

At trial, the drunk driver was present with his attorney at counsel table. State Farm adjuster, Charles Matthews (not his real name), was in the gallery watching the trial. Allstate had a pretty face sitting at the counsel table pretending to be the corporate representative from Allstate. She was not the adjuster on the file and had no say regarding settlement of the case.

The first thing we did was call the police officer onto the stand and showed the jury the video of Mr. Garcia failing the field sobriety test. The video showed that he was staggering and slurring his speech, and he was also rather belligerent at the scene. I could have not choreographed it better.

The police officer testified that onlookers had subdued Garcia before the police arrived. One of the good Samaritans who had seen the crash and then tackled Garcia testified to what he saw and did. We put on our client and her husband, as well as the other witnesses, including Dr. Engebretsen and Dr. Fox. The orthopedic surgeon who treated the neck injury also testified.

For the defense, Dr. Sullivan was the usual suspect who testified. He was the defense doctor who never found anything wrong with anybody in these defense exams. Dr. Sullivan did a credible job for them, but of course, he had experience. There were no surprises for us. Dr. Sullivan said that Angela had not received a permanent injury to her neck in the accident. We were able to show the jury the financial relationship between the defense doctor and the insurance company.

All in all, I felt we had an excellent chance of obtaining an excess verdict. The jury was in the jury deliberation room for a magical just about two hours and came back with a total verdict of $98,902.00. I was over the moon with the result. We saved a day of trial by dismissing our punitive damage claim since Garcia had nothing.

Shortly after the trial, State Farm paid the drunk's $10,0000 coverage as well as their portion of the cost judgment rendered. Allstate paid us their $25,000 coverage plus their portion of the costs and disputed whether or not we were entitled to bad faith damages.

Chapter 36

After we obtained the verdict, I went into the hall and telephoned my good friend, Jeffrey Liggio. Jeff was the past president of the Academy of Trial Lawyers, and one of his specialties was handling bad faith litigation. Jeff confirmed that we had properly filed a Civil Remedy Notice. He asked if I could get the clients down to his office in West Palm Beach later that week, and I arranged it with my clients. Jeff promptly filed the bad faith suit and proceeded to take discovery from the defendant, Allstate.

Since we were pursuing a bad faith claim, we were entitled to see the entire Allstate file on the case which would ordinarily be barred to us. There were some very interesting items in the file. The chief smoking gun in the file was a computer printout from a computer program which Allstate used then, and is still, in fact, uses today. The program was called Colossus. Under Colossus, the person entering the data types in all the information they have regarding the plaintiff's injuries, liability. and other factors. Once that's typed in, the operator presses a button, and sometime later, a computer printout comes and lets them know what the machine believes Allstate's exposure is in the case. In this case, the printout said that Allstate's exposure for Angela Hogan's injury was $15,600.00.

Jeff Liggio scheduled the Allstate adjuster's deposition to be taken in Bradley Pierce's office, and I was happy to attend. Jeff, at first, established the authenticity of the documents he had from Allstate, and he proceeded with the main portion of his deposition. He first asked the Allstate adjuster whether or not in Florida, there was a code of ethics an adjuster had to follow. The adjuster answered that all insurance adjusters are required to follow the code of ethics. Jeff read from the code of ethics that an adjuster's first allegiance in the case should be to the policyholder. In this case, the policyholders were the Hogans, and they should have treated them fairly in all their dealings.

Then Jeff Liggio asked, "You had this printout in your hand early in the case. Why did you only offer your insureds $5,000.00 to settle the case?"

The adjuster stammered and said, "I felt that was appropriate."

Mr. Liggio asked him why, after the Hogans had obtained an attorney, Allstate had only increased their offer to $15,000 and not $15,600, which Colossus indicated was appropriate. Once again, the adjuster had no response to that statement, and that was particularly damning, especially in a bad faith case.

All cases had to be mediated before they were reached for trial. In this case, the mediation occurred, and Angela and Kenny and I, along with Jeff Liggio, attended. It was held in Jeff's office in West Palm Beach. There was a real representative present from Allstate, along with Bradley Pierce. I cannot tell you what happened at the mediation. I can tell you that sometime after the mediation, probably as a result of progress made at the mediation, Mr. Liggio obtained a one-hundred-seventy-seven-thousand-dollar settlement for our clients, and his attorney fee was paid by Allstate. The Hogans were delighted.

Epilogue

Chapter 37

Not long after the settlement in question, Larry Hogan and Kenny Hogan invited me to go fly fishing with them on their airboat over on Lake Okeechobee. At that time, waters in Lake Okeechobee were much cleaner than now, and there was an abundance of fish. We were particularly going for panfish like bream and shell cracker, and I had a very nice time. Both Larry and Kenny Hogan told me that they felt the citrus industry may be suffering a downturn because of certain diseases among the trees, including canker. They said they thought it might be a good time to sell the business and move to another place. They had lived in St. Lucie County all their lives but did not like the way it was changing. It had been agricultural community most of their lives, but development was getting ramped up, and the Hogans did not like the change. They told me that they were thinking of moving to Missouri, where the fishing and hunting was better than in Florida, and told me that their business and homes were up for sale.

The Hogans sold their business at the top of the market and sold their homes. There had always been a rusty sign in front of the business that said, "Hogan Brothers Welding." I lost track of these nice people for many years.

After they left, the welding company that bought the business and the location went belly-up because of the downturn in the citrus industry.

Approximately ten years, later I was driving from Port St. Lucie up to visit with my mom and extended family near Tallahassee and attend a Florida State game on a long weekend. I decided to not go the whole way on the interstate but to take surface roads (US Highway 27) from Ocala, Florida, west to Highway 19 and then north toward Tallahassee. The road intersected with Highway19 at Chiefland Florida in Levy County. I wanted to go that way because just north of Chiefland, before you get to the Suwannee River, there was a vineyard. The vineyard sold all types of wines but also specialized in producing scuppernong wine. The scuppernong is a muscadine grape with a very distinctive taste. Every place I lived as a child growing up, we had a very large arbor of scuppernongs in the backyard, and we all loved the taste. The vineyard also sold large bottles of scuppernong juice, which was definitely a taste from the past. My sister Ann told me that she was enamored with that juice, and she had discovered this vineyard sometime before when she had been traveling. I pulled into the vineyard and ordered a case of juice (twelve bottles) so I could give some to my sisters and mother and take one bottle back home so I had some of my own.

As I was pulling out of the driveway to get back on Highway 19, I looked left to see if there was any traffic, and then I looked right. Staring me in the face was a sign that said, "Hogan Brothers Welding." It was the same sign I had seen west of Fort Pierce ten years before. I decided to pull into the business. When I got there, Larry was making modification to a golf cart. He came out and shook my hand and had a broad smile on his face.

I said, "I thought you guys were going to Missouri."

Larry explained that before they could make the move to the "show me" state, they discovered Levy County, and it was much like old Florida. It was very conservative (they were Republican), and the fishing and the hunting in the area was over the moon. I asked him how the business was going, and he had a broad smile and said, "We're the only shop doing propellor work within ninety miles. We do all the work for the Florida Game and Fish Commission in the area, and the reward for that is in addition to being paid nicely, the game wardens tell us where the good fishing and hunting is located." Larry also explained they had another business where they bought used electric golf carts cheaply at a golf retirement town about sixty miles east of them known as "the villages." They converted these carts into silent hunting carts with new heavy-duty transmissions and camouflage paint. These were advertised on the internet. Larry said they could not build them fast enough and sold each one at a huge profit. He showed me a half dozen golf carts waiting for the conversion and said all of them were already sold.

I asked him how Kenny and Angela were. He said Kenny was out sick that day, but Angela was working at the school board for Levy County where she was a high official. He said that their two boys had grown into strapping young teenagers and were doing well in school. He said this was the greatest move they made in their entire life. He thanked me for helping him and for helping Kenny's family. I drove on to Tallahassee with a big smile on my face.

BOOK 13

Health Insurance, Bad Faith

Chapter 38

Melissa Riggs was a lady who had just gone through a divorce. A few days after the divorce was final, she went out driving alone at night, and no one is sure what happened. She was on a dirt road in western St. Lucie County when she seemed to have struck a mound of sand. Her Jeep CJ rolled over, and she was horribly injured. She was not discovered until the next morning when a fisherman came by and saw her lying in the ditch, covered with ants.

Melissa was airlifted by trauma hawk to St. Mary's Medical Center in Palm Beach County in an unconscious condition. At the time, St. Mary's was the only level 1 trauma center in the area. She was diagnosed with a "fractured aorta," which was leaking blood into her body cavity. This is an injury which is fatal in well over 90 percent of cases. Eight hours of herculean surgery saved Melissa's life. Unfortunately, because of a cutoff of the blood supply to the lower spine, Melissa was paralyzed from the waist down. Her motor nerves were gone. However, she still could experience pain and pleasure. Melissa had been hospitalized for over six months, attempting to regain her life.

I was at my office in Port St. Lucie when I received a call from Sandy Shaw (not her real name). Ms. Shaw was a paralyzed former client of mine who was now working to counsel other newly paralyzed victims. Ms. Shaw asked if I could drive over to her friend Melissa Rigg's home, as Melissa was not able to get around with a car yet. I said I would be happy to see her. I called Melissa and made an appointment to get by her house that afternoon. I went to the address given and was shocked that from her backyard, you could see the home of one of my closest friends, Bill Majewski. I had visited Bill at his home on several occasions, and I knew this neighborhood. There was a large boat in Melissa's yard, and the house looked relatively neat and clean.

Melissa was an attractive blond lady who was slightly overweight. She kept a warm smile. Melissa explained to me that her parents had come down from the north and stayed in the home for three or four months until she got out of the hospital. They had now returned to their lives, and she was not unhappy that they were gone. There was a lot of friction between Melissa and her mom and dad.

Melissa was distraught. She explained to me that she had little memory of the accident but knows that she was driving west of Port St. Lucie in the county and that her Jeep CJ had rolled over.

There had been several cases around the country of deadly rollovers of the Jeep CJ, and in fact, there had been one verdict here in St. Lucie County against Jeep for several million dollars a year or two before. Out-of-town lawyers handled that case. I immediately thought that we might have a products liability case against Jeep, but I was unsure. I asked Melissa where the Jeep was, and she said, "I don't know. I do know that my mom and dad, shortly before I got home, gave the keys and the title to the towing company which was coming to collect their tow and storage bill. They had agreed to take the salvage value of the car in return for wiping out the bill." Melissa had no say in what was done, according to her. I realized that I needed to chase down the subject vehicle, fast.

That day, I contacted the tow yard, and they informed me that the vehicle had been sold for salvage. They told me who they sold it to. I was finally able to get through to that company the next day. I told them I was willing to buy the vehicle in question. They told me, "Too late!" They said that the vehicle had been crushed by their machine two days before and was being loaded on a truck to send to the metal recycling center.

Without the actual vehicle, a products liability case could not be won, in my opinion.

Chapter 39

At my first meeting, Melissa told me that her main problem, however, was her medical bills. At that time, they were over $800,000, mostly to St. Mary's Medical Center. PIP had paid the first $10,000 of the bill, and no one else had been paid anything. Melissa said, "What really pisses me off is that my health insurance carrier is refusing to pay any of the bills." I was shocked.

I asked, "Why are they refusing?"

She replied, "They won't tell me."

She gave me the phone number for the health insurance adjuster, and while at her home, I called the adjuster and asked her why they had not paid the bills. I explained that they had had most of the bills for more than four months, and under Florida law, they had to pay the bills within the four months or otherwise provide a statement in writing as to the reason they're not paying. The insurance adjuster replied, "We're not in Florida. We're in Illinois."

I explained that the accident happened in Florida, the insurance policy was purchased in Florida, and the medical bills were incurred in Florida, and that given those three facts, Florida law would apply. I asked the adjuster just what reason she thought they did not need to pay.

She said, "We have reason to believe that Mrs. Riggs was driving under the influence of alcohol. And under the terms of our policy, if our insured is guilty of a felony during the time they receive an injury, we don't have to pay."

I explained to this adjuster that there were a few problems with their theory. The first one was that Melissa Riggs had never been charged nor convicted of DUI. In addition, I explained that DUI in Florida was a misdemeanor, not a felony. I asked when they would make a final decision and give us a determination.

She said, "We've got it under advisement. It's still under investigation."

After we hung up, I spoke with Melissa and asked her to tell me when and where she bought the insurance policy. She explained that one day, this particular insurance salesman came to the place where she worked. Her employer had allowed all the people working to take an unpaid hour when they could go down and visit with this salesman and decide whether or not they wanted to personally purchase the health insurance policy or not. The employer did not participate in any way in the conversations, nor did the employer pay anything toward the insurance for its employees. These facts were important since if this was an employer-controlled operation, a federal law called ERISA applied, and we would have to file the case in federal court under the ERISA statute. This was problematical for a couple of reasons. First of all, if you sue your insurance company in Florida because of their failure to reasonably pay your bills and you win, you're entitled to attorney's fees to be paid by the insurance company. There was no attorney's fees provision in the ERISA statute, and you must sue them in federal court. In addition, ERISA in federal court was handled by a judge, not a jury. If you get a conservative judge, good luck in getting much on your case. I had seen ERISA liens before and was not totally cognizant of what it was about. I decided to research it before proceeding further.

I noted that the Academy of Florida Trial Lawyers was holding a seminar on the subject of ERISA to take place at the Tampa Airport later that week. Unfortunately, I had a 4:30 p.m. hearing in West Palm Beach the day before the seminar. West Palm Beach is an hour south of us, and I would be quite tired when I got home, had dinner, and drove the roughly three hours to the Tampa Airport. I decided it would be more reasonable for me to hop a flight from West Palm Beach directly to Tampa on the "puddle jumper" that would fly back and forth between those airports. After my hearing in West Palm, I went to the airport and boarded the plane. The flight had about fifteen passengers aboard. I had a small briefcase, and I was planning on taking copious notes at the seminar. I also had a small suit bag. I spent the night in the airport hotel.

The seminar was being presented by one of the officers of the Academy of Florida Trial Lawyers, Jeff Liggio. Jeff was slated to be the president of the Academy within a couple of years, and he was well respected in the profession. I did not know Jeff before that day. He put on an excellent seminar, and I took notes and also took all the materials from the seminar and put them in my briefcase. I then proceeded back down to the concourse in the airport and got on the puddle jumper for the trip back to West Palm Beach and my automobile. I was shocked when Jeff Liggio followed me onto the plane and sat next to me. We struck up a conversation.

I told him that he had given a great seminar, and I was particularly concerned about ERISA and the fact that it was raising its ugly head in several cases lately. He thanked me, and I asked what kind of practice he had. He said he mostly dealt with bad faith from insurance companies, and he explained to me what insurance bad faith was. He said if I got a bad faith case, he would be happy to look at it and perhaps get justice for our clients. I thanked him.

From what I had learned in the seminar, I believed that Melissa's claim against the insurance company was a simple contracts action which could be filed in circuit court here in St. Lucie County Florida. I was sure that ERISA did not apply and could avoid at trip down to federal court. At that time, the closest federal courthouse was in West Palm Beach.

Fairly soon after making that determination, I filed suit in St. Lucie County Circuit Court attempting to enforce the contract and require the insurance company to pay all the outstanding bills and to pay our attorney's fee for the trouble Mrs. Riggs had gone through in making them do the right thing.

Twenty days after I filed the suit, I received an answer accompanied by a petition to have the case removed to federal court. There was a memorandum of law of over twenty pages attached to the petition outlining why the defense believed this was an ERISA matter. I read all twenty pages and initially thought, *This ain't ERISA*. I then read it again and again and began to doubt myself. I decided to call the expert, Jeff Liggio, and I got him on the first try.

I explained the facts of my case to him, and he said, "This ain't ERISA."

I answered, "I know, but we're now stuck in federal court, and getting out of there is going to be like pulling eye teeth." I asked him if he would help me on the underlying case and any bad faith case that might result. He said that he would. He said that he would be in charge of getting it removed back to state court, along with my help, and would also assist me in negotiation or, if negotiation did not work, the trial of the case.

The insurance policy called for a maximum benefit of $1 million.

One of the reasons that it stunk to be in federal court was the fact that the judges in that court were inundated with criminal drug trials from all the drug busts the local authorities as well as Coast Guard were making on the east coast of Florida. There were weekly reports of drug busts, though it was obvious that more drugs were getting in than were being kept out. Many of those drugs came through the Port of Fort Pierce as well as the Port of the Palm Beaches. Therefore, there were lots of such cases in the US District Court for the Southern District of Florida, West Palm Beach Division. The judges were required, under the speedy trial rule, to get criminal defendants to a trial in an expedited manner. Civil cases took a back seat and were gotten to whenever the court could get around to it. It took us nine months before we could get a hearing on our removal petition.

On the day of the hearing, I went with Melissa Riggs down to the federal courthouse and met Jeff Liggio. We went in the courtroom and sat down. The defense was there with an army of attorneys, at least six, who were from the States of Florida, Alabama, and Illinois. The defense had filed an extensive brief in opposition to our petition for removal, and Jeffrey had filed a further brief that explained why ERISA did not apply.

The judge entered the chambers, and it was Chief Judge Norman Roettger. Judge Roettger was impressive looking. He was tall, and he had a very long waxed handlebar mustache and a head full of flowing gray hair. He had a reputation of being a fairly straight-shooting judge with no obvious bias.

At the start of the hearing, the judge looked at myself and Mr. Liggio and our client and said, "I don't know why you're here in my court trying to go back to state court. ERISA is a good law, and it ensures that contracts such as this one are complied with if the factual evidence will support that." We thought we would have an uphill battle.

The hearing lasted all day. In the morning, the judge was asking hard questions to us, but none of them to defense counsel. A miracle happened at the lunch hour. Apparently, over lunch, the judge had researched the ERISA law. After lunch, the judge repeatedly asked Jeff Liggio what the law was on certain points. He came down hard on the defense. When the case was over, Judge Roettger indicated that he was entering an order within the next few days explaining his decision.

Later that week, Judge Roettger entered his fifteen-page order which not only sent the case back to state court but also eviscerated most of the affirmative defenses that had been filed by the insurance company. We would be able to go forward with our complaint in state court and would be able to seek attorney's fees. I was sure we would win at trial.

Once the case was back in the circuit court in St. Lucie County, it moved very quickly. There had been a delay of about a year caused by the trip to federal court. At that time, the trials were set according to the date the lawsuit was filed. Judge Kenney was generally efficient in getting his cases to trial.

A trial order was entered requiring us to disclose witnesses, have a deadline for completion of discovery, and most importantly for us, a requirement that the case be mediated before trial.

By this time, there were obviously two insurance companies involved. One had underlying coverage of $1 million, and the other was a "secondary" insurance company which paid if the award was greater and liability was found. Therefore, we needed a bigger space than my humble conference room to hold all the attorneys, clients, and insurance adjusters necessary to have an effective mediation.

We scheduled mediation to take place at a hotel which was conveniently located for me, approximately one mile from my office. The mediation took approximately four hours. A settlement was reached in the amount of $1 million. In addition, the defense paid $600,000 for the costs and attorneys' fees involved in getting this matter resolved. Melissa was extremely pleased with the result. I told her not to get too excited. There was still a matter of a lawsuit filed by St. Mary's Hospital seeking payment of their $800,000 medical bill. I told her that we needed to escrow out the money while I was fighting that battle.

Within less than a month, I had been able to negotiate the St. Mary's bill down to less than $300,000. Melissa Riggs got the balance of the $1 million.

Epilogue

Chapter 40

In the months following the settlement, Melissa went through extensive rehabilitation. She was taught to drive a car with hand controls, and she purchased such an automobile. She was working hard to improve her mobility, including her ability to transfer in and out of her wheelchair. She then developed, very quickly, strong shoulders and arms, as those were the means of her movement.

Melissa got a job with the VA Hospital as a medical record transcriptionist. She was a friendly visitor at my office and let me know how she was progressing.

Melissa got involved with a special project ongoing at University of Miami, Jackson Memorial Hospital. The project was named for Hall of Fame football player Nick Buoniconti's son, who was paralyzed in an accident. The purpose of this project was to see if paralyzed people could be retrained and, through rehabilitation, obtain some of the use of their legs. Melissa sent me pictures of her on the machine where you hold your weight with your arms while "walking" on a treadmill. In the picture, she was sweating and obviously had been working on this quite hard. Melissa told me that there was no way she was going to spend the rest of her life in a wheelchair.

Melissa would take daily trips around the neighborhood in her wheelchair and met most of the neighbors. She actually bonded with Barbara Majewski, Bill's child, who had suffered from cerebral palsy and also had a great deal of trouble walking. The two of them became friends.

Melissa had been out on the boat a couple of times and was developing a tan, although she had put on some weight as a result of the lack of walking or running. She was still a nice-looking lady.

Melissa came to my office and asked me to do a will for her. I prepared that gratis. The will left most of her assets to the Buoniconti Project at the University of Miami Medical Center at Jackson Memorial. Melissa's parents received the home and the car, which were worth considerably less than Melissa's financial investments.

Melissa had suffered from asthma as a child and still received asthmatic treatment. Unfortunately, approximately five years after the case settled, Melissa was riding her wheelchair around her block and was about halfway home when suddenly, she had a massive attack of asthma. She died from that attack.

I attended the memorial service for her, along with the Majewskis. The service was held by her parents at Melissa's home and, there were perhaps twenty-five or thirty people present. Melissa was a fine and noble individual. The world is less without her.

BOOK 14

A Lawyer Goes Down

Chapter 41

As I indicated, when I moved my offices to Port St. Lucie, there was only one other attorney in that city who was doing, almost exclusively, personal injury and wrongful death work. The young attorney's name was Aaron Browner (not his real name). Aaron was a little younger than me, though he was going prematurely bald and was not in very good physical condition. I had once seen Aaron in action in a jury trial in Fort Pierce, and he seemed to have some skill in front of the jury. However, when the jury went out and he was waiting for the verdict, he was the most hyper individual I had ever seen. He was jumping around outside the courtroom and could not sit still. He was extremely wired. I told him, "Aaron, settle down. You did a good job, and the verdict is going to be okay." He said that he was always like this when he was not in court and that he was naturally hyper. Aaron had a reputation for chasing girls and running with a difficult crowd. One of his friends was an attorney who had an office on the second floor of the office building where my office was located. My office was on the fourth floor. That man had lost his law license because of a confirmed cocaine habit. Cocaine caused that young lawyer to neglect much of his duties.

In addition to that individual, Aaron had been seen around town with a few other people of notoriety. I believed Aaron was partying way too much and with the wrong crowd.

Sometime in the mid-nineties, I got a call from Aaron Browner. He said, "Roger, you have to help me. I've got a case which I need to refer out, and it needs some work done immediately." He assured me it was a very good case and asked if he could bring the case file over to my office for discussion with me that morning. I reluctantly agreed to see him.

Shortly thereafter, Aaron showed up with a banker's box full of paper that this particular file had generated. I asked him why something needed to happen right away. He told me the statute of limitations was going to run in less than a month. I was extremely reluctant to take the case, but he said that he had no other choice.

He asked me to look at the facts of the case, which I did. When I read about the case in the records that he had, I couldn't believe that Aaron had not filed suit or otherwise settled this particular case as it appeared to me to be a slam dunk. He had the file in the case for over three years. The client, who was extremely injured, had been hit by a drunk driver at an intersection in Stuart, Martin County, Florida. He had spent a considerable amount of time in the hospital and had large medical bills. The client still suffered from a back injury which caused him to walk with a limp the rest of his life. This case should have been settled for a large amount less than a year after the crash.

While I was looking at the file, Aaron excused himself to go to the restroom, which was located in the hall outside my back door. Aaron went through the kitchen area of my office, which he was familiar with. When he returned a while later, he apologized. He said he had stopped and looked in my cabinet in my kitchen and had taken out the small portion of rum that was in the bottom of a bottle there. That rum bottle had been used in my office to spike the punch that we had at our Christmas party. We always held a Christmas party for our clients and friends in December of every year, and I had neglected to bring that bottle back to my liquor cabinet at home. I was shocked that Aaron would do such a thing without at least asking.

He told me that he "needed some courage." He said the Bar was supposed to be meeting with him that afternoon and that he was in trouble with them. He said he wanted to make sure that this client was not damaged by his screwup. I said I would talk to the client.

It seems that Aaron had a serious drug and alcohol problem which had been out of control. I called the client and made an appointment to see him that afternoon and told Aaron I would see that client. If I got along with him okay, and if the client agreed, I would take over the handling of the case. Aaron said that they would agree, that he had already discussed the case with his client and his family. However, I wanted to hear it from the client and get their signature on the line. Aaron told me that he was not going to take a referral fee in this case as he felt guilty for what he had not done.

In perusing the file, I discovered that Aaron had, early on, made a nice demand on the insurance company for the drunk driver's employer. The drunk driver was a construction worker. He was doing a job down in Stuart, Florida. The company he worked for was from the State of Kentucky. That employee, together with three other employees of that company, had come down to Stuart to do a job which the company had bid for. The vehicle they used to come down was a vehicle owned by their company from Kentucky.

When Aaron had sent the demand to that insurance company for that company, they had mailed him a letter back and told him that the owner of the vehicle was not responsible for the damage in this case since the owner had not given permission to the driver to drive the vehicle at the time of this accident. They had enclosed a signed agreement that the at-fault driver had made with his employer which said the vehicle could only be used for business purposes in Florida for the transportation to and from the job and the motel in Stuart. Of course, the injured party did not agree to this, and that paper was useless.

In Florida, we have something called a Dangerous Instrumentality Rule. This rule states that the owner of a motor vehicle is equally responsible with the driver of the motor vehicle for that driver's negligence. This was particularly true when the owner knew, or should have known, of the purposes for which the vehicle was to be used, but this was not essential.

The company sent these four guys to Florida with only one vehicle. Just how were they to go buy groceries? How could they go to the beach on their day off? The idea that they would not be using the company vehicle was absolutely ludicrous. I did not believe that the company, or the driver, had much of a case and felt this matter was a slam dunk.

The first time the company in Kentucky heard my name was when I filed suit within a couple of days. I did not wait to demand any settlement since the statute of limitations was about to run.

Before the tortfeasors (defendants) had filed their answer to the suit, it had been settled for around $450,000. This was the easiest money I'd ever made, but I did not want to handle any other of Aaron's cases which might ultimately get me in trouble. I had been warned by my malpractice carrier in the past to look out for cases where the statute was about to run as. If the case was dismissed, we might have a problem filing a new complaint.

Epilogue

Aaron Browner lost his license to practice law. He had a major drug and alcohol problem and could not function in his duties as an attorney. Many of his clients were damaged as a result of his spiral downward, which had been lasting a couple of years when it caught up to him.

A few years ago, Aaron died in an assisted living facility. He died young and totally broken. Cocaine and alcohol are a lethal mix for anyone trying to practice law or anyone else in society, for that matter.

I have been meticulous in my practice to be ethical for all my clients. I'm proud to say that no client of mine ever filed a complaint with the Florida Bar over any of my actions (knock on wood).

BOOK 15

Relationships

Chapter 42

The key to my law practice success is based upon relationships which I have established over the years with extended families who I am in contact with. An example of this is the Antonelli family (not their real name).

In 1980, I was representing two of the Antonelli brothers, Lennie and Patrick. They had been driving their automobile down US One near Fort Pierce, Florida, when a drunk driver swung across in front of them and collided head-on. Lennie, particularly, had movie star good looks. The only blemish he had was a three-inch-long ugly scar down the left side of his face which he had sustained in the accident in question. It was probable he would have some plastic surgery to lessen that, but the scar would be forever. Lennie was a student at Florida State University and was home for the summer visiting his family.

The injury to his brother, Patrick, was more serious, in my opinion. Patrick had suffered a lacerated liver in this accident and had been hospitalized for quite some time, though he was recovering nicely. Patrick was by far the larger of the two of them. He was around six three tall and weighed probably 275 pounds, which all appeared to be muscle. Patrick worked out religiously. He was a fireman down in Martin County to our immediate south. Lennie was particularly interested in closing out this case before he had to go back to Florida State. Early on in this case, I was able to work out a reasonable settlement for the two boys. They did not have transportation and wanted me to come to their house to sign the settlement statement outlining just what everyone was getting. Their house was on the edge of the country very near Fort Pierce. It was in a more or less rural area. The Antonelli house was a very nice ranch-style home with probably four bedrooms. Lennie and Patrick told me that they had two brothers, one of whom was living in the home at that time as well. I had not met that brother, nor had I met Lennie or Patrick's father or mother.

When I entered the Antonelli home, I was showed into the living room. I was impressed. On all walls, there were numerous beautiful game trophies. There were three of the largest white-tailed deer heads I'd ever seen. There was a mount from an elk, a mount from a mule deer, one for a bear, and, interestingly, several birds, including turkeys and pheasant. Every mount had underneath the mount an arrow which was attached to the mount. I asked my clients if they had actually shot all these animals.

Lennie blushed and said, "No, that was our dad. He is the Robin Hood." Lennie explained that his father had won the archery championship in the State of Ohio five years running before moving to St. Lucie County. His dad was retired on some sort of disability. I explained to the boys that I liked to hunt, but I did not bow hunt. I told them that I was fascinated by the idea of the compound bow and that you could take large animals with a stick and a string in one hand and an arrow in the other.

Just at that time, walking up behind me was the Antonelli father, Richard. Richard said, "I heard that. If you're serious, I will appreciate your meeting me at the bow shop tomorrow at five p.m., and I will fit you with the equipment that you need in order to do that. I will then train you how to shoot such a bow." I could not resist the offer.

We finalized my work on Lennie and Patrick's case, and I was promptly at the bow shop the next afternoon.

Mr. Antonelli fitted me with the latest compound bow and showed me the kinds of arrows I would need. He then brought me back to his house, which had a barn in the backyard. On the side of the barn was a large target, perhaps six feet by six feet. We stepped off twenty paces from the target and drew a line in the grass. I was told to stand behind the line and see if I could hit the target.

Even though the poundage on the bow was set at only thirty-five pounds, I had a very difficult time drawing the bow. I finally got it to full draw. I immediately fired the arrow. I thought I had the site properly lined up. The arrow almost missed the target but settled in the lower righthand corner about three inches from the bottom.

I said to Mr. Antonelli, "That's not very good, is it?"

He replied, "Actually, most people I teach to shoot the bow cannot hit the side of the barn on the first attempt." He showed me how to properly draw a bow, and it was quite easy once you knew the method. Knowledge is everything. Brute strength is not necessary.

Three or four months later, I was fairly accomplished with a hunting bow, and I could hit an area of about three square inches at thirty yards or less. Richard invited me to go with him and friends up to Pennsylvania on a hunt that they did every year. They shared a motor home from here to Pennsylvania where they hunted on "Uncle Louie's" property. The first day there, I killed a deer, while no one else in the group killed one. We had plenty of meat for the camp.

My relationship with the father, and to a certain extent with the sons, continued for several years. Once I learned how to shoot, I invited Richard to come up to North Florida with me to go hunting on some property I had there with my cousin, Jim Glisson. He was in love with the place.

I had met Richard's wife, Gigi, and she was very nice. Being Italian, she had straight black hair, brown eyes, and olive complexion. She was not petite, but she was still rather attractive.

Richard was a noted snook fisherman. The snook is perhaps the best tasting fish that grows in the Atlantic, and they fight like the dickens. The first time Richard took me out on his boat, I landed a snook that weighed approximately forty pounds. My back was sore for days thereafter.

Richard later traded in that boat and bought another one. He had a special chair put on the front of the boat so that he could run the trolling motor with foot pedals while still fishing. The chair in question rotated 360 degrees on its base. It was twenty-three inches above the deck on the end of a pedestal.

One day, while fishing, Mr. Antonelli turned the boat seat in one specific direction. When it hit one magic spot, the seat jumped out of the plastic holding device, and Mr. Antonelli was launched across the deck, where he struck his neck and head area against the fish box. Richard was injured with a herniated disc in his neck, which was very painful. He called me to see if he had a case. I went out and looked at the boat. When I put the seat back on the top of the pedestal and rotated it for 355 degrees, it was as solid as the Rock of Gibraltar. The remaining five degrees rotation, when it hit that spot, the seat would always fall off the pedestal. The pedestal would fall onto the deck very quickly. I told Richard not to get rid of the boat as I thought we had an excellent products liability case on our hands. This was a new seat with a new housing device which had been recently installed by a local shop. We sued the seat manufacturer as well as the local distributor. The local distributor was brought into the case because we wanted to keep the case in the State of Florida and not in federal court. The manufacturers were out in California, and if we had sued only them, they could have had the case removed to federal court, which I personally disliked.

Soon, Mr. Antonelli came into my office. He brought with him a device which turned out to be the seat in question. He apologized to me and said that he had sold the boat when someone offered him more money than he thought it was worth, and he was purchasing a new boat. He said prior to giving up the boat, he had removed the housing and pedestal and chair in question and had mounted them on a large plastic crate, which I believe in the past held milk jugs. I went over to the device, and it still failed in the same location where Richard had now put a small mark on the platform to show the area which was dangerous. Richard had taken video of the boat, together with the chair, before the sale had been finalized. The video showed the failure of the chair housing.

The case progressed nicely. We took the deposition of the distributor, who testified this was the best fighting chair on the market and that they had had no problems with it in the past. Likewise, the manufacturer indicated it was their belief it was a sound device, which, when properly used, could not malfunction as we had alleged.

Finally, the day came for mediation of the suit. There were representatives from the manufacturer as well as their attorney. The local distributor was also there along with his attorney. We had a mediator. I brought into the room the device that Mr. Richard Antonelli had prepared, and I placed it on the conference table. After discussing how the injury occurred, I put a demonstration of the actual chair, which was the subject of the suit. I made sure that the affected spot was pointed in an area that was not occupied in my conference room. I showed how strong it was at most points in the compass, but when it reached the critical area, the slightest pressure on the seat caused the seat to violently jump from its housing and slide across the table. It seemed to scare everyone present when that happened.

Needless to say, that mediation resulted in a large settlement on behalf of Mr. Antonelli. This case happened in the early 1990s. In 2000, Richard and his wife, Gigi, came to my office with a serious problem. It seems that some years before, Gigi's father had died, and he was a fairly wealthy man from Ohio. He had left his money in a trust and named Gigi's brother as trustee to take care of his and his sister's money. There were only two children in the family.

The trustee did not regularly provide Gigi with reports as to what investments he was making or what returns on the money he was receiving. He sent her a small stipend every month from the trust to help Gigi financially.

It turns out that the brother was investing all the money in the trust as if it were his own. He also made some very unwise investments. In one case, he had purchased a run-down golf course in Jackson, Mississippi, with the idea that he could turn it around. Most of that investment was lost.

In another investment, he bought a relatively nice golf course in northern Ohio, which, because of the weather, could only be used effectively as a golf course approximately seven months out of the year. Needless to say, that investment also failed to have a decent return. Gigi's interest in the trust was initially right at $2 million. In just a few years, Gigi's brother had managed to lose over $1 million of that money.

Gigi's brother resided in Stuart, Florida, in an upscale community.

I sued him in circuit court here in St. Lucie County, Florida, and alleged that he had defrauded his sister and further alleged that he had violated his fiduciary duties as a trustee.

Discovery in the case was carried out in Florida, Mississippi, and in Ohio. In Jackson, Mississippi, I took the deposition of a bank official who had with him several banker's boxes of records from his dealings with Gigi's brother. Not long before I got this case, my son had graduated from Stetson Law School and had joined our practice. I assigned him the task of going through every banker's box to see what evidence was useful in the case. My son, Steven, has an almost photographic memory. He only needs to read something once, and he knows where it is.

Next, I went to the State of Ohio, unfortunately in the dead of winter. It was fifteen degrees, and the wind was blowing when we arrived in Cleveland. When I left the Orlando Airport that morning, it was seventy-five degrees and balmy.

I had packed up in my bag hunting coveralls for my first day in town, as that was the warmest garment I had. I also had a coat and a sweater. When I got downstairs from the baggage area of the airport, I opened my bag and put on my coveralls before going out into the elements. I took a shuttle from the airport to the hotel nearby. The next morning, I took the shuttle service into the city, and it pulled me up to the curb next to the building I was seeking. I was wearing a suit and had an overcoat. I stepped out of the vehicle, and suddenly, my foot was in the gutter, which was full of salt and ice water from the treatment of the snow from the day before. It was bitterly cold. I realized then why I really did not like living in the north.

I went upstairs and had a productive day with the bank officer. There were literally about one dozen more bankers boxes of materials involving the case. I looked at several of them and verified the only things in these boxes were related to the investments made by the trust. I subpoenaed all those boxes and obtained copies of the same from the bank. These were shipped back to Florida to join the approximate four boxes I had previously received from Mississippi. The boxes consumed most of the floor in my conference room.

Steven proceeded to read every piece of paper in those boxes. There were many thousands of pages. He read very fast, but it took him the better part of a month to go through every box. He had found at least one gold nugget of evidence in each box, which really brought home the breadth of the fraud. There had been no disclosure to the banks of the existence of the trust, and Gigi's brother had simply invested the funds as if they were his own. This was a clear violation of fiduciary duty.

I took the deposition of the trustee/brother, and he verified that he was the trustee and that he understood there were fiduciary duties which he claimed to have met. He also testified that he believed that these were excellent investments which would pay off "in the long run."

The case was set for trial. However, the court had ordered us to mediation. By that time, Buck Vocelle had become a Supreme Court certified mediator. The mediation would take place in his office in Vero Beach, Florida. At the mediation, the brother and sister barely talked with each other. They were obviously estranged by this time. At some point in the process, the brother asked to speak with his sister (my client) in private. She assented to the meeting, and the two of them went elsewhere while the attorneys stayed in the room awaiting their return. The two of them agreed on a settlement, which my client insisted on. I believed there was some threat to her involved but was unable to figure it out. Still, a million dollars is nothing to sneeze at.

The brother ultimately made Gigi an offer "she couldn't refuse." It was implied by the brother that if there was any more, he would be filing bankruptcy, which would tie up the case for years. Everything that takes place in a mediation is typically confidential. This conversation which he had with his sister and her husband took place on a short break and was outside the mediation conference room.

The offer the brother made was $1 million. Gigi Antonelli reluctantly agreed to accept that offer and dismiss the case.

This case concluded in 2002. I had known and represented the Antonelli family in there different decades. We had become friends, and they trusted my advice. They had been a referral source.

Epilogue

Chapter 43

By the year 2002, Lennie had completed Florida State University with a business degree. He moved to Colorado to help his brother, Mark, as a manager in a home building business his brother owned. His brother, Patrick, had moved to Ocala with his wife and child. Shortly after Gigi's case was completed, Richard and Gigi sold their local property and bought a very nice place near Chattahoochee in North Florida. It was eighty acres and had lots of wild turkeys and deer on it. When I would go up to visit my family, I would go by and say hello. I had contact with Richard perhaps once or twice a year. One year, he had requested permission from me to hunt on my property, which I gladly gave. That day, Richard took the largest deer which was taken in Florida that year. Usually, Florida deer are not that big, but this had obviously migrated down from Alabama, where they have better stock. Richard had the animal's head mounted, and it was on his wall next to three others he had gotten in the State of Ohio which I commented on earlier. The four deer all looked like brothers.

Gigi died about three years ago as I write this book. Last fall, I visited with Richard Antonelli in his home in North Florida.

When I had met Richard back in 1980, I was impressed that he had a solid head full of white hair. His age was hard to determine, though I later found out he was only in his fifties when I first met him. All his shooting buddies at the archery tournaments referred to him as "the old man." When I represented Richard around 1990, he did not seem to have aged a day and still was referred to as "the old man." When I saw him in 2021, I observed that his appearance had not changed, even though he was well into his eighties. He still hunted and fished and shot a competition bow with great steadiness. Richard was one of the most amazing people I had ever met, and I will miss him when he is gone.

Book 16

Good Neighbor?

Chapter 43

Donnie Arnold (not his real name) was an attorney who advertised heavily with billboards located throughout the Treasure Coast area of Florida. The attorney, whose picture appeared on the billboards, looked to be in his late twenties. He was handsome, with thick black hair and white teeth. These ads included a smiling photo of Donnie holding his young beautiful daughter and an indication that his law office handled all kinds of personal injury cases, including such things a medical malpractice, slip and fall, and automobile accident cases. Some of his ads claimed he used to work for the insurance companies and "knew their tricks." I had never met Mr. Arnold, but I was pretty sure he didn't handle medical malpractice cases personally. I also doubted he had very much expertise in handling the other types of cases he advertised. I had never seen him at a docket call with all the attorneys who actually try cases.

It is a dirty secret that some "lawyers" don't actually practice law but only run a law-related business called a referral service. These "lawyers" sign their unfortunate clients to the highest contingency fee allowed by law. Often, these attorneys will seek a fast settlement with the insurance company, which often is not in the client's best interest. Unless these guys can reach a quick settlement, they usually refer the cases to lawyers from such places as Miami or Ft. Lauderdale. They send the cases a hundred miles away so as not to build up local attorneys who might take future business away from the referrers by getting good results. "Lawyers" like Donnie get 25 percent of the legal fees for doing, oh, about three hours of work and investing none of their money. I had believed that Donnie Arnold was one of these "lawyers" because I had never seen him in court, even for a routine motion, nor had I ever heard of him actually trying a case. To say I had no respect for Donnie Arnold is an understatement.

Out of the blue, one morning, I received a call from Donnie. He said, "You don't know me, but I have a case I want your help on. I understand you aren't afraid of going to trial and that you love trying cases against Bradley Pierce [not his real name]."

I explained to Donnie that my own malpractice insurance company had warned me about getting involved in other attorneys' messes. Donnie assured me I could make some serious money on the case and asked that I meet the client before I made any decision about representation.

Donnie Arnold told me that I knew the family of his client and would love the case if I looked at it. He said he was desperate as the case was on next week's trial docket before Judge Scott Kenney in Fort Pierce. Donnie also admitted, sheepishly, that he was not prepared to try the case and had, in fact, never before tried a personal injury case to a jury. He said the client was Josephine Lewis (not her real name), and she was in town from Connecticut for another week, staying with her folks. Her mother was Monica Lewis (not her real name), who used to cut my wife's hair. Her dad was John Lewis (not his real name), a retired Florida Highway Patrol traffic homicide investigator who I had met earlier in my career and genuinely liked. My wife, Betsey, and I were also friends with Monica Lewis's sister, Stephanie. Fort Pierce is a pretty small town.

I asked Donnie Arnold just how unprepared he was for trial. He stated that Josephine had undergone emergency spinal surgery up in Connecticut as a result of her injuries from the accident. Mr. Arnold had not yet taken the deposition of her treating neurosurgeon. The good doctor could not come to Florida for the trial, and discovery was closed, so it was impossible to take his video deposition at the last minute. Of course, the surgeon was perhaps the most important witness in the case. I asked Donnie how he could let such an important matter slide for so long, and he said he thought State Farm would settle without going to the expense of a doctor's deposition in Connecticut.

I did know the family of Josephine Lewis and felt sorry for her and her family. However, I was still reluctant. I had other cases I was working on but told him I would not decide until meeting the client. If I agreed to help with the case, it would be only if we could get a continuance from Judge Kenney. Continuances are routinely granted by the courts, especially when a new attorney is hired in a case. I had never heard of a court not granting a continuance in this circumstance.

The next morning, Josephine Lewis and her six-year-old daughter, Ashley, were in my office, along with Donnie Arnold. Josephine was only five feet, two inches tall at most. She weighed perhaps 170 pounds. Josephine had short brown hair, nicely done. Despite her chubby appearance, she had a pretty face and a nice disposition. She seemed quite intelligent. Her little girl, Ashley, was a beautiful child with a wide smile and an obviously sharp mind. She seemed to understand everything that was going on.

Josephine was only about twenty-four years old but looked over thirty-five. She had obviously been through an ordeal. I asked her about her past and how she got to where she was that day.

Josephine told me she had been adopted as a baby and raised by wonderful parents in Fort Pierce. After she grew up, she had met her birth mother, who lived in the northeast. Josephine had been very athletic at Westwood High School in Fort Pierce. She starred on the girls' soccer team and was drum major for the marching band. Her grades had been excellent, and she had attended Indian River Community College on a scholarship. She majored in dance and music. Shortly after starting college, Josephine got married and pregnant. I'm not sure in which order, though it is not important. Before Ashley was born, Josephine Lewis's marriage had already ended in divorce. Ashley's father lived in Fort Pierce and worked in the computer installation and repair business.

When Ashley was born, Josephine moved back in with her parents and got a job. After a year or so, she started at IRCC again on a part-time basis. While in school, she also worked part-time as a cashier and helped support herself and Ashley in that way. For fun, Josephine participated with the local theatre group, the Pineapple Theatre, as the music and dance director. She had also been the featured dancer in several productions at the theatre.

A month or so before the collision, Josephine had graduated from IRCC with an associate of arts degree and had earned a scholarship to Palm Beach Atlantic College in dance. She could complete her bachelor's degree in a couple of years if she worked at it. Josephine had been involved romantically with a young man who had recently relocated to Connecticut for a job, and she had mixed emotions about what she wanted to do when the crash happened and her life changed.

Chapter 44

On the date of the crash, she had picked up Ashley from day care and was headed home. Josephine was driving an older model Volvo which had been purchased for her by her father. She had stopped for a red light at US One and Gardenia Avenue in Fort Pierce and had been sitting there for a minute or two. Suddenly, a large white pickup truck slammed into the rear of her car, bending the frame of the Volvo and injuring Josephine Lewis's neck. Even though they were wearing seat belts, Josephine Lewis had instinctively reached out her hand to protect Ashley right before the crash and was in a twisted position at impact.

The Fort Pierce Police came to the scene and noticed that Josephine was in some distress with a painful neck. Though she was advised to take the ambulance to the emergency room, Josephine Lewis refused. She told me she did not like Lawnwood Regional Medical Center's emergency room. She told me her aunt worked at Lawnwood and, in the past, had told Josephine some horror stories. She did not want to wait for hours in the emergency room while heart attack victims, those with gunshot wounds, and other patients were treated ahead of the less injured folks, such as her. The EMTs told Josephine at the scene that she probably did not have a fractured spine. However, she was told to seek medical treatment. Josephine had a friend of the family who was a chiropractor and whose office was right down the street from the accident scene. She decided to see Dr. Kenneth Schwarz first.

Josephine's damaged Volvo could not be safely driven from the scene of the collision. Josephine's parents came to the scene. Her dad took charge of her car while her mom drove Josephine down to Dr. Schwarz's office.

Dr. Schwarz took x-rays of Josephine Lewis's cervical spine, which confirmed there were no fractures. The x-ray did show, however, that the spinal column was in severe spasm. In a normal neck x-ray, there is a curvature in the shape of a C. In a neck in severe spasm, there is a straight up-and-down appearance to vertebrae, often referred to as a military spine. The spasm was confirmed by the doctor's manual examination of the neck muscles. The chiropractor diagnosed a cervical strain/sprain with a possible herniated disc. Dr. Schwarz did not perform chiropractic adjustments on Josephine. He did apply ice to the swollen neck and thereafter treated the neck daily with moist heat and massage. Fairly soon, Dr. Schwarz referred Josephine to a neurologist, Dr. Hooshang Hooshmand of Vero Beach, Florida, for treatment.

Josephine had been a patient of Dr. Hooshmand in the past. When she was about eighteen years old, she hurt her lower back while working a Christmas job with the local UPS office. Workers' compensation had referred her to Dr. Hooshmand at that time, so she and the doctor knew each other.

When Dr. Hooshmand saw Josephine a few weeks after the collision, he confirmed Dr. Schwarz's diagnosis. In addition to the persistent spasm, Josephine Lewis now had pain and tingling down both arms and into the hands. This is a medical condition called radiculopathy, which is symptom of a pinched nerve, or more seriously, it might be a sign of spinal cord compression. Dr. Hooshmand ordered an MRI of Josephine's cervical spine. The report came back from the radiologist as positive for a herniated disc between the fifth and sixth cervical vertebrae with some stenosis (narrowing) of the area around the spinal cord.

Almost a month post-collision, Josephine was experiencing serious symptoms in addition to her pain. Dr. Hooshmand wanted to refer Josephine to a neurosurgeon here in Florida. By that time, Josephine had decided to relocate to Connecticut, where her boyfriend lived. She had also been offered a job there. Dr. Hooshmand asked his patient where in Connecticut she would be living and gave her the name of a prominent neurosurgeon near her new home. Josephine took her MRI films with her when she moved. About a month after arriving in Connecticut, she met with the surgeon suggested by Dr. Hooshmand. That neurosurgeon performed emergency anterior cervical discectomy and fusion surgery soon after first meeting Josephine in New Haven, Connecticut.

Before moving north, Josephine Lewis signed a contract for Donnie Arnold to handle her personal injury case. Donnie told me that he learned the driver of the white pickup truck was uninsured. Florida has no mandatory bodily insurance coverage law and up to 30 percent of drivers in the state are uninsured. These uninsured drivers account for a high percentage of collisions statewide. A Florida resident's only protection against these people is to purchase uninsured motorist insurance. Donnie immediately started trying to settle Josephine's case with the UM carrier, State Farm.

Josephine lived with her parents at the time of the crash. Since they had stackable uninsured motorist coverage with State Farm on their autos, including the car driven by Josephine, total insurance coverage in this case was $225,000. Donnie Arnold had this information when he tried to settle with State Farm for $30,000. State Farm's response was an offer of $6,000 total. I asked him how he arrived at the $30,000 demand value for the case. He had no answer to that. I thought to myself that it was a number easily divisible by three.

From the medical records brought by Donnie Arnold, I learned that within a month or so of moving to Connecticut, Josephine had emergency neurosurgery performed by Dr. Richard Sabshin of New Haven. Dr. Sabshin was a clinical professor of neurosurgery at Yale University. His credentials were impeccable. Dr. Sabshin performed an anterior cervical discectomy and fusion at the C5/C6 level of the spine. In layman's terms, the doctor made an incision and entered the neck from the front, eased the larynx to one side, removed the herniated disc, and performed a fusion of the fifth and sixth cervical (neck) vertebrae. The surgery had been performed at St. Rafael's Hospital in New Haven, and we had the hospital and medical bills which, by themselves, greatly exceeded the $6,000.00 State Farm had offered Donnie to settle. Josephine's recovery had not been perfect. She went through extensive physical therapy, which helped relieve some, but not all, of the pain. This was expensive too. Even after State Farm received all the medical bills and records, including those of the surgery and rehabilitation, their position regarding settlement remained unchanged.

In a dream case, a plaintiff's personal injury attorney looks for several factors:

1. Clear liability. We had that here.
2. A definite and provable injury. We had that.
3. A nice client with a pleasant personality. We had that.
4. A defendant with ability to pay. We had that too.
5. Time and resources to prepare for trial. That was the only problem.

I told Josephine and Donnie Arnold that I would agree to help with the case only if we were able to get a continuance. I asked Donnie if he had filed a Civil Remedy Notice against State Farm. He answered, "That's about the only thing I have done right." He produced the acceptance letter from the Department of Insurance, and it actually was okay.

Under Florida's Bad Faith laws, to hold an insurance company responsible for their actions of bad faith, it is necessary to notify them with a Civil Remedy Notice and also indicate to them that there is bad faith going on. The insurance company has only sixty days after receipt of the Notice to do the right thing and settle. If not, there might be serious consequences for the carrier later. Under the law, if you succeed and can prove that there was bad faith, the insurance company may be responsible to pay 100 percent of any verdict together with attorney's fees and costs. In that scenario, there is no policy limit. If we won big, State Farm would likely pay the excess verdict, plus attorneys' fees and costs.

I worked out an agreement with Donnie Arnold. We were to share equally in the advancement of all costs necessary to properly prepare for and try this case. I would receive the lion's share of any fee earned (60 percent), though he was to receive a larger amount than the usual 25 percent referral fee (40 percent). He was allowed to attend trial and pay attention to get some experience. Donnie was also to help in any way I asked. He was to particularly take notes during voir dire and during defense counsel's opening statement. He was to consult with me regarding these notes during the process. However, I would be responsible to make all decisions relative to the trial and would handle any settlement negotiations with regard to the case, with proper consultation with Josephine Lewis. I was to be the attorney who was to consult with the client when necessary. Donnie Arnold, as well as the client, understood these conditions and agreed to them.

The case could not possibly be won if it had to be tried in the next few weeks. We agreed to try to obtain the continuance and work like hell to get ready in a few months if that was all the time the judge allowed. In addition to not taking Dr. Sabshin's deposition, Donnie had not taken the deposition of the rehabilitation doctor or physical therapists who had worked with Josephine Lewis up in Connecticut. The time had expired to take such depositions. There were several other holes in the case as well. Donnie was sure that Judge Kenney would give us a continuance, as there had been none in the case before. I was not so sure.

I prepared and signed a contingency fee contract with Josephine Lewis. I also had a signed agreement with Donnie Arnold regarding the division of fees and responsibility for costs in the case. Then I quickly drafted a notice of my appearance on behalf of the plaintiff in the case. I also prepared a motion for a continuance to give me time to prepare for trial. We forwarded a copy of both to opposing counsel, along with my letter withdrawing Donnie's offer to settle for

$30,000. I believe this was on a Thursday, and the docket call was scheduled for the following Monday

On Friday morning, I received a phone call from Wally Smith, the supervising adjuster of the State Farm Regional Office in Fort Pierce. He and I knew each other, as I had settled and litigated numerous cases against State Farm over the years. Wally said, "Roger, you need to stay away from this case. The client is a fraud, and we're going to run Donnie Arnold out of town on this case."

I responded that Josephine Lewis was certainly not a fraud. Her injuries were real, and liability was clear. I said, "The fact you hold some kind of grudge against her attorney should not be a cause for vengeance against your State Farm policyholder."

He said, "Well, if you get involved with this case, it is going to cost you too." He also said, "Your client is a fake, and we have videotape evidence to prove it."

I thought, *What is Wally afraid of?* After that conversation, you could not have run me off this case with a shotgun.

Chapter 45

On Friday afternoon, I attended the docket call with Donnie Arnold. My client was also in attendance. A docket call is where perhaps fifty lawyers are in the courtroom together, and one by one, the cases on the docket are called up, and the judge assigns the trial dates. The first case called on the docket was *Josephine Lewis v. State Farm*, even though we were not the first case on the list. Judge Kenny said we were to start trial Monday. I spoke up and informed the judge that I had just been retained as trial counsel and that I had filed a motion for a continuance so that I could prepare for trial. I indicted we would need several months to get up to speed and properly represent my client. I pointed out that no continuance had been previously taken in the case, and as a general rule, continuances are routinely granted. Josephine Lewis would be prejudiced if I were not allowed to prepare. I had case law on hand to prove these points.

Bradley Pierce spoke up and told the judge that State Farm would not agree to a continuance and argued that they would be somehow prejudiced by any delay. I knew that Judge Kenney and Bradley had been close friends before Kenney ascended to the bench. They were rumored to still be close and had been seen sharing cocktails at local Fort Pierce bistros from time to time. I should have not been shocked when the judge denied my motion for continuance and said we would be starting trial Monday morning.

I asked the judge if I could have one minute to confer with my client and cocounsel. He said yes. I then huddled with Donnie Arnold and Josephine. I asked Donnie whether this case had ever been voluntarily dismissed. He answered, "You can do that?"

I told him, "Yes, if the statute of limitations has not run and the case had not been previously dismissed." He said we were okay on that point. I explained briefly to Josephine what I was doing. I then turned to Judge Kenney and announced, "Your Honor, in view of your ruling two minutes ago, the plaintiff is taking a voluntary dismissal without prejudice. I will be refiling the case before the end of next week."

Judge Kenney hit the roof. He became louder. He stated, "Mr. Messer, you realize that if you dismiss and refile the case, you will have to pay the costs of the defendant."

I told the judge I understood we would be responsible for reasonable costs before we could proceed but told him his ruling on the motion for continuance left me no alternative. I said, "I assume we will receive a fair hearing on the defense motion for costs."

The judge said we would and called the next case.

Chapter 46

On Friday of that week, I filed the new *Josephine Lewis v. State Farm* case and paid the filing fee and cost of service of process. Donnie sent me a check for his half of this. Shortly thereafter, I received a motion to tax costs filed by Bradley on behalf of State Farm. It was accompanied by a short affidavit signed by Bradley alleging he had received certain cost bills from State Farm relating to the case. The amount sought was almost $10,000. This was a huge amount for the defense for a case where trial had not yet occurred, and no expert witnesses had been paid by the defense except for a retired orthopedic surgeon who had supposedly performed an "independent" medical exam on Josephine.

I filed a motion to allow me to take discovery on the issue of costs. It was granted. I demanded and received copies of all bills and much correspondence between the State Farm adjuster and such providers as the surveillance company from Connecticut which had run up huge bills in following and filming Josephine. At first blush, it appeared that either State Farm or the surveillance company might be double billing. I demanded and received copies of all videotapes of the surveillance—literally hours of it. I also demanded proof of all other expenses State Farm claimed it had spent in the case.

We scheduled depositions in Connecticut of the investigators who took the surveillance. One cold week in March 1999, I journeyed to Madison, Connecticut, Josephine Lewis's hometown. Madison is a beautiful seaside village hard up against Long Island Sound. It is a quaint little New England town with fishing boats in the harbor and neat homes done in early colonial architecture. The depositions took almost a day as I watched a ton of videotape.

It turns out the surveillance company had used three teams, sometime simultaneously, to stalk and film the actions of Josephine and her daughter, Ashley. They had talked with Josephine's landlady and told her they were investigating possible insurance fraud. The landlady had rented them an apartment across the courtyard from Josephine's home so they could easily snoop. Amazingly, they had no video of Josephine doing anything in her own yard. One of the bills they submitted to State Farm was for renting that apartment.

I watched all the videotapes while asking questions of the investigators. The longest and dullest videotape showed Josephine attending one of Ashley's girls' soccer games. For the entire time at the game, Josephine stood on the sideline like an unmovable object, never smiling. She never clapped her hands nor showed any emotion. Josephine neither jumped up and down nor ran down the sideline to follow the action like other parents were doing on the film. She did give her daughter a small hug at the end of the game, but she looked in pain in doing so. The tape ended with Josephine and Ashley getting into her car.

The second and best video was of scenes taken at the Connecticut Firemen's Picnic. The investigators said they tailed Josephine's car from her apartment over to a public park in the next town where the event was held. It was a multicar tail by the surveillance team and sounded quite cloak-and-dagger. The investigators were sure they had not been seen by Josephine. Two separate video teams were on the scene at the park and followed Josephine around, taking snapshots and videotape.

The video showed Josephine attending the event with her boyfriend and her daughter. There was a scene with Josephine eating an ear of corn. I assure you, no one looks petite or attractive while eating an ear of corn while facing a camera. A lot of time at the picnic was spent just walking around. On the film, Josephine always moved very slowly. Toward the end of the tape, Josephine and Ashley were shown in an egg toss contest with other mothers and daughters. In the game, moms and daughters stood in a line facing each other. They tossed a whole raw egg to each other. After each toss, they took a step back. The winners were those standing last with an unbroken egg. Lots of laughing was going on. State Farm's gum shoes filmed this scene from two directions simultaneously, and we had both takes. On the film, the game was progressing when suddenly, and without any apparent reason, Josephine fell on the ground with a pained look on her face. In ten seconds, she got up and brushed herself off and walked away with Ashley. This scene was repeated from another angle on another videotape.

After viewing the videotapes and asking questions of the videographers, I took the deposition of the owner of the investigative agency and had him produce his billing records to State Farm. We now had proof that State Farm was attempting to double bill for the surveillance. Of course, under oath later, State Farm's lead adjuster on the case would claim it was an honest mistake.

Before returning to Florida, I took the opportunity to visit with Dr. Richard Sabshin in New Haven, which was only fifteen miles west of Madison. I was pleased to learn that Dr. Sabshin was a clinical professor of neurosurgery at Yale University. The doctor taught future spine and brain surgeons at one of the premier medical schools in the United States. Dr. Sabshin had privileges at Yale University Hospital but was also chief of neurosurgery at Saint Rafael's' Hospital in New Haven and said he liked the operating room staff and facilities there better.

Dr. Sabshin just looked like the brilliant neurosurgeon, which he was. He spoke clearly and concisely like a teacher. The doctor was tall and thin and wore dark rimmed glasses. He had wispy thinning hair and appeared to be about forty-five years old. He had a pleasant manner about himself that I thought would go well in front of a jury. I asked Dr. Sabshin why he performed what he had referred to in the records as an "emergency anterior cervical discectomy and fusion" on Josephine Lewis.

He stated, "Sir, first of all, we had the MRI from Florida and a new one from here at Yale which showed the disc herniation, the stenosis, and probably cord compression." He said he had personally viewed the MRI films and had consulted with a top neuroradiologist at Yale, and he had agreed with Dr. Sabshin's assessment.

He continued, "Also, and more importantly, there are four signs of cord compression. First, there was numbness in the extremities, especially the hands. Josephine had that. Secondly, there was urinary incontinence—that is, an inability to control the bladder resulting in a person occasionally wetting themselves. Josephine had that. Third, there was falling down for no apparent reason or an inability to walk easily. Josephine had that. The fourth sign is paralysis. Did you want me to wait for that fourth symptom to happen?"

At that moment, I knew the case was a lock. State Farm's video of the egg toss contest and Josephine's unexplained fall, along with the doctor's testimony, was all the evidence I thought I would need to get a good result from a jury. I thanked Dr. Sabshin for meeting with me and told him I would schedule a videotape deposition for use at trial at a later date at a time when defense counsel could attend. He said he would be happy to help in any way he could as Josephine Lewis was one of his favorite patients. She was still under his care for follow-up evaluation.

After returning to St. Lucie County, I took the deposition of the State Farm adjuster. Thereafter, I filed an objection to the defense cost motion. After a hearing, Judge Kenney reduced the amount of costs from the first *Josephine Lewis* case to which State Farm was entitled to about $7,200. He ruled that the discrepancy in the billing was an apparently honest mistake. I paid half of the $7,200, and Donnie Arnold paid the other half, though he bitched and moaned about it. Donnie was also unhappy about paying half of the costs of my trip to New England, even though I had flown coach. His complaints about the costs of the case were a continuing theme throughout the case.

Ninety days after filing suit, I filed a Proposal for Settlement (PFS) in the case, offering to accept $160,000 to settle all of Josephine

Lewis's claims. Florida's PFS statute and the applicable rule of civil procedure is designed to push parties toward settlement. Under the law, a plaintiff may file such a proposal, and if the defendant refuses to settle and net judgment after a jury verdict exceeds the offer by at least 25 percent, the plaintiff would be entitled to attorneys' fees and costs as of the date of the PFS forward. The defendant has thirty days to accept the offer and pay the demand. Thereafter, the offer is of the table and no longer enforceable.

This PFS law is a double-edged sword. The defense can also file a PFS. That offer is also on the table for thirty days. If the plaintiff rejects the offer and ultimately receives a net judgment of less than 75 percent of the proposal, the plaintiff must pay the defense attorney's fees and costs. The law is very unfair because the insurance companies have limitless ability to pay any attorney fee award, while such an award could routinely bankrupt many plaintiffs.

How did I arrive at $160,000 as a proper amount to demand in the PFS? I performed a study using a publication called the Florida Jury Verdict Reporter. I looked at the last ten reported cases in South Florida from Orlando to Key West wherein the following facts existed:

1. There was clear or admitted liability in a rear-end auto crash case.
2. There was an injury requiring one-level anterior cervical discectomy and fusion surgery.
3. There had been a trial to a verdict.

Interestingly, there were eight cases out of the ten that fell in the $200,000–$250,000 range.

Two cases were outliers. One was low at about $140,000 while the other was high at about $450,000. Ignoring those two cases, it was obvious to me that the jury value of these cases was in the $200,000 to $250,000 range. By filing a PFS for $160,000, all I had to do was hit the low end of the probable range to kick in my client's right to have State Farm pay her attorney fees. I was certain State Farm would not pay the PFS as their official offer only stood at about $30,000. I was quite happy when thirty days had passed from my filing the PFS and State Farm had not accepted the offer. From that time forward, I fully expected a trial.

While Donnie was still handling the case alone, the defense had sent Josephine Lewis to retired local orthopedic surgeon Dr. John Sullivan for an alleged "independent" medical evaluation. Under the law, a personal injury plaintiff can be required to attend a physical examination by a physician hired by the defense. Nowadays, we call those a compulsory medical examination. It is certainly not "independent." In these cases, the examining doctor is always chosen by the insurance company and can be trusted by them to issue a report denying the seriousness of the injury. Usually, the report will find no causation between any obvious injury and the collision, which is the subject of the lawsuit. For his report and later testimony at trial or deposition, the doctor is paid handsomely. As a semiretired orthopedic surgeon, Dr. Sullivan "earned" over $100,000 per year from the insurance industry for his one-sided conservative medical opinions of otherwise seriously injured people. Dr. Sullivan passed away some years ago. May he not rest in peace.

I have always thought there is a special place in hell reserved for medical professionals who took the Hippocratic oath to, among other things, "first do no harm," and then for lucre did their best to prevent injured people from getting justice. Since the *Josephine Lewis* case, I have noticed the quality of the defense doctor witnesses has improved, and their annual earnings for their services has sky-rocketed, but that is for a later story in this book.

Dr. Sullivan was a tall man with wispy gray hair, big ears, high cheekbones, and a craggy face. I had taken his deposition in numerous cases over the years, and in all the hours I had been with him, I had never seen him smile. He was very old-fashioned in his practice of medicine. Back in the mid-eighties, MRIs were new technology. I recall a case where Dr. Sullivan testified that the technology could not be trusted and was "just some electromagnetic hocus-pocus." He did believe in x-rays.

In Josephine's case, she had attended the examination unescorted. Donnie did not think anything was wrong with that. I usually like to either have someone from my office (sometimes me) go with the client or have the exam videotaped. Otherwise, as here, the only proof of what happened there is the doctor's report. I always carefully read these reports as sometimes, though rarely, the physicians actually tell the truth. Dr. Sullivan's report stated he had "reviewed the reports of the two MRIs." In another section of the report, it indicated he had reviewed the reports and the actual films of the x-rays taken in Dr. Schwarz's office the day of the crash as well as the later x-rays. He had also reviewed all the other medical records. From his physical examination of Josephine, along with that record review, Dr. Sullivan had the astounding opinion that Josephine Lewis never had a herniated disc in the cervical spine. According to his expert medical opinion, she suffered from "an osteophyte," which is a bone spur on the edge of the vertebrae which Dr. Sullivan indicted had been present for many years before the car crash. According to Sullivan, that was the cause of all her problems, not the car crash. The fact that symptoms arose right after the collision was just coincidence. Dr. Sullivan expressed doubts that the condition had been serious enough to require surgery.

Dr. Sullivan had been listed on State Farm's witness list as an expert medical witness in the second *Josephine Lewis v. State Farm* case. By rule, the defense is usually limited to one such witness, and they could not hire another one later in the case. I took Dr. John Sullivans's deposition. At first, I established his credentials. He was a "board-certified orthopedic surgeon." He had practiced locally for many years. The doctor had not graduated from any Ivy League medical school, though he listed training at Harvard on his CV. I asked him about that, and he testified that he had attended one continuing education course in the subject of public health at Harvard. The course had nothing to do with orthopedic surgery. I got the doctor to agree that he had not performed an anterior cervical discectomy and fusion in many years. He also agreed that he had done this kind of medical expert work for State Farm for years and was paid a nice income for his testimony on their behalf.

I asked him about what he had reviewed before reaching his opinion in this case. He repeated, word for word from his report, that he had, among other things, "reviewed the reports of the two MRIs." I then asked him if that meant he did not actually review the MRI films themselves. He answered that he didn't need to review them. He had the x-rays which he said provided the proof of the alleged osteophyte, or bone spur, discussed in his report. I smiled and ended the deposition fairly quickly. It does an attorney little good to challenge the medical expert at his deposition. It is much better to wait and maul him in front of a jury.

We took the deposition of the driver of the pickup truck which struck Josephine's Volvo in the collision. He admitted the crash was entirely his fault and that Josephine was lawfully stopped at a red light when he crashed into the rear of her car. I was certain that the defense would admit liability on the eve of trial and attempt to have this case be all about Josephine's believability and not about anyone else's negligence.

Josephine was visiting with her folks in Fort Pierce that summer before the trial began, and I scheduled an office visit with her. We discussed the need to find "before and after" witnesses who knew the injury had changed Josephine. I told her I preferred these witnesses were not family members, though they might do in a pinch.

Josephine said her best friend, Karen Bukea (not her real name), was visiting Fort Pierce that week from Jacksonville and could probably come by that afternoon. I said I would love to meet with the two of them. Later that day, Josephine introduced her friend and fellow dance student at IRCC. The young lady had also been Josephine's choreographer at the Pineapple Theatre and had known her for years before and after the collision.

Karen Bukea told me Josephine was the best dancer at the school and was a star of all of IRCC's dance productions. She said, "You wouldn't believe how Josephine could tumble and pirouette and leap across the stage so effortlessly."

I said it would be nice if we had video of those performances.

Josephine said, "Yes, it would be, but we don't."

Karen Bukea said, "I think we do." She asked Josephine, "Don't you remember? The dance professor took videotapes of all the live performances with a still camera mounted in the middle of the auditorium. He said it was to help him with grading. I bet you he still has the tapes."

I called the professor immediately and learned that he did, in fact, have the videotapes in his attic. He was only too happy to let me have them. Josephine and her friend left to go and pick up the videotapes. They promised to return to my office the next morning.

By ten the next morning, the three of us were huddled over a video monitor trying to view the small figures bouncing across the stage. I was shocked when the young ladies pointed out the dancing Josephine to me. She was a sprite, appearing to be no more than ninety-five-pounds, and she was a pretty amazing dancer. Some of her movements reminded me of gymnastics. The film I was watching was taken about six weeks prior to the crash, and the dancer, Josephine, I was watching appeared to be half the weight and half the age of the Josephine I knew.

Josephine said that her continuing pain and lack of regular exercise resulted in her present appearance. She blamed the collision for everything and blamed State Farm, her own insurance company, for not taking responsibility. Josephine told me she did not want to settle the case until they paid her the limits, plus paid her costs and attorneys' fees. I didn't want to settle the case either.

I explained to Josephine that I wanted to send the videotape to my good friend Jim Young's office at Legal Video Inc. I would ask Jim to try to enhance the film and to blow it up so the jury could see Josephine better. I also wanted to see if he could make her more recognizable.

While she was in my office, I called Josephine's physiatrist, her medical rehabilitation doctor. Dr. Andrew Yuan's office was in Bridgeport, Connecticut. Dr. Yuan said he very much wanted to visit Florida for the trial as it looked like a November trial date, and he hated the cold weather in the northeast. The good doctor said he would plan a vacation around the trial and only charge us for the time he testified. He would pay for his own flight. I couldn't believe how nice he was. He said he would visit with me in Connecticut when I came up there to take Dr. Sabshin's deposition. I told him that would be great.

My office scheduled Dr. Sabshin's video deposition as well as the deposition of Josephine's physical therapist to take place in Connecticut during a two-day period. Of course, the dates were coordinated with Bradford's office as he would attend also. We also scheduled a court-ordered mediation in the case for shortly after our return from the depositions.

Before I left for the north, I heard from Jim Young. Jim had already digitized the videotape. He said blowing up the film was easy and could be shown on his large-screen equipment in front of the jury. He also figured out how to place a spotlight image around the dancing Josephine Lewis on the video. The spotlight would move as she moved around the stage. He had shortened the performance to about eight minutes and said he had edited it down to just the best parts. We amended our exhibit list for the trial to include the original videotape as well as the edited version and sent copies to Bradford's office.

In anticipation of Dr. Sabshin's video deposition, I had ordered a medical illustration exhibit from a group out of Atlanta known as Medi-Visions Inc. This exhibit showed, in detail, all the steps of the anterior cervical discectomy and fusion which had been the surgery performed on Josephine Lewis. Before paying to blow up the exhibit, we sent a copy to Dr. Sabshin for his review. He made a couple of small suggestions, which were forwarded to the medical illustrator. She made the revisions and sent them back to Dr. Sabshin for his approval. When he was happy, we had the exhibit blown up to power size. Because the time was tight, I had the blown-up exhibit shipped from Atlanta directly to the hotel in New Haven, where I would be staying.

When I arrived in Connecticut the evening before the video deposition, I was ecstatic at how the exhibit had turned out. The next morning, I arrived at the doctor's office at Yale University well before the deposition was scheduled. We reviewed the exhibit as well as what I thought the doctor's testimony would be. He had given deposition testimony in the past and was not nervous. We were ready.

The videotaped deposition was taken in a conference room there at Yale. Dr. Sabshin went over his impeccable credentials. He explained in detail all the symptoms which Josephine had exhibited at the time of his first examination of her—the numbness in the hands, the urinary incontinence, and the falling down. The doctor explained the importance of all these findings. He explained why he had to perform the surgery on an emergency basis to prevent paralysis.

He then placed the actual MRI films on a view box there in the room. In front of the video camera, he pointed it out the large herniated disc which had been causing Josephine Lewis's symptoms. It was touching the spinal cord. The doctor reviewed the neuroradiologist's report from Florida and the one from Yale, where those experts also found the herniated disc. I asked him if he reviewed the x-rays, and he said he did. He said they don't show much because x-rays do not show soft tissue, only bone. I asked the doctor if he knew the difference between a herniated disc and an osteophyte. He said he did and explained the difference. Dr. Sabshin's opinion was that the bony growth on the edge of Josephine's vertebrae was very tiny and could not be symptomatic. He noted the original radiologist who read the x-ray did not even comment on the osteophyte as being a significant finding.

Dr. Sabshin then took the jury painstakingly through the entire surgery, using the blown-up medical illustration. He said the exhibit perfectly portrayed the surgery that was performed. He noted that besides the disc material that he removed from between the vertebrae, Josephine also had "sequestered" disc material floating freely in the spinal fluid near the spinal cord. This had to be very carefully removed so as not to irritate the spinal cord.

I asked Dr. Sabshin if he had to have an MRI machine on during the surgery to see the herniated disc. He laughed and said that herniated discs are visible with the naked eye, but "I use those large Coke bottle glasses so we don't miss anything." I asked the doctor what he did with the disc material after it was removed. He indicated it was sent to the lab at Yale and then showed the laboratory report that confirmed it was of human herniated disc material. I had blown up a copy of the lab report and had Dr. Sabshin comment on it in front of the video camera.

We closed the deposition with the doctor's testimony that Josephine did not make a complete recovery. He said she was still in rehabilitation, and she would need follow-up care in the future. He testified that Josephine had a permanent impairment according to the AMA Guides. Dr. Sabshin testified that within reasonable medical probability, Josephine's injury and permanent impairment was caused by the automobile collision, which was the subject of this case. He said Josephine would have real though lessened pain throughout her life.

Defense counsel Bradley Pierce attempted cross-examination of Dr. Sabshin. It was ineffective and did not shake the doctor from his opinions. Yes, the doctor had met with me right before the deposition and once before that. Yes, I had agreed to pay him a reasonable fee for his time in giving the deposition and had paid him for the time used in our prior conference. Yes, he really hoped Josephine would be successful in her lawsuit, as she deserved it. I must say I love it when defense lawyers ask questions which are easily fielded by real medical experts who care about their patients.

The deposition lasted a little over an hour. I was smiling as I drove through heavy midday traffic over to Bridgeport and Dr. Yuan's office. Dr. Sabshin's testimony was extremely powerful, and it was "in the can" and could not be changed.

Bridgeport is an industrial city just east of New York. I stopped for lunch to review Dr. Yuan's records before I spoke to him. How did we ever get along without GPS? I found Dr. Yuan's office with some difficulty but arrived in time for our 1:00 p.m. scheduled meeting. No patients were waiting in the outer office, and the doctor explained that they were all scheduled for after 2:00 p.m. that day.

The first thing that struck me about Dr. Yuan was the fact he had only one arm. I later found out that he was also missing a leg. The double amputation had been caused by a horrible subway accident in New York City. Dr. Yuan volunteered all this information at the beginning of our conversation without being asked. I think he thought it might put me at ease. Dr. Yuan was nicely but casually dressed. The doctor was not a tall man. He was thin and had Oriental features with straight black hair and a warm smile.

I asked him to go over his credentials with me. He gave me a copy of his CV and then went, in length, into his training in Oriental and Western medicine. The doctor had a DO in physical medicine and therefore was a "physiatrist." He also was trained in medical acupuncture and acupressure. I asked the doctor what the difference was, and he jokingly explained that insurance companies in Connecticut and New York would pay $25 per needle for acupuncture but nothing for acupressure. He said the treatment methods worked in much the same way, and he personally preferred acupressure for his patients. "But, of course, I have to get paid, so I routinely use the needles," he said with a wry smile.

I said, "Excuse me for asking, but how do you administer acupressure with only one hand?"

He said, "Easy. Do you want me to show you? I noticed you don't look comfortable. Do you have a neck condition?"

I was shocked. I had suffered for years with a herniated disc in my own neck and was considering going ahead with surgery myself. Dr. Yuan said he could relieve my pain temporarily and wouldn't charge me for it. The doctor had me lie down on a low table. About ten minutes later, after sharp and intense pressure being applied to certain points in my neck and some of the areas of my back, I felt 100 percent better. I was a believer.

Dr. Yuan explained he could relieve Josephine Lewis's pain just like that, but it was only a temporary fix. Other long-term modalities were needed for her to live a somewhat normal life in the future. He said Josephine would probably need this type of nonnarcotic pain relief for the rest of her life.

The doctor asked me lots of questions about our area of Florida. I told him we would put him up in the nicest hotel in St. Lucie County, though it was not *that* nice. We would make sure he ate at good restaurants while he was here. He said that was all he wanted—that and his desire to help Josephine, who he genuinely liked.

That evening, I had driven back east over to Madison. I met with Josephine over dinner at a local restaurant and discussed the progress of the case. The mediation was scheduled for a week or two later in Florida, and the trial date looked like it would be in early

November 1999. I asked her how she was doing. She said that physically, she was still in pain, but it had improved.

I told Josephine that after Dr. Sabshin's deposition earlier that day, I expected State Farm to begin in earnest to try to finally settle the case. She said she would only accept the policy limits, along with all my costs, including the $7,200 we had to pay for the first aborted case. She said she might waive the right to attorney fees if the case was settled without much more of a fight. She was a tough lady, and I respected that. Josephine had a great deal of courage and had already been through a lot. She told me that she was furious that State Farm had spied on her and Ashley in her own backyard. She said she felt violated.

"Is this what I paid them all the premiums for?" she asked. Josephine wanted this trial to happen. I wanted this trial to happen. It was likely to happen since State Farm was unlikely to meet her reasonable demands.

I asked Josephine how she was doing financially. She said it had been tough. For six weeks after the surgery, she had not been able to work. Josephine had no savings and was forced to borrow some money from her parents so that she and Ashley could get by. Josephine had promised to pay them back as soon as she got some money from State Farm. She told me her parents were not that well off either. Josephine valued her independence, and it was embarrassing for her to need her parents' assistance. A huge advantage the insurance companies have in these cases is the financial stress serious disabilities place on injured people who must somehow continue to pay their bills during the litigation process. Puny settlement offers may look enticing to folks who find themselves in desperate financial straits.

The next morning in Madison, Connecticut, we held the videotaped deposition of the physical therapist. It only went okay. This physical therapist seemed to be sure she could completely cure any condition. The lady talked on and on about what great progress Josephine was making and how, with her help, she should make a great recovery. She liked that Josephine worked hard to get better with physical therapy. The future assessment of the therapist, however, was, as I thought, a little rosy. This wasn't the most important witness anyway.

Before catching my flight home, I met with another friend of Josephine's who had been listed as a witness. This nice lady worked with Josephine there in Madison. She said she would be happy to come to Florida to testify "on her own nickel." She had witnessed Josephine falling down at least two times after she arrived in Connecticut and before her surgery. She had also seen the pain on Josephine Lewis's face during recovery from the surgery. This is the kind of five-minute witness that jurors love in a personal injury case, and the defense hates.

Shortly after I returned to Florida, State Farm made what I considered their first serious attempt to settle the case. They made an offer of $100,000. My guess was that they thought my Proposal for Settlement for $160,000 (which had expired) was still in effect as our bottom offer. The defense soon learned that was not the case. We indicated that the policy limits, plus all costs expended by our side, might be able to settle the claim. We would consider waiving our entitlement to attorney's fees if there was a prompt settlement.

A couple of weeks later, Josephine flew down to Florida to attend the court-ordered mediation. In our circuit, the court required all litigants to meet with a mediator agreed to by both sides. Both sides are required to attend and attempt settlement. The mediator has no power to force a settlement. He or she can cajole and push, but ultimately, either side has the right to say no. In theory, the mediator is chosen jointly by the attorneys for both sides. Either side can veto a mediator. In practice, at that time, State Farm was notorious for insisting on using one of a limited number of civil mediators. These were typically individuals who State Farm was sure would back them up and try to push a plaintiff toward the result State Farm wanted. I didn't object to the mediator suggested by Bradley, as I believed it wouldn't make a difference. We weren't going to settle without huge concessions from the insurance company anyway.

Not surprisingly, this was the shortest mediation I ever attended in my career. No one is permitted, me included, to say exactly what happens at any mediation. Suffice it to say, the case did not settle in a very short time. As I was leaving the mediation, their mediator stopped me and asked me to reconsider their "fair" offer. He said he would bet me that Josephine would get less from a jury than the State Farm offer. I asked him how much he wanted to bet and asked if $1,000 would be appropriate. I said I would make it tax deductible. The loser would make out the check to the winner's favorite charity. The mediator said that was too rich for his blood.

I said, "Okay, how about a hundred?"

He replied, "How about fifty?"

I said all right, and we shook on it.

About five days later, I was driving down Interstate 95, returning from a hearing in Vero Beach on another case, when my cell phone rang. I thought only a few close friends, family, and my office employees knew my cell number as I valued my privacy. I was quite surprised to hear Wally Smith on the other end of the line. He said, "Roger, I know you really want to get $200,000 out of this case, but I can't get it for you. I know we offered $150,000 to settle. If it will settle it, I'll see if I can get $185,000."

I replied, "Wally, I am required to discuss your offer with my client but can assure you that $200,000 is quite a bit less than she wanted to settle the case. I'll get back to you, but you should get some more authority if you want to avoid a jury trial."

When I got back to the office, I called Josephine and relayed the offer to her. She agreed with me that we should stick by our decision to accept nothing less than the policy limits of $225,000 plus all costs. I called Wally back and rejected his offer.

The trial was rapidly approaching. One of the last depositions scheduled by the defense was of Dr. Hooshang Hooshmand in Vero Beach. Bradley had subpoenaed all of Josephine's records from the doctor, not only of the neck injury but also of the worker's compensation lower back injury from several years before. At the deposition, the doctor was a good witness for Josephine Lewis. He said Josephine had no neck injury before the automobile collision. Dr. Hooshmand testified he had treated Josephine Lewis for a lower back injury when she was about eighteen, and she had gotten better. He said he always checked for neck injuries too, and she had none from the worker's comp accident.

Dr. Hooshmand reviewed the MRI of the neck which he had ordered before Josephine left for Connecticut. He agreed with the reading neuroradiologist that Josephine Lewis had a herniated disc at C5-C6 which was causing her symptoms. He said he had referred Josephine Lewis to the best neurosurgeon he knew of in the State of Connecticut. Dr. Hooshmand said he was sure Josephine would need surgery when she left his care to move north. Bradley took the doctor painstakingly through every scrap of paper in the doctor's files. It was a long deposition, but I believed it was helpful.

After the deposition was over, I stayed behind to chat with the doctor. He agreed to come down to testify live at the trial. He asked me how Josephine was doing and how she had made it through the surgery. I was sure Dr. Hooshmand would make a good impression on the jury. He was a big bear of a man with thick silver-gray hair. He spoke with an interesting Iranian Farsi accent but was an American citizen who had practiced medicine in Vero Beach for many years. Dr. Hooshmand told me he absolutely hated Bradley and State Farm. They apparently had a history.

Chapter 47

The trial was to begin at 9:30 a.m. on a Monday in early November 1999. I entered the courthouse lobby and noticed Bradley and the State Farm adjuster, Charles Matthews, standing there. As I entered the elevator, both of them jumped on behind me. After saying good morning, Bradley said, "Roger, you win. We're going to pay you $200,000 to settle this case."

I told him that I doubted my client would accept the offer. I explained she had incurred heavy costs in this case and would be entitled to costs plus attorney's fees if the verdict was over the $200,000, as we expected. Charles Matthews spoke up and said the $200,000 was only on the table until the trial began. I said I would discuss it with my client and cocounsel but doubted we would settle on those terms.

Josephine and Donnie Arnold were waiting in the hall next to the courtroom. I took them aside and recited, word for word, my conversation with Bradley and the State Farm adjuster. Josephine immediately indicated that nothing short of the limits, plus costs at this time, would settle the case. She said as an olive branch, she would agree to waive entitled to attorney fees if the case settled right now. Donnie Arnold spoke up and indicated he thought the $200,000 was a good offer. He thought we shouldn't be so hasty in turning it down. I told Donnie I had waited a few years to get Bradley and the State Farm adjuster in this position and was looking forward to kicking some butt. Josephine and I both believed we would do better with a jury. I had tried around thirty trials against Bradley over the years, and he was unpleasant for me to work with. We really disliked each other.

I entered the courtroom and walked over to defense counsel's table and turned down the offer. Charles Matthews spoke up and said, "Okay, but the offer is off the table." He then walked out of the courtroom. The "face of State Farm" who would sit with Bradley at counsel's table during the trial was a young attractive female junior adjuster from the Fort Pierce State Farm Office who had absolutely no say in whether the case settled or not.

Right before the jury panel was to enter, Bradley stood and announced to the court that the defendant, State Farm, was admitting liability, and the trial would be on the subject of damages only. This was totally expected. We would have had no problem proving liability anyway.

The trial was expected to last at most a couple of weeks, and it began quite slowly. It took almost all the first day to pick a jury. I believed the voir dire went okay. While I was not completely satisfied with the jurors, there were no horrible members on the panel at the end. A couple of more peremptory challenges would have been handy, I thought. Both sides completed opening statement before the end of the day.

After that, the trial seemed to fly along. Everything went well on Tuesday and Wednesday of the trial. The high point of the first two days of testimony had been the appearance of Dr. Yuan, the physiatrist from Bridgeport, Connecticut. When he came forward to testify, the clerk asked him to place his right hand on the Bible and repeat the oath.

Dr. Yuan stated, "I don't have a right hand."

The jury jumped to attention and really paid attention to everything he said after that. It was great testimony from a witness who had been there before. I believed we might finish by the middle of the next week if everything continued to go as scheduled.

On Thursday morning, Dr. Hooshmand was due to testify. Everything went according to Hoyle during my direct examination of the good doctor. He first gave the jury an outline of his extensive credentials. Early in his career, Dr. Hooshmand had been a medical school professor at the Medical College of Virginia. He was board-certified in both neurology and psychiatry. He had hospital privileges and had practiced medicine in Vero Beach for many years. He was a published author of medical treatises and had written several chapters of medial textbooks.

The doctor then told of his treatment of Josephine, both when she was eighteen and later when the injury occurred. He testified he believed her neck injury was only caused by the rear-end collision, which was the subject of the lawsuit. He said Josephine was permanently impaired as a result of the crash. Dr. Hooshmand used the AMA Guides to Impairment to spell out the seriousness of the injury. He stated he was sure Josephine was going to need surgery when she left his care to move to Connecticut. He confirmed that he had referred Josephine to Dr. Sabshin at Yale University.

On cross-examination, Bradley inquired on whether the injury to the neck could have been a longstanding osteophyte. Dr. Hooshmand replied he was "one hundred percent sure that was not the case." And he stated, "I can prove it." The doctor reached into his coat pocket and retrieved a report of a cervical (neck) MRI report from the time of her workers' compensation injury when Josephine was eighteen. He told Bradley the report showed Josephine Lewis had no abnormalities in the cervical spine just a few years before our accident. Bradley almost fell down behind the podium.

He stammered to Judge Kenney that he was moving for a mistrial. The judge sent the jury to the jury room to hear argument on the motion. Neither Bradley nor I had received this important document from Dr. Hooshmand when a records request was made. The defense was probably entitled to a mistrial because of the surprise. Judge Kenney asked Dr. Hooshmand when he had discovered the evidence.

The doctor replied, "Last evening when I was reviewing all the records getting ready to testify. This record was lying at the bottom of the box." The doctor also said he had not shown the document to me before he let everyone in the courtroom see it that morning. He said he would have produced it earlier if he had found it.

I don't know if the good doctor was telling the truth or if he had laid a trap for his old enemy Bradley. At least he sounded believable. Judge Kenney pondered the situation for a couple of minutes and then stated, "Gentlemen, we can do one of three things. First, the plaintiff can withdraw the evidence, which they shouldn't do since it absolutely wins the case for them. Second, State Farm can get out their checkbook and settle the case. Or third, I can grant the mistrial, which I do not want to do."

The judge asked if State Farm's adjuster on the case was in the room. Bradley said he was not. Bradley explained that State Farm had made a "reasonable" settlement offer before the trial started, but the offer had been rejected and was off the table. Judge Kenney asked if the adjuster had a phone, and Bradley said he did. The judge then said, "Well, get him here right now. I've got a jury waiting."

Thirty minutes later, Charles Matthews entered the courtroom and chatted for a couple of minutes with Bradley. He then told the Judge the $200,000 offer was back on the table, but just for today, but it was not negotiable. Judge Kenney shook his head in disbelief. I told the judge we would see him on the next available court docket. The judge called the jury back into the courtroom and announced the mistrial. He thanked them for their service. I asked the judge when the next docket was to begin, and he said it would be after the first of the year. He also said he might be reassigned to a different post in the circuit by that time, and a new judge might try the case next time.

Before Josephine left to go back to Connecticut, we had a talk in my office. She told me not to settle for less than the coverage, plus costs and attorneys' fees. Josephine told me her parents had paid to fly her down for this trial, and they would pay to bring her down for the next. I told her I anticipated a February trial date. She told me that was great for her as she liked to come down to the sunshine during the dead of the northern winter.

Not a week later, I was in my office in Port St. Lucie when Josephine called me. She said, "I'm going to kill him. I'm going to have his law license." I asked who she was talking about, and she said, "Donnie Arnold."

It seems Donnie Arnold had taken it upon himself to call Josephine's parents and discuss the $200,000 settlement offer with them. He had apparently asked them to see if they could change Josephine's mind about accepting the offer. She said they were now refusing to assist her financially in any way from that point forward since she could have "reasonably settled" the case and paid them what was owed. Josephine asked me what the procedure was to bring a Bar complaint.

I gave Josephine the address of the Florida Bar in Tallahassee and told her I would help her with such a complaint, if necessary. However, I asked her to please wait until after the trial to take any such action. I told her I would call Donnie and read him the riot act on this. I explained I did not want any more unnecessary crap hitting the fan this close to trial. She said she did not want Donnie Arnold to be able to say a word during the next trial. I said I would handle it.

I immediately called Mr. Arnold and said, "What the hell were you thinking? She wants your license and would probably get it from the Florida Bar. It's not bad enough that you failed to prepare for trial, but now you are going against the specific instructions of your client and have taken actions adverse to her. You ought to kiss Josephine Lewis's feet and pray she doesn't bust you."

Donnie apologized to me. I told him the person he needed to apologize to was our client. Donnie said he couldn't afford his portion of the costs of the upcoming trial. He said I spent more money than he thought I would on preparation, and he said he wouldn't have signed on to the deal had he known what the costs would be. I told him we would get all of that back when we won. I also told him he should spend a little less on advertising and more on the costs necessary to service client cases.

I explained that Josephine did not want him to take an active role, at all, with regard to the next trial. He said that was okay with him. He repeated he couldn't pay his portion of the costs and said he wanted to rework the deal. I told him I would pay all the costs from this point forward, but my fee would be greater. He said he only wanted a 25 percent of my fee like he would get from a straight referral. I said, "Fine, but please don't screw up any more." I also told him that Josephine Lewis could still file a Bar complaint against him if she desired, and he should bend over backward to be nice to her. I said, "Hopefully, when we get a large verdict, Josephine will be in a forgiving mood."

Chapter 48

The new judge assignments became official on January 1, 2000. Judge Kenney was reassigned to the Juvenile Division. We drew Judge Robert Hawley, a very bright and young jurist who had only been on the bench for a few years. I was delighted. I had known Judge Hawley when he was a defense attorney for the Paxton Crow Law firm. We had several cases against one another over the years and got along, not as friends but as respected adversaries. I liked that he was an experienced civil litigator.

Judge Hawley assigned us a trial date in late February. Before the trial, Bradley filed a motion to show an edited version of the hours of video surveillance they had of Josephine. I objected, and we had a hearing. After argument, Judge Hawley ruled Bradley could show an edited version but also told me that I could show the jury as much of the surveillance video as I liked.

As in the first trial, I worked with jury consultant, Dr. Melissa Pigott, in preparing for voir dire. Jury selection is extremely important, and in a case of this magnitude, use of an expert is essential. I definitely wanted to not leave any bullets in the gun. The entire weekend before the trial was spent honing the voir dire questions and finalizing my opening statement. We were very prepared when the trial day finally arrived.

On the first Monday of the trial, I once again entered the courthouse lobby. This time, Bradley and Wally Smith from State Farm were there. Charlie Matthews was absent. They once again jumped on the elevator behind me. Bradley said, "Roger, you win. We'll pay your client the limits of $225,000 to settle."

I answered, "Plus all reasonable costs and attorneys' fees to be awarded by the court. By settling now, State Farm can save the costs and attorney's fees for this trial." I said those were my instructions from my client but indicated I would relay the offer to Josephine immediately to see if she had changed her mind.

She had not. Also, State Farm rejected our counteroffer, so the second *Josephine Lewis v. State Farm* trial began.

Why does the voir dire portion of trials take so long? The purpose of the jury selection process, as I see it, is to weed out those folks who have their own personal agendas. I call them the haters. These people may hate the jury system because it encroaches on their lives and makes them give up some of their personal time to serve on a jury. They may hate plaintiffs and their "greedy" lawyers who, in these folks' minds, are only out for quick and undeserved buck. They may hate all chiropractors and believe all members of that profession are "quacks." They hate medical doctors who treat injury victims and view them as "overpaid and overeducated snobs." They may hate the entire system because sometime in the past, they or a family member may have suffered an injury and the system did not compensate them. Oftentimes, these potential jurors have preconceived ideas about "tort reform" and believe that no case is worth more than an arbitrary amount set by law regardless of the evidence.

There are prior appellate court decisions which indicate that if any of these biases are brought out in voir dire, the sitting judge must remove those potential jurors for cause. The trick for a trial lawyer is to get these potential jurors to let down their guard and reveal their true beliefs.

The judge can remove a limitless number of potential jurors for cause. Also, each side has a limited number (usually three) of peremptory challenges and can remove that number of jurors for no reason that has to be explained. These challenges are jealously protected. Good lawyers will try to get as many biased jurors removed for cause as possible. There are always folks remaining on the panel that you are not comfortable with, however.

In the Lewis trial, Judge Hawley properly removed for cause a relatively large number of "bad apples." We were selecting a jury of six members with one alternate who serves through the trial except for jury deliberation. The alternate is there in case something happens to one of the first six. My favorite juror in the panel would up as the alternate. Melissa Pigott agreed with me that this nice lady was our ideal juror. If I had used my last peremptory to get her on the panel, Bradley would have used his last to bump her, and the next potential juror in line after her was, I thought, poison to us. The jurors were sworn in, and we were to begin opening statements and start presenting testimony the next morning.

On the second morning of the trial, something interesting happened. One of the six jurors was unable to continue, and the alternate moved onto the main panel. We smiled but were worried we might lose another juror during the two-week trial and suffer a mistrial. If that happened, we would have to start over. It's called "working without a net."

In my opening statement, I tried to explain in brief detail what the evidence would show during the trial. I went over the names of the witnesses and the important things I expected them to testify to. I particularly discussed at length the surveillance videotape which State Farm had taken of Josephine that I intended to show them. I told the jury it was hours long, and most of it was uninteresting. However, I told them that near the end of the tape, there was something important going to happen. I said I would raise my hand just before that occurred and requested they pay close attention. I told them that Josephine would suffer a fall, and it would be filmed from two directions. I asked the jurors to ask themselves what caused the fall to occur. I told the jury that the videotaped testimony of Dr. Richard Sabshin would answer that question for them. I did not tell them what Dr. Sabshin would say. You must leave something out to build interest in the jury.

The trial, from our viewpoint, went flawlessly. Dr. Hooshmand did not screw up this time. He made valid points about Josephine Lewis having a "pristine" cervical spine just a few years before this collision. Dr. Hooshmand showed the jury the cervical MRI report from before the collision and the one taken after. He also said Josephine Lewis had been injured and had a permanent impairment from the collision.

Dr. Schwarz, the chiropractor who had treated Josephine on the day of the crash, and Dr. Yuan also appeared live and did admirable jobs. Josephine's father, John Lewis, testified to his daughter's being in pain at the collision scene and all the time since. He also talked about the damage to the Volvo and showed pictures he had made of the bent frame. Josephine's coworker from Connecticut testified about Josephine's problem falling in the first month after she arrived in the state. Josephine's precious then eight-year-old daughter testified to the severity of the crash and the way her mom's life was affected. It was ten minutes of sweetness.

Several days into the trial, we had a video day for the jury. We turned off the lights in the courtroom and, on a big-screen television, showed the several hours of surveillance. I raised my hand right before Josephine Lewis fell on the video, and the jurors sat up and paid attention. They looked surprised. We also showed them the same fall from a different point of view which had been taken by State Farm's videographer.

I then showed the jury Dr. Sabshin's video deposition where he went into detail about the symptoms of spinal cord compression, which included numbness in the hands, urinary incontinence, and falling down for no apparent reason. There was a look of understanding on the juror's faces.

Josephine's friend, Karen Bukea, took the stand. She explained how great a dancer Josephine was before the collision and how the injury had caused Josephine to put on weight and age. She described how the professor at IRCC had filmed Josephine's dance performances, and she narrated the video. She said she had seen the video and that her friend Josephine was the girl in the spotlight. She told the jury that the filmed performance had occurred only six weeks before the collision. I then showed the jury the edited dance video of the pre-collision Josephine dancing, leaping, and spinning across the stage.

My last witness was Josephine. I was afraid that with the case going so well, she might say or do something to cause a mistrial. I had coached her for hours about what not to say. Even though she wanted to, she was not allowed to tell the jury that because she paid the premiums, she was entitled to win against State Farm. She could not tell the jury how furious she was that State Farm treated her like a fraud instead of the honest, injured person she was. She felt violated because her own insurance company had her and her daughter followed and had slandered them to the landlady. State Farm had treated her shabbily. However, the issues for our trial were (1) how badly Josephine Lewis was injured in the collision and (2) the economic and noneconomic damages that flowed from that injury. All the other matters she wanted to scream about were irrelevant and inflammatory and could earn us a new mistrial.

I should not have worried. Josephine was a smart lady who held in her anger and just told her life story to an interested jury. I was so proud of her. I then rested the plaintiff's case.

At this point in the trial, the defense made the usual motion for a directed verdict. With such a motion, the defense argues that the plaintiff's case lacks some essential element of the cause of action sued upon. The defense also argues there is insufficient evidence to submit to a jury. Almost always, these motions are denied, and of course, the directed verdict motion was summarily denied in this case as well. Bradley then presented his case.

Bradley's principal witness was Dr. Sullivan. The doctor first went over his credentials and told the jury he had performed many anterior cervical discectomy and fusion operations over the years. He then parroted the written report he had filed in the case over a year before. He indicated it was his medical opinion that Josephine Lewis's injury was not caused by this collision. He indicated his doubt about the propriety of the surgery. The doctor said all her symptoms were caused by "an osteophyte" or bone spur, which, in his opinion, predated the collision by many years.

My cross-examination was pretty simple. I established the financial relationship between Dr. Sullivan and State Farm. The rest of the cross-examination was from the facts established in his deposition. Dr. Sullivan was forced to admit that he had not performed an actual ACDF surgery in many years. The clincher was Dr. Sullivan's admission that he had not actually reviewed Josephine's MRI films in this case prior to reaching his medical opinions. He had only reviewed the radiologist's report on the MRI, which had said there was a large herniated disc.

State Farm had no surprises for us during this trial. State Farm did not share their edited version of the video. When Bradley rested their case, I was confident of a win.

Closing argument was the easy part. I spoke for about thirty minutes, having reserved fifteen minutes for rebuttal. I carefully discussed the high points of the testimony of our witnesses. I reviewed the ACDF surgical demonstrative exhibit from Dr. Sabshin's deposition. I showed the jury the lab report from Yale, which indicated that the material Dr. Sabshin had removed was "human herniated disc" material. A nice chart had been prepared showing the past medical bills, which were large. I talked about the cost of future medical care. Then the holes in Dr. Sullivan's testimony were pointed out. I asked the jurors to do justice and return an amount that they thought was fair. I suggested something in the $300,000 range.

Bradley's closing argument was pretty weak. He started by stating, "Now we know why we are all here for so long. Mr. Messer wants way too much money." He told the jury that the evidence showed that Josephine Lewis had not suffered a herniated disc. He said, "She only had an osteophyte. You should give her only a token for the aggravation to that preexisting injury."

On rebuttal, I started by stating "A *token*? State Farm wants you to give Josephine Lewis, their policyholder, a *token*?" I told the jury that a token would get a person a ride on the New York City subways. I indicated that State Farm had taken the truth for a ride in this case. I told the jury they should return a verdict showing what the truth was in this case They should answer the first question on the verdict form that "Yes, Josephine had sustained a permanent injury in the collision that was the subject of this case." They should then give truthful and just answers to all questions regarding the value of the case. I asked them to do their duty and be fair. I then sat down.

The jury retired to the jury room to consider its verdict. I went into the courthouse hall and telephoned my friend Jeffrey Liggio to discuss the case. I told Jeff that I anticipated a result, including costs and attorneys' fees of well above the $225,000 limits. Yes, we had properly filed our Civil Remedy Notice, and the instances of bad faith were well-documented. Jeff asked me to call when the jury returned with a verdict, no matter how late. He said that if the case turned out as expected, he wanted to see me and Josephine Lewis in his office in West Palm Beach the next day, and certainly before she returned home to Connecticut.

I then opened a good book and began to read to take my mind off the pressure of the situation. In what seemed like no time but was actually about two and a half hours, the knock came on the jury door. The jurors were pretty expressionless as they entered the courtroom. They returned a verdict in Josephine Lewis's favor of $265,520. We would also be entitled to all our costs plus attorneys' fees to be set by the court. The jury smiled at us as they left the courtroom, after they were thanked for their service by Judge Hawley.

Judge Hawley then thanked Bradley and me for a case well tried. Court was adjourned. Hugs were had all around. Donnie Arnold apologized to Josephine and me again and said he was sorry he didn't believe in us enough. Josephine said she accepted his apology. Josephine called her parents to let them know the news, and they insisted on taking Josephine Lewis; her daughter; my wife, Betsey; and myself out to a nice French restaurant for dinner. I called Jeff Liggio about the verdict and scheduled the next day to meet him in his office in West Palm Beach. We gathered our materials and finally got out of the courthouse about thirty minutes after the jury had gone.

Right outside the courthouse, one of the jurors was waiting for us. It was the alternate juror who had been promoted to the panel.

She was the lady I thought would be our best juror. She came up to Josephine and said she wanted to hug her neck. She said, "We were not going to let them get away with it." The lady was crying. We all thanked her. The juror asked me for my card.

Josephine and I met with Jeff Liggio the next day. Jeff told me he would make us a deal. He would write one letter to State Farm outlining their bad faith behavior to them. The letter would indicate his willingness to sue them for the bad faith. He told me that if the case settled as a result of that letter, he would only charge us $1,000. If, however, he was forced to file suit, there would be a contingency fee applied to the case. He explained that under the law, attorney's fees would probably be paid by State Farm at the end, but those could make settlement difficult. Jeff understood that Josephine needed her money. Jeff said he would wait to write the letter until after I had filed my Motion to Tax Costs and Attorney's Fees.

I filed those motions fairly quickly. The hearings occurred about three weeks later. Judge Hawley awarded almost $80,000 in costs, which included the $7,200 in costs we paid from the first abortive case filed by Donnie Arnold and all the costs from the two trials I was involved in. Because of the proposal for settlement, we were entitled to all our costs, including such things as travel expense up to Connecticut for depositions. Usually, the court would not award those types of costs unless a successful proposal for settlement had been filed.

Over the objection of Bradley, Judge Hawley ruled that my proposal for settlement had been filed in good faith and that we were entitled to a reasonable attorneys' fee as well as a multiplier. A hearing was scheduled to determine the amount of the fees. Each side was to retain expert witnesses (other trial attorneys) who would review the file and give an estimate of a reasonable fee. Judge Hawley would enter an order setting the final amount of the fees. A final judgment for all the amounts would be entered by the court after that hearing.

Of course, State Farm had the right to appeal up to thirty days after entry of the final judgment. They made some noises about that possibility.

Jeffrey Liggio wrote a brilliant letter concerning the bad faith activities of State Farm in this case. He pointed out that State Farm would be ultimately responsible for all appellate costs, including attorneys' fees. They would also be responsible for Jeffrey's fees for handling the bad faith lawsuit. He gave them thirty days to work the matter out with me.

In May 2000, I received a phone call in my office from Wally. State Farm made a substantial offer to settle the entire case, including cost and attorneys' fees. There was no mention of bad faith, but Josephine would have to dismiss the lawsuit before any judgment was entered. This offer was rejected. What we considered a much more reasonable settlement was actually reached prior to the end of May, however. Less than two months from the date of the verdict, State Farm agreed to drop any appeal. They agreed to pay Josephine Lewis and our office $530,000, which made Josephine and me very happy. It was well above the jury verdict, attorneys' fees, and costs.

I will tell you the result was fair and a hell of a lot better than the $30,000 Donnie Arnold had demanded to settle the case pre-sit about three years before.

Epilogue

Chapter 49

The verdict in *Josephine Lewis v. State Farm* was entered on March 1, 2000, which was, I believe, a Monday. It was the conclusion of a two-week trial and I, personally, was exhausted. Because I had not been at my desk in over fifteen days, it was stacked pretty high with work, and taking time off was impossible. My fiftieth birthday was coming up on the next Saturday, a fact I hoped my wife and office staff might forget.

My good friend, Sheriff's Deputy Bill Hardman, called me on Tuesday and said he had tickets for four to see a country and western star who was appearing at the St. Lucie County Fair that Friday night. I had forgotten the county fair was going on. I told him Betsey and I would love to come. Bill and I had been friends since about 1985. We had coached Little League baseball together and had worked as volunteer umpires in the local leagues. We had even umpired a state championship Little League series. Bill had been the DUI deputy for St. Lucie County for a five-year stretch back in the nineties, and I had ridden along with him on his shifts many times.

Betsey and I had sold Bill and his wife, Zandra, our home on Greenwood Drive in Fort Pierce when we built our new home in Port St. Lucie. I had been best man at their wedding. Bill and I had been to several out-of-state college football game trips together over the years. I had enjoyed a meal or two at his mother's table, and he had done the same at my mom's. We were that close, and it wasn't strange for him to assume we would go to a concert with them. I suspected nothing.

Betsey and I were supposed to pick Bill and Zandra up at the Greenwood Drive home in the early evening. As we turned onto Greenwood Drive, I noticed cars and trucks lining both sides of the street, all the way around the block. I said to Betsey, "It looks like someone is having a hell of a party." I didn't realize until a minute later that the person having the party was me. I was busted. As I arrived in front of the home, I was waved into a parking space of honor. Over a hundred folks were milling about the front yard, where my former client, Rick Gosser, was manning a large barbeque smoker grill. Everyone there was either a present or former client, present or former neighbor, friends, our office staff and their families, and colleagues from the legal or medical profession. Many of them wore black hats celebrating my fiftieth birthday. I was saying hello to everyone and shaking lots of hands and getting my back patted. Bill Hardman came out of the house and told me I was wanted inside. He had someone there he wanted me to see.

We went into the house, and on the couches in the front room sat my seventy-five-year-old mother along with two of my sisters. My two children were there. Everyone was sitting with Josephine Lewis and her parents. I had been led to believe that Josephine had returned to Connecticut. I had no clue my mom and my sisters were driving the seven hours from their north Florida homes to be there. My daughter, Johanna, had also secretly driven down from Florida State in Tallahassee, where she was in school. My son, Steven, was there, having driven over that day after classes at Stetson Law School in St. Petersburg. Everyone from my paralegal staff to my wife, my extended family, and closest friends were in on it, and I was in shock. I admit shedding tears of happiness that evening.

Bradley was not at the party. His picture was, however. Donnie Arnold had made up a poster with Bradley's picture on it. A cartouche above his head read, "It's an osteophyte. Give her a token."

I saw Josephine a few years ago when she came down to Port St. Lucie to visit her parents. She had lost a great deal of weight and really looked good. Josephine Lewis still resides in Connecticut. She had a seven-year-old daughter, Isa. Her much older daughter, Ashley, earned a college scholarship in soccer. She graduated with a degree in journalism and now lives in the northwestern United States. Josephine's parents moved from Fort Pierce and now reside near my office in Port St. Lucie. Betsey and I see them around town occasionally. They are nice folks.

In a way, State Farm did "run Donnie Arnold out of town" on the *Josephine* case. Donnie apparently decided that personal injury plaintiff's tort law was not his thing. He moved with his family to Colorado, and the last I heard, he was in the real estate business. Josephine never filed the Bar complaint.

State Farm was also apparently "run out of town," though not necessarily because of the *Josephine Lewis* case. For the next couple of years after the trial, I was able to reasonably settle almost all my State Farm cases with the local Fort Pierce claims office. However, State Farm, apparently in a cost-saving move, closed all its regional claims offices in the state and relocated them to one central location in Winter Haven, Florida. State Farm got rid of most of their old adjusters, and that was a bad thing. Relationships we built up with adjusters, like Charlie and Wally, after a while, did result in obtaining efficient justice for our clients. These were pretty smart guys who did not give away State Farm's money. They were generally conservative in their assessments, but you knew who they were and could usually negotiate with them.

The *Josephine Lewis v. State Farm* trial was, I believe, one of the last jury trials as a defense attorney by Bradley. He opened his solo practice handling plaintiff's personal injury cases in Fort Pierce, later in the year 2000. He and I had slugged it out in over thirty jury trials since I first crossed swords with him back around 1982. Bradley was a tough competitor who I did not personally like. I believe that since then, we have been able to put aside our differences and do a good job for each of our clients. I can't say I miss trying cases against him.

BOOK 17

Broken Wheelchair Spoliation of Evidence

Chapter 49

In late 2002, I was in my office doing routine paperwork when the receptionist buzzed me and said, "Roger, there is a paralyzed man in a wheelchair in the waiting room. Can I show him in?" I was only too happy to see him and asked that he be shown in immediately. I had handled paralysis injury cases before. I got up and held the door open for the gentleman.

Carl Gressman was accompanied by his friend, Richard Spang (not his real name), a former client of mine whom I had successfully represented in a difficult case a few years before. Carl was in a great deal of pain and had his shoulder in a harness.

I learned that Carl had called his friend while lying on the floor of his home. The friend had gone to the house and assisted Carl by helping him from his house, after which the friend drove Carl to the emergency room. Carl couldn't get out of the chair and had to be lifted by his friend. Carl had never had a problem with that type of transfer before. Carl had fallen from a broken wheelchair and injured himself.

Carl Gressman was an interesting-looking guy. He was in extremely good physical shape, except for his paralysis. Carl was tall and thin. Because of his haircut and beard, his facial features looked very much like Jesus's in the biblical illustrations. His chest and shoulders looked very muscular. He was a very soft-spoken individual and quite pleasant to be around. Carl spoke with a slight lisp.

Carl Gressman had been injured in a motorcycle accident about twenty years before, somewhere around 1980 when he was eighteen years old, and he was paralyzed as a result of that accident.

I discussed that injury with Carl and learned that prior to his paralysis, he was extremely active physically, playing sports, etc. Initially, he had a very hard time coping with his disability. He was extremely depressed and abused drugs and alcohol and was always engaged in a "pity party." This "down" period in his life lasted several years.

Carl had a daughter who was born a couple of months after Carl's paralyzing injury occurred. He indicated the daughter lived in Maryland, and he had not seen her in many years, but he wanted to very much. They wrote to each other. Carl explained that had he turned his life around and got drug-free after going through rehab. He then enrolled in several college courses. He had gotten a job and considered himself self-sufficient. He had moved to Florida. Carl paid his taxes like everyone else. He got by with the earnings he had but didn't have much savings.

Carl had remained active physically once he relocated to Florida. He was involved in wheelchair basketball and was an avid swimmer. He owned a Jet Ski and liked to take it out on the Indian River on a fairly regular basis. He also owned a riding lawnmower that he used to cut his grass. Carl was gifted mechanically. He was in the process of rebuilding a classic motorcycle. His early model Mercedes automobile had been refitted so a person could drive it with only hand controls. He enjoyed having a live-in girlfriend and having what he told me was a normal sex life. Carl accomplished all of this without the use of his legs.

Carl explained to me that he preferred a standard nonmotorized wheelchair because he found it easier to get around if he pushed himself and also found it kept him more physically fit. It required his upper-body strength to transfer in the chair so he could carry on his activities of daily living. He could, by use of his very strong shoulders and arms, lift himself from the chair and onto the toilet, or a chair or couch, and generally used the wheelchair mostly for his transportation around his home and also for use in playing basketball. Because he was so active, he preferred a wheelchair without arms, as he considered those easier to maneuver. The loaner wheelchair he was using that first day in my office had armrests, which Carl did not like.

A year or two before this latest injury, Carl had visited Capak Inc., a company in Vero Beach, Florida. That store sold and leased medical equipment, including wheelchairs. He went to their showroom and picked out a Quicky III model, which was on the showroom floor, that met his needs. Capak leased it to Carl. He was told that the chair was new, but, in fact, it had been sitting there on the floor, untested, for several years. We learned of this fact later on in our investigation. Carl leased the chair with the proviso in the lease that Capak would be responsible for any upkeep of the chair and any repairs.

How did the accident happen? I asked. Carl said that while rolling across the floor at home earlier that day, the right axle on the wheelchair broke, dropping Carl onto the floor, where he landed on his right shoulder with all his weight. Carl's rotator cuff was severely injured, and his supraspinatus muscle, a muscle running on top of the shoulder blade up to the arm, was completely torn. The supraspinatus muscle is the largest muscle in the rotator cuff and works to enable us to raise our arms above our body.

The injury was devastating to Carl. All Carl had to move with were his two arms. His arms and shoulders were like anyone else's legs. After this latest injury, Carl was now, essentially, a triplegic.

When Carl fell to the floor, he did not want to call 911. He did not want to be horsed around by a group of EMTs. Instead, while on the floor, he called Capak Inc. and told them that their wheelchair was broken and requested that they bring him a substitute that he could use until they repaired his old wheelchair, which he liked very much.

Capak sent a van and a loaner wheelchair to Carl's home, and they helped him get into the wheelchair. Carl's pain in his shoulder was pretty intense. He called his friend, Richard Spang, and asked him to help him. Spang had driven him to the emergency room and later brought Carl to my office without an appointment.

At the emergency room, they x-rayed Carl and gave him a CT scan of the shoulder. He was unable to raise his right arm over his head at the hospital. They gave him something for pain and made an appointment for him with a local orthopedic surgeon.

When the Capak employee left the Gressman home, he had taken with him the defective wheelchair and took the broken axle piece with him. Carl told him that he wanted to have the broken parts back, and the Capak employee assured him there would be no problem with that. The first thing we did in the office that day was call the president of Capak Inc. and request the return of the broken axle. The president of the company, Mr. Capak, assured us it would be returned with the repaired wheelchair. We then wrote a letter for Carl to sign requesting the return of the broken part. We mailed it certified mail, return receipt requested.

Two weeks later, Carl Gressman gave me a call. He was obviously crying on the other end of the phone and told me that Capak had returned the wheelchair to him but told him they had "lost" the parts that had been broken. I had previously told Carl that we needed those parts to get them to a metallurgist so that we could consider filing a products liability case against the manufacturer of the wheelchair. I told Carl to come into my office immediately.

When Carl came to my office that second time, he was distraught. I told him that I would handle it. He was in the office when I called Mr. Capak and got him on the phone. I said, "You returned Mr. Gressman's wheelchair to him, but you failed to return the broken axle which he had requested."

Mr. Capak said, "I know. We lost the broken parts. Without the parts, you can't sue anyone."

This was a product liability case. I filed suit the next day against Capak Inc., alleging initially the distributor (Capak) put a faulty and untested product into the stream of commerce when they knew, or should have known, that it was dangerous for use as a wheelchair. We also had a count in the complaint for something called spoliation of evidence. Spoliation is a cause of action which arises when a defendant, either intentionally or negligently, acts to destroy known relevant evidence, particularly after being placed on notice of the need for the evidence. A major advantage to filing against Capak, and not the wheelchair manufacturer, was that we could keep the case here in the State of Florida. My certified letter to Mr. Capak was going to be exhibit "A" in the spoliation case.

We knew that the insurance company for Capak was Progressive. Progressive used Attorney Joseph Graves to represent Capak. Joe was a very nice guy. Mr. Graves was, in actuality, a salaried employee of Progressive Insurance and worked in their local office. His nominal law office was actually an adjunct of Progressive. I had always considered it a conflict of interest for an attorney to be representing a party defendant while in total allegiance to the insurance company, whose interest may not be identical to that of the insured. Progressive had a $1 million insurance policy they told us about.

Approximately twenty days after the service of the lawsuit upon Capak, Mr. Graves filed an Answer and Affirmative Defenses to the case. In response to every allegation relative to count one and two of our complaint, there was a general denial. As an affirmative defense, they alleged the accident was caused by Carl. There was also an allegation by Mr. Graves that the real party of interest in this case was the manufacturer from California, and as such, it was a case that should be removed to the federal courts since there was, in his mind, diversity of citizenship, and the total damages in this case greatly exceeded $75,000.00. Graves had filed a third-party suit against the manufacturer. Graves filed a petition to remove the case to federal court. I was sure we were being wrongfully removed to federal court. Unfortunately, when an appropriate motion is filed by a defendant alleging that there is cause to have the case removed to the federal court, the case is automatically removed, and it is up to the non-moving party to come into federal court and prove that the case should be remanded back to state court.

I tremendously disliked federal court and decided to call in my good friend Jeffrey Liggio, who had just finished a term as president of the Academy of Florida Trial Lawyers. We discussed the case at length, and I reached an agreement with Mr. Liggio's office for the two offices to work together and split fees in the case, if any were earned. We would also split costs. I had worked with Jeff on a few other cases, and we are friends. I knew this was a large case. Mr. Liggio was to handle the remand motion back to state court, with my assistance. He also assigned one of his partners, Jeannie Williams, to help me in the underlying case. Jeannie was an accomplished attorney in her own right. I also discovered that she was dating a friend of mine, who was also a plaintiff's attorney from a different law firm in Palm Beach, Freddie Rhodes. I must say that Ms. Williams and I worked very well together. By the way, after the case was over, Jeannie and Freddie got married. They now practice law together with their own private litigation practice in Palm Beach County.

Our prosecution of the underlying case had delays. It took us forever to get the remand motion heard in federal court. Meanwhile, Carl Gressman's life began to completely deteriorate. The first loss for Carl was that his girlfriend moved out of the house. The next thing he lost in his life was his job.

Mr. Gressman worked in the office of a local company where he did work in a call center as well as did other things for them. He had been with that company for several years and had been named Employee of the Month as well as Employee of the Year on one occasion with them. He lost his job there because he suddenly had tremendous problems making transfers from the wheelchair onto the office chairs, and, more troubling, he also had problems transferring from the wheelchair onto the toilet, even using the handicapped bathroom facility. On more than one occasion, Carl had gone to the restroom and attempted to lift himself off the chair to sit on the throne. Repeatedly, he was unsuccessful and actually soiled himself. After that happened, he would be sent home by his boss to get cleaned up and come back another day. This happened several times. Eventually, the company let him go. I called his boss at the company about this, and he told me "Carl was a great employee who we love very much. Everybody liked him. Unfortunately, he was not able to take care of his daily needs, including, principally, going to the bathroom. We had to let him go, reluctantly."

After he lost his job, Carl's income went down the tubes. He was entitled to social security disability benefits, which came to just over $750 a month. Unfortunately, rent and utilities cost about that much, and there was no money left for food, clothing, or the other needs that everybody has.

When he lost his job, he also lost his health insurance and his prescription drug card. Paraplegics routinely have large drug bills because of the drugs they take for their condition. With a prescription drug card, his expense for drugs would be about $30 a month. After he lost his job and his insurance, the prescriptions alone were approximately $680 per month. After paying for the necessary drugs, Carl was left with less than $70 a month to live on. The rent was a lot more than that by itself. He lived on that $70 as well as charity from his friends and family.

His daughter sent him what she could from up in Baltimore. More importantly, she sent Carl pictures of her new baby girl, Carl's granddaughter. Carl showed off the new baby's picture to me. He was so proud of that little girl.

To pay for his day-to-day needs, Carl sold his Mercedes. He sold his Jet Ski. He sold the lawnmower and any other things which he had which had any value whatsoever. Carl was evicted from his home.

Local orthopedic surgeon, Dr. Norman Palmeri, of Port St. Lucie, Florida, had performed reconstructive surgery upon Carl's right shoulder, including the rotator cuff problem and the torn supraspinatus. This was done relatively soon after the injury occurred, while Carl still had health insurance. Unfortunately, that surgery was not successful in returning any strength or usefulness to the shoulder. To make matters worse, Carl was right-handed.

Carl Gressman needed prompt medical treatment that he could not afford. Because of his inability to properly transfer in the chair, he developed decubitus ulcers that became infected. When infected, if decubitus ulcers are not treated, the infection travels deeper in the tissue, causing great damage. Carl's decubitus ulcers were on his buttocks and legs. Eventually, the infection can reach the bone, and as a result thereof, the patient could die. Early on in the case, Mr.

Gressman's medical bills were huge, for which he had no insurance. Carl had several extended stays at the hospital with these decubitus ulcers. I visited him there on a couple of occasions.

It took about nine months to get the case in front of the federal judge on our remand motion. This was mostly because at that time, the federal court was inundated with drug cases as the east coast of Florida was a major point of entry for all kinds of illegal drugs. Whenever the Coast Guard or other authorities made an arrest of the drug importers, the case would be immediately taken up in federal court. Criminal defendants are entitled to a speedy trial. Civil litigants are not. When we finally got a hearing, the case was remanded to circuit court in St. Lucie County in fairly short order.

I alleged in my complaint that Capak failed to properly inspect and maintain the wheelchair and also alleged spoliation. One of the major problems in the plaintiff's case was that we had neither the broken axle nor photos of the broken axle. However, in deposition testimony of the Capak repairman, it was stated that he had, in fact, seen the broken axle and had taken it to his employer as directed by the employer. He explained that the metal dowel in the axle had sheered. He said the parts were thrown away when the repair was complete.

Capak had sued to bring in as a third-party defendant, the manufacturer from California. We retained an expert in wheelchair engineering, Farhad Bocheshaghi, from Tallahassee Florida. He was of the opinion that no products liability case would lie against the manufacturer because of the lack of physical evidence from the broken axle. The California manufacturer was let out of the case through summary judgment, as we thought they would be. Mr. Bocheshaghi's deposition testimony really solidified our spoliation case.

Before the case was ready for trial, Carl came under the care of Dr. Craig Lichtblau, a physiatrist from North Palm Beach, Florida. A physiatrist is an osteopathic physician and generally has the same hospital and surgical privileges as someone with an MD degree. A physiatrist is a treating physician. Dr. Lichtblau, in addition to attempting to treat the patient with physical therapy and medication, also prepared a life-care plan for Carl outlining the medical care that he would need in the future and outlining the cost of the same. We also retained a vocational rehabilitation expert, Roe Baltayan, who was willing to testify to the lack of employability of Carl. Lastly, we hired a Palm Beach County economist, Bernard Pettingill, to testify relative to the economic loss in this case. The defense also hired experts in various fields. Depositions of experts were taken by both sides.

After the case was remanded back to state court, it was set for trial around Christmastime in 2002. We went through a mediation process where we were unsuccessful in settling the case. At that time, every case which we handled had to go through mediation before a trial could be set. We settled a fairly high percentage of cases that way, but this one did not settle at that time.

Before the start of the mediation, Carl told me that he only wanted to make sure that he had enough money to pay his medical bills and then visit with his daughter and new granddaughter, either in Florida or in Baltimore. I assured him we should have enough money for that when it was over. His daughter had just given birth to her first child, and that was a granddaughter which Carl urgently wanted to meet and hold. The mediation failed because of the intransigence of the defense. After the case was over, Joe Graves told me he wanted to settle, but Nationwide wouldn't let him. It turns out this was the last case Joe handled for Nationwide. He now has a successful plaintiffs personal injury office in Vero Beach.

When the judge finally scheduled the case for trial, the defense indicated a willingness to discuss further potential settlement of the case and wanted a settlement conference.

By that time, Carl Gressman was living in a friend's garage as he was essentially homeless. The friend's wife did not allow Carl to come inside the house. However, there was a bathroom with access to the outside which had a toilet and a sink. Carl did not have a shower. Carl got by the best he could. I would go down to talk with him and always stop and bring some fast food and tell him that I'd had some lunch and wanted him to have some too, as long as we were talking. The garage had no air-conditioning, and it is hot in the summer and autumn in Port St. Lucie.

The defense requested we talk settlement again. A time was set for a telephone negotiation more or less on the eve of trial. Carl was to meet with me in my office in Port St. Lucie on speakerphone. A friend drove him to my office. Jeff Liggio and Jeannie Williams were in their office in West Palm Beach and were speaking directly to Joe Graves and a representative of Progressive. Carl and I heard this in real time. Only the client can settle the case. The attorneys cannot settle without the client's approval.

Settlement negotiations lasted several hours. It started shortly after lunch with our demand at $2 million and defense offer at barely $500,000.

By approximately 5:00 p.m., the defense raised their offer to $1 million. When he heard that, it was all I could do to prevent Carl from jumping through the phone and demanding the case settle for that number. I told him, and Jeff Liggio told him, that it was likely that the insurance company had more money but was trying to save a dollar. We assured him the insurance company would not take the $1 million off the table and allow us to go to trial in this matter as their potential exposure could totally ruin the insured, who would then have an awesome claim for bad faith against his own carrier.

About forty-five minutes after the $1 million offer, the defense agreed to settle for a structured settlement which cost them $1.6 million. It was set up through a program that enabled Carl to keep his disability benefits. Carl may not have lived through the trial and the appeal that was bound to happen.

Epilogue

Chapter 50

I assisted Carl in his reentry into life. He had already been in the hospital several times with decubitus ulcers, and those cases often had been handled as a charity matter. Carl had some bills that had to be paid. Carl obtained health insurance. Carl now had funds for appropriate care, and Carl was able to go back into the hospital for intensive treatment.

In addition, Carl took some of the money, and he purchased a home in Port St. Lucie, roughly five miles from my office. He then spent roughly $50,000 to make major changes in the home, such as widening the doorways to enable Carl easy access with his wheelchair. The roof trusses had to be strengthened for the specific purpose of installing a rail system. When this was set up, a Hoyer lift was installed at his bedside. There was a Hoyer lift in the kitchen and a Hoyer lift in the bathroom. The lift would raise Carl up to the chair attached to the rails. Using the rails and the Hoyer lift, Carl was able to lift himself out of the chair and use the rail system to transport himself around the house and do everything necessary to carry on his life. He had plenty of money for food and clothing. Daily nursing care was arranged for him, and a special bed was brought in to avoid decubitus ulcers. The bed was specially made with interior rollers, which changed the position on its own on a periodic basis.

Once he got moved in, Carl invited me over to his house to visit with him and several friends of his who were sharing simple drinks. While there, I also met his nurse, who was seeing him daily. She was a fairly attractive RN who seemed very attentive to Carl's needs.

Two or three weeks after my visit to Carl's house, he made an appointment to come in and see me. He was accompanied by his daughter and granddaughter, who had flown down from Baltimore (at Carl's expense) and were spending time with him at his house. Carl was delighted. He also told me that he was now dating his nurse, and they were getting serious.

Some months later, I received an invitation to attend their wedding, which I enjoyed. Carl sent me a video of him taking his bride across the threshold in his house, with him sitting in the wheelchair and the nurse sitting on his lap. Carl was extremely happy and still sexually active, which was extremely important to him.

About ten years later, tragically, Carl died. I attended his funeral and was one of the people to give a eulogy. Carl's daughter thanked me. After the settlement, I had prepared a will, for free, for Carl. The will left everything to his daughter.

Carl Gressman was a very special person and became a good friend through this process. We were able to reach a fine result for this man, which greatly improved his quality of life in his waning years.

You do not necessarily have to go to trial to get justice!

BOOK 18

Tractor Trailer Crash

Chapter 51

Richard Clark (not his real name) was a dump truck driver for a company called Dickerson Inc., which was a huge construction company which had contracts for working on Interstate 95. The work on the highway was always done at night. In 2006, Richard was working on the Dickerson project down in Martin County, Florida. When he emptied the asphalt from his dump truck around 4:00 a.m., there was no time for him to make another run back to the plant north of Fort Pierce for more asphalt. He was free to drop the truck off at the yard and go home and sleep. Unfortunately, he did not make it home.

I did not know the Clark family before this matter came to me. I had seen in the newspaper a story about the crash which had taken place on I-95 less than two miles from my office. I did not read everything about the case, but it looked like it was a severe collision. I knew that one person had died in the collision.

Richard's wife worked in the Tax Assessor's Office here in St. Lucie County Florida. At that time, the tax assessor was Jeffrey Furst, the realtor who sold us our first house in Fort Pierce. It turns out the house they sold us was the one he and his wife and kids were living in. We had become, very quickly, close friends. I was active in the

Democratic Party. When Jeff decided to run for the school board, I supported him. Later, when the school board gig had run out, he ran for property appraiser, and I supported him. Our friendship went beyond politics, however. We had been known to fish together on Jeff's nice motor yacht. Our kids were friends with each other.

Anyway, Jeff told Mrs. Clark that she should come to my office and talk to me about the case. It turns out that Richard was not able to come in because he was lying in a hospital bed in Palm Beach County, seven weeks post-accident. He had been airlifted to the trauma unit at St. Mary's Hospital in a coma.

The crash occurred, as I said, on Interstate 95, traveling north. The dump truck, which was being driven by Richard, was the largest model dump truck that Dickerson used in their business. It was huge. It came equipped with a speed governor, which prevents the vehicle from traveling more than sixty miles per hour. Richard was heading north with an empty truck when he was slammed in the rear by an eighty-thousand-pound loaded tractor trailer traveling approximately one hundred miles an hour.

We know the speed of that vehicle because there was a witness who, while he did not see the accident, saw the actions of the tractor trailer driver. This was another semi-tractor trailer driver, and he told the highway patrol, "Look, I was breaking the law. I was speeding at approximately eighty miles an hour because there was no traffic on the road. Suddenly, this other semi almost blew me off the road when he went by me at a high rate of speed, estimated at one hundred miles an hour. That guy was weaving from one lane to another." He had observed the speeding semi-tractor trailer about three miles from the crash scene.

The dump truck had been totally demolished. At the scene of the crash, there was a fatality. The passenger of the semi-driver was asleep in the sleeper birth of the cab and was thrown from the vehicle and wrapped around a pine tree. The police were initially unsure as to whether or not that person had been the driver of the dump truck as Mr. Clark was nowhere to be found. When they began to move the debris, including when they moved the body of the loaded trailer off the ground, they saw Mr. Clark lying underneath, in a coma. He was taken by trauma hawk to St. Mary's Trauma Center in Palm Beach County, where he remained in a coma for over a week. He also had numerous injuries, including, most significantly, several fractures in his spine, particularly his lower back.

Mrs. Clark indicated to me that she was sure they were going to use my services, as I came highly recommended from Jeff. She was to get Richard out of the hospital within a couple of days and would come into my office at that time with him to sign the necessary paperwork.

When he got to my office, Mr. Clark hired me, and I began to gather the medical records and other records. I had an extensive conversation with Richard, who was an extremely pleasant person. He was certainly mild mannered. He was nice to be around and would make a very good presentation in front of a jury, if that were necessary. He was married to his high school sweetheart and had one adult daughter. Richard was sixty-two years old.

Richard explained to me that he did not know how he had been thrown from the vehicle. He said that he "always" wore seat belts, but for some reason, he did not put the seat belt on that evening. It turns out that the workers' comp carrier paid 25 percent less in the medical benefits and other workers' comp benefits because of this failure on the part of Mr. Clark. This increased the money burden on Richard and his family. The workers' compensation law seemed so unfair.

I obtained the accident report from the highway patrol, which was very interesting reading. From it, we obtained the name of the semi-tractor trailer driver witness who testified to the speed and unsteady driving by the defendant semi-tractor trailer driver. That witness told the highway patrol that while he was doing eighty miles per hour, "the other truck nearly blew him off the road." Three miles after that happened, Mr. Clark was struck in his large dump truck. It was very likely that the offending semi-tractor trailer driver was asleep at the wheel.

I also learned that at the scene, the highway patrol found two different sets of logbooks in the cab of this semi-tractor trailer. It was obvious that the defendant trucking company was deliberately violating the Federal Motor Carrier Safety Act, which limited the miles and hours that a person could drive in a day. Those rules also required that a driver have ten hours of rest after a day of work before he was legal to drive.

We also learned of the name of the other deceased passenger and were somewhat fearful that we might be seeking the same target for recovery as the decedent's estate.

Mr. Clark came into my office, and we discussed what we needed to do. I felt it was appropriate to immediately file suit to get in line ahead of the deceased party.

That decedent's estate also filed a suit against the trucking company and driver for wrongful death shortly after we filed. Unfortunately, for that individual's family, the autopsy showed that that gentleman had troubling levels of cocaine and opioids in his system. I felt this would greatly reduce the value of the deceased party's family's claim.

Amazingly, the tractor trailer driver, a Cuban American who could barely speak English, was not injured in the accident.

I had called Dickerson Inc. to see if I could get in and view the wreckage of the dump truck. I arranged a time for me to meet with Dickerson's representative at their yard, north of Fort Pierce, to view the damage. This gentleman told me that he was in charge of salvaging all parts possible from any wrecked vehicle that Dickerson had in their inventory. He said this was the first wreck that he had examined where there were no salvageable parts. The dump truck had been demolished. The salvage man told me that no one had ever found the front axle on this truck. Near the accident scene was a canal roughly twenty-five yards away. They did not drag the waters to see where those parts were, and I assume they still are out next to I-95 in the canal.

I looked at what was left of the cab. The windows and windshields were all broken, and the cab was so smashed up that it would be impossible for a cat to sit on the seat. I wondered how Mr. Clark had survived. I took pictures of the damage to the dump truck and returned to my office.

This was a rare occasion when a seat belt being worn in the crash would have been a bad idea. In the vast majority of cases, having a seat belt would offer the rider some protection. Because of the lack of seat belt in this case, Mr. Clark was thrown from the vehicle before total destruction of the cab took place and landed in the grass on the shoulder of the road. The soft body of the semi's trailer was over him, but it had not crushed his body. Thankfully, Richard Clark did not appear to have a permanent brain injury.

We got the pictures from the highway patrol that were taken the night of the crash, and they were fairly gruesome.

Early in the case, in fact, shortly after the defense had filed their general denial answer, I was contacted by the insurance adjuster and attorney for the defense and asked to appear for a "global" settlement conference, along with the personal representative of the estate of the deceased person from the accident.

Through discovery, we found that this trucking company had exactly one truck and one driver. The corporation was owned by a Cuban American, and the existence of the corporation made obtaining funds from the company in excess of their insurance policy quite difficult. There was only a $1 million insurance policy on the truck in question.

It seems that the owner of the corporation may have had several such companies and had spread them out to try to avoid liability in case there was an accident. If we got a huge excess verdict, we planned on going after the owner since we believed it as actually a large trucking company working together with all the smaller companies.

We got the true logs that this driver had in his possession and which logs were used to pay him by the company. We also got the fake log which showed compliance with the Federal Regulations.

From the true logs, we were able to determine that the driver had been driving the day before from Boston to Miami with one stop along the way to rest for about eight hours. He was hauling a truck full of Maine lobsters for delivery at Miami. He dropped his truck off at the loading dock to have it unloaded and reloaded. The dock reloaded the trailer with fish for Boston. He got to Miami that day around 8:00 p.m., dropped the truck off, and went home to bed. The defendant driver slept a couple of hours and then went back to the loading dock in Medley, Florida (central Miami), and proceeded to drive north on Interstate 95 at about 2:00 a.m. He arrived at the crash scene about two hours after he left Miami.

Shortly after we obtained this information, the defense contacted us for a "global" settlement conference, and it was scheduled.

Meanwhile, we discovered there was an excess policy of insurance for another million dollars. We met with the mediator and with the personal representative from the estate of the dead man. After a lengthy mediation, we settled our portion of the case for $1.68 million. That was after settlement of the workers' compensation lien. The balance of the insurance coverage was paid to the decedent's estate to settle that claim.

My client was over the moon with happiness. He had been told that he was not ever going to be able to drive a truck again. He was already sixty-two years old. After the settlement, Richard's wife retired from the Tax Collector's Office, and they continued to live quietly in their Fort Pierce, Florida, home.

Epilogue

During my representation of Richard Clark, I came to appreciate what kind of person he was. He spoke softly but intelligently. He was a rabid Penn State Football fan, having grown up near Happy Valley in Eastern Pennsylvania. He told me that he followed the team on television and was hoping to go watch a game in person. The year after the case was settled, Florida State was playing a bowl game against Penn State in Miami. I got tickets and invited Richard, and we had a wonderful time. I do not remember which team won, and that's strange for me not to remember that. I know that the two legends, Bobbie Bowden and Joe Paterno, were present before and after the game, shaking hands and carrying on an animated conversation with lots of smiles.

Over the years after this accident, Richard would be a frequent visitor to my office. He referred a minor case to me. Unfortunately, about a year ago, Richard's wife passed away. Then about one month later, he joined her in death. He is survived by a daughter.

I have handled about five tractor trailer crashes from 1978 until now, when I have a case pending involving a brain damaged fifty-year-old woman. Those cases included a death, a broken back, a severe herniated disc requiring surgery, and two brain injuries.

When an eighty-thousand-pound semi-tractor trailer traveling at maximum highway speeds crashes into a passenger car, the results can be devastating.

How can you figure how much force is involved in such a crash? Physics taught me that force equals half the mass times the velocity, squared. That is about all I remember from the freshman physics course I took at Florida State University. The Federal Motor Carrier Safety Administration rules are there for a reason. Unfortunately, unscrupulous trucking companies continue to break the rules and violate the statutes.

I understand that there are law-abiding trucking companies out there, but I haven't run across any. Of course, we only get these cases when there is a screwup. Good companies are likely to cause less mayhem.

Book 19

Drunk Driver vs. Pedestrian

Chapter 52

Anna Badillo called us for an appointment to discuss an injury case that she might have. Anna was familiar with our office as my partner and son, Steven, had represented her and her daughter in a minor (nonpersonal injury) matter some months before, and she was pleased with the result. Anna looked pretty banged up when she came in to see me. She was walking with great difficulty because of an injury to her back. Anna came into my office, and she appeared to be a relatively attractive fifty-year-old lady. She was a rather slim brunette. She told me she had been hit by a drunk driver. I was taking copious notes.

It turns out that Anna Badillo worked every day in the admissions office at JFK Hospital in West Palm Beach. Her typical day was to get up around 3:30 a.m., have a quick shower and breakfast, and drive down before daylight to West Palm Beach well before the admissions office opened at 6:00 a.m. She lived in extreme southern Port St. Lucie, and therefore, it would take her about forty-five minutes to get from home to the job. Anna explained that she was normally in very good physical condition.

I asked her how the accident happened. She told me of her routine every day. When she got home from her job about 3:00 p.m., she would change into her jogging outfit and go for a run. Anna had a planned route around her neighborhood which was exactly three miles long, and she ran it every day, rain or shine.

On the day of her injury, Anna completed about half of her run and was jogging eight to twelve feet from the paved shoulder off the road when she was suddenly hit in the back by a Chevy Camaro being driven by a drunk driver. Her back was slammed into the hood of the car. She slid up the hood until her shoulder struck and broke the radio antenna from the vehicle. Anna then fell off the hood to the ground. The driver of the vehicle, Stephanie Ann Knox, backed up, got back on the road, and began to drive away at a fairly slow rate of speed.

Two nice ladies who had witnessed the collision stopped to try to give Anna some assistance as she was in obvious distress. Anna was attempting to call 911 when they showed up. The two ladies asked Anna what they could do to help her, and Anna said, "I would appreciate it if one of you would stay with me until emergency people arrive, and could the other one of you follow that car that hit me?"

One of the ladies drove down the road behind Ms. Knox's vehicle. At the end of the block, Knox turned right and then turned into the first driveway that she came to. When the police arrived, this nice lady was perhaps a quarter mile down the road from the accident scene and was pointing to the car and the home in question.

A couple of police officers went down to the home to make an arrest for what they thought was just a simple hit-and-run accident. When they got there, they found Stephanie Knox along with her fiancée and her baby boy. The police officer separated the fiancée from Stephanie and questioned the two of them separately. At that time, Stephanie had a distinct odor of alcohol on her breath.

Her boyfriend indicated that Stephanie had arrived about ten minutes earlier and looked very worried. She had told him, "Honey, I think I hit someone with the car. You need to hide the car." "Honey" refused to move the automobile. Stephanie told the police she thought she hit a garbage can. Stephanie Knox was arrested for DUI and leaving the scene of an accident with injuries. The police had a nice video of her failing the field sobriety test at the jail.

Meanwhile, Anna Badillo was taken to the hospital with various injuries, principally, to her lower back and shoulder. She was treated at the hospital for several hours and released with instructions to see an orthopedic surgeon.

As Anna worked at JFK Hospital, she knew all the doctors who were affiliated with that hospital, and one neurosurgeon particularly that she admired was Dr. Dutcher. Ultimately, this doctor would perform back surgery on Anna.

I learned early on that the drunk driver had no insurance coverage and further learned that Anna did not have substantial uninsured motorist coverage. She had a $25,000 uninsured motorist policy with Nationwide Insurance. Her daughter, Nicole, who lived with her, also had a $25,000 Nationwide policy. Both UM policies were stackable.

I assured Anna that if we were able to easily settle the case, we would reduce our fee tremendously, and I did not anticipate a problem settling the case given the seriousness of her injury and the small amount of coverage. I sent Nationwide all the hospital and doctor records that we had, along with the bills, and asked them to pay us the $50,000 limits. Three weeks later, we received a check in the mail for $25,000, along with a letter. The letter from Nationwide indicated that there was, in fact, $50,000 in coverage. However, it was in the insurance company's opinion that the case was only worth "the first $25,000" and was not worth the second $25,000.

After receiving this offer from the insurance company, we filed a Civil Remedy Notice with the State of Florida and notified Nationwide that we believed they were dealing with us in bad faith. The sixty days expired on the Civil Remedy Notice, and our offer to settle was withdrawn. At that point in time, we filed suit not only against Nationwide Insurance but also against Stephanie Ann Knox and alleged we were seeking punitive damages against her. Stephanie had no money and was represented by the public defender's office in her criminal case.

I attended the criminal trial of Stephanie Knox, both to listen to the testimony of Anna Badillo and to discover what penalty Ms. Knox would receive from the State. Ms. Knox was found guilty and sentenced to four years in the State Penitentiary. As Ms. Knox had no legal representation for the civil case, I was free to talk with her, both before and during the litigation. After I served her with a subpoena and summons, I had visited with her at the county jail while she was awaiting transfer to state prison. She was extremely apologetic. She said she "didn't know what she would do" about a reply to the punitive damage count of the suit, let alone the rest of the suit. Of course, I didn't tell her this, but I didn't really care about the monetary value of the punitive damage count. I only wanted to be sure that the trial would be mostly about Stephanie Knox's liability and, to a smaller extent, about Anna Badillo's damages. I urged Stephanie to file some kind of reply to the lawsuit as I did not want a default against her.

Later, Stephanie signed and filed a handwritten answer to the suit, denying all key elements.

Once the case was ongoing, I visited with Ms. Knox at the Broward Correctional Institution where she was serving her prison time. We had scheduled a deposition for the case, and I came early to talk with Ms. Knox. She was still very apologetic and did a lot of crying. She told me she had not seen her child since the day of the accident and that the boy was being taken care of by his father, who was refusing to talk to her. Nationwide's attorney, Ansley Ellmyer, was defense counsel for Nationwide and was an extremely pleasant and nice lady and a good lawyer. She attended the deposition on Nationwide's behalf and ultimately was the trial lawyer for the insurance company.

Dr. Dutcher performed a fusion operation on a couple of vertebrae in Anna's lower back to alleviate the pain and return her to a more or less normal life. Of course, Anna would have a permanent injury as a result of the injury received in the crash. There was a small scar on her lower back.

Nationwide hired Dr. Michael Zeide to examine Anna and testify to his opinion that no lower back surgery was necessary and that the injury was not really a herniated disc. Dr. Zeide was a semiretired orthopedic surgeon who still maintained an office in Palm Beach County, even though he had not done back surgery in a few years.

All the plaintiff's bar referred to the doctor as "Zero Zeide," as he almost always testified in a way that would prevent his insurance company client from paying anything. Dr. Zeide had a reputation among the plaintiffs' Bar of being slightly less than truthful when he was testifying on behalf of insurance companies and their clients. He did not testify, except on extremely rare occasions, on behalf of an injured person. For his services, Dr. Zeide had earned between $500,000 and $1 million a year for several years. I had seen Dr. Zeide in numerous cases before this one, and he still today is plying his trade as an insurance company expert. In addition to testifying regarding medical issues, he tries to indicate that bills for hospitals and doctors are somehow inappropriate.

I took Dr. Zeide's deposition in preparation for trial. I asked him about his practice involving back surgery. He indicated that he was very skilled at that and had gone to extensive training within the last year at a major university. I asked him about the training, and he told me that the students (all practicing doctors) were taught the latest techniques on lower back surgery. They were allowed to practice on several different cadavers. Dr. Zeide believed that by going to the course, he was able to testify that he knew everything about lower back surgery and had performed lower back surgeries.

Dr. Zeide, at deposition, testified that Anna Badillo did not have herniated discs in her back but instead had something called a tarlov cyst, which he indicated had nothing to do with any injury in the accident but was preexisting.

After the deposition, I went to Dr. Dutcher, and he discussed the surgery with me. I had never met this doctor before as he did not routinely go into court and testify regarding any injured person and apparently had tried to stay out of court. However, he was a friend of Anna and had done the surgery for her even though she had a legal claim pending. Dr. Dutcher explained to me that the herniated discs were large and were obviously of recent creation. He showed me the MRI film which proved this, in his mind. In addition, he said there was a "tiny tarlov cyst" one or two vertebrae down from the herniated discs. He explained to me that tarlov cysts often are produced as a result of trauma. He said, however, that the tarlov cyst was not the cause of Anna's symptoms.

I felt we were ready for trial, and I filed my Notice for Trial.

We received the trial order, scheduling the trial in the spring of 2008. This order was entered by Judge Ben "Buck" Bryan. Judge Bryan had been a fairly good judge but was extremely upset in 2008 because the state was forcing him to retire because he was reaching the age of seventy. He became a total curmudgeon on the bench. I had been his friend before he became a judge. That didn't matter. Judge Bryan was nasty to all lawyers in 2008. At the end of 2007, a real estate "bubble" suddenly burst, dragging down the economy. Judge Bryan was swamped with all the foreclosures that flowed from that. He looked harried.

I filed a routine motion to have the sheriff of St. Lucie County go down to the prison and pick up Ms. Knox and bring her to the St. Lucie County Jail to await the trial in the civil case. This was a very routine motion that I had never seen denied. We had a pretrial hearing where Knox was attending by telephone. A civil defendant, such as Ms. Knox, is not entitled to a court appointed attorney. Ms. Knox would appear pro se at the trial and, in effect, represent herself.

Ms. Ellmyer and I were perfectly willing to start the trial as scheduled in March of 2008. Judge Bryan asked Ms. Knox when would be the earliest time she would be able to get out of jail so that she could easily come to trial to represent herself. She explained that with good behavior, she would be out in February of 2009. Judge Bryan, then, on his own motion, continued the case until the first of March 2009. This was despite the fact that this delay had not been requested by the plaintiff or Ansley Ellmyer or Ms. Knox. The judge also said that this case would be someone else's problem as he was going to be retiring in December. As I indicated, Judge Bryan had become a curmudgeon in the last year of his stay on the bench.

In January of 2009, Judge Burton Connor took over the civil division in St. Lucie County. I had known Judge Connor when he was in private practice over in Okeechobee, Florida, and I respected him. I thought he would give us a fair trial.

Chapter 53

As soon as the first of March rolled around, we inquired and discovered that Ms. Knox had not gotten out of prison for good behavior and was still to be there for about six more months. We noticed the case for trial, and Judge Connor scheduled the case to take place in May of 2009. We filed the same routine motion with the judge to have our local sheriff's office transport Ms. Knox from the Broward County Correctional Institution to the St. Luce County Jail on Rock Road west of Fort Pierce. The judge signed the order, and the transfer was made shortly before the trial was to begin.

On the first morning of trial, there was a great commotion when Stephanie Knox walked into the courtroom from the holding cell and was accompanied by a large female officer from the Department of Corrections as well as a local sheriff's deputy. Knox was dressed in a prison jumpsuit. Ansley Ellmyer and Nationwide were very upset. They asked the court to delay the start of the trial until Ms. Knox could become appropriately dressed. The judge denied that motion but said that defense counsel could have her appropriately dressed for the afternoon session.

Then Ms. Ellmyer asked the court to relocate the trial to another courtroom as there was not sufficient room at defense table for the representative of Nationwide, Ms. Ellmyer, and the defendant, Ms. Knox. Judge Burton Connor denied that motion and asked, "Just where were you during the pretrial, and why wasn't this brought up at that time?"

Ansley had no reply to that statement. She then requested that Ms. Knox be required to sit at the far end or head of the table so that she could face the jury and requested that there be an appropriate modesty curtain placed under the table for privacy when Ms. Knox was to appear later in the trial in a dress. The curtain would hide the leg chains.

The court granted that motion and told defense counsel, "This is the defense table, and all defendants are entitled to sit there." We had staked out the plaintiff's table well in advance as it was the closest table to the jury box, and I felt that was an advantage.

Ansley Ellmyer asked that the leg chains and handcuffs be removed during the trial. It was okay with us. The judge asked the state prison guard if she had objection. She did, but not to the handcuffs. The handcuffs were removed before the jury panel was shown into the courtroom.

Voir dire went well for us, I thought. In opening statement, I explained the accident to the jury and further explained that liability was not going to be particularly challenged by the defense. I explained that the testimony which showed that Anna's jogging route, which she performed every day, was generally on the sidewalk facing oncoming traffic. However, at approximately the halfway mark, there was a small canal which was covered by a bridge. On the left side of the road, there was no way for a pedestrian to cross the bridge without being in the roadway. There was ample room on the other side of the bridge for people to walk even four abreast. Anna's planned route caused her to cross the street at a stop sign about two hundred yards before the bridge. Her routine was to change to the other side as soon as she reached a crosswalk after passing the bridge.

I explained that approximately fifteen yards beyond the bridge, Mrs. Knox had suddenly swerved off the road and struck Anna Badillo with the front of her Camaro. I discussed the impact involved, including the back injury and the injury to her shoulder which was caused by the radio antenna.

Ms. Ellmyer, in her opening statement, said that this was a comparative negligence case and that some of the injury was caused by Anna Badillo's negligence. She said that Anna had been running on the wrong side of the road at the time of the accident and said the court would advise the jury of the law on which side of the road a person should run at the close of the case. She said that the facts of this case were clear that at least some of the injury was caused by Anna Badillo. She also questioned the seriousness of the injury.

We called the two eyewitnesses to the crash, and they were very forthcoming with their testimony. The lady who had followed Stephanie's car to the corner was Hispanic and had a fairly thick accent. She was obviously pleased that she was able to help cause the arrest of the drunk driver.

We called Anna's daughter, Nicole, to the stand, and she talked about her mother's commitment to physical fitness as well as the fine relationship the two of them had. She said that Anna never had any pain-filled days before this accident but had been racked by pain since then. Some of the pain had been lessened by the surgery Anna had gone through, but the pain was not totally eliminated.

Dr. Dutcher testified to his opinion based on the MRI films that he went over that the accident caused two herniated discs in Anna's back. He also noted the presence of a tiny tarlov cyst a couple of vertebrae down the column from the two herniated discs. He explained that this tiny cyst should not have been symptomatic at the time the picture was taken, although it might be in the future. Dr. Dutcher explained that while he was in her lower back performing the laminectomy discectomy and fusion, he also carefully removed the tarlov cyst from the spinal column.

The police officer was present as a witness and explained the physical evidence which showed the location of the impact and the place that Anna was lying when he arrived at the scene. The officer then told them about picking up the broken radio antenna at the scene and taking it with him down the street where our witness was pointing out the location of the defendant. He said that the first thing he did was compare the radio antenna with the remaining unbroken portion of the antenna on the Camaro. He said it was a perfect match. He then knocked at the door, entered, and spoke separately to the two adults in the room.

I had the officer tell the tale about Ms. Knox asking her boyfriend to hide the car and admitting that she thought she hit a person. On deposition, Stephanie Knox indicated that she had hit a garbage can. We read a portion of the deposition. I called Stephanie's fiancée, and he testified honestly.

The last person I intended to call to the stand was Stephanie Knox. I asked the court for a short continuance so I could speak with the witness and explained that one of the things I intended to talk about with the witness was something which could greatly shorten the trial. I requested that Nationwide's attorney not be allowed in for that discussion. Thankfully, Judge Connor agreed and said he would allow us ten minutes while everyone else was having a water break to have a private conference.

I spoke with Ms. Knox, who was extremely apologetic and admitted her fault. I told her that we decided that at the end of the case, we were going to drop the claim for punitive damages, and that would save the court a day of trial going over her financial condition and going over her horrible driving record before the accident. She looked extremely relieved and thanked me. She said, "What do I need to do?"

I said, "You don't have to do anything. However, you indicated repeatedly that you were sorry for what you did. I would appreciate your getting on the stand and explaining that to the jury."

She looked very nervous, as she had never testified in open court, with the exception of her criminal trial. However, she said that she would do the best she could. I also explained it would be nice if she repeated that at closing argument.

I went back in the courtroom, and I called this lady to the stand before the jurors came in. We had previously had the handcuffs taken off Ms. Knox, but she still had on a leg chain. The jury would never see nor hear the chains. Ms. Knox went up to the witness box while the jury was still out so they could not see her walking in chains.

Ms. Knox testified that she was totally responsible for the accident. She said, "This poor lady did not do anything to cause the accident. It was all my fault. I'm so sorry that it happened. I paid a tremendous price, and I have not seen my child since this occurred. I have been locked in prison, but I only wish Ms. Badillo the best." I sat down and felt extremely confident.

For the defense, Dr. Zeide came on and testified that Anna Badillo's herniated discs were not that bad and were not caused by the accident in question. He also said that the discs were not the cause of her pain in her back but that it was, instead, caused by the tarlov cyst which he said could not have been related to trauma. On cross-examination, I asked Dr. Zeide if he still performed herniated disc surgery in his practice. He answered that he had performed "several of them last summer." I asked him when that took place, and he told me the date, which was interestingly the same day he was attending the class on back surgery.

I responded, "No, Doctor, isn't it true that all of those surgeries that you did last summer were in a class, and all of them were performed on cadavers who could not complain or sue if you screwed up?" Dr. Zeide sheepishly agreed with that statement.

Before closing argument, I informed the judge that we were dismissing our claim for punitive damages and saving the court some time. Judge Connor was very thankful of that.

The closing argument began, and I emphasized the pain and suffering that Anna had gone through and also had a chart with all the medical bills outlined. Thankfully, Anna had nice insurance through the hospital where she worked, but she still had some out-of-pocket expenses for co-pays. I talked about how this accident had changed her life and her relationship with her daughter, and I repeated what Ms. Knox said that Ms. Badillo was not, in any way, responsible for the accident. I sat down.

Ansley Ellmyer concentrated on the comparative negligence in her closing argument. She also asked for an award of much less than we had requested. Under the law, had the jury determined that Anna Badillo was, let's say, 10 percent at fault for the accident, the jury would enter its verdict for the total damages, and then the court would reduce the total damages by 10 percent. This is the law in Florida regarding comparative negligence.

While there is a statute that says that "where applicable" a pedestrian should be facing oncoming traffic, we pointed out that this was not applicable in this case as it was not reasonable for Ms. Badillo to have to run across the bridge on the actual pavement when facing oncoming traffic.

During the trial, Judge Connor had, after each witness was about through, asked Ms. Knox if she had any questions. She always replied sheepishly, "No, Your Honor."

Ms. Knox had also been given an opportunity to speak every time either side made any objection or a sidebar conference. She always said, "No, Your Honor." When Judge Connor asked her if she wanted to make a closing argument, Ms. Knox replied, "Yes, Your Honor." The jury and judge looked surprised. Stephanie Knox said, "This nice lady did nothing to cause this crash. It was my fault. I was drunk and shouldn't have been behind the wheel. I urge you to treat Mrs. Badillo fairly." She then sat down.

The jury went into deliberation and were only out for about an hour when they came back and rendered a verdict in our favor for $534,693.84. The judge reduced that verdict by the amount of $25,000 to reflect the $25,000 Nationwide had paid initially in the case. After the jury retired, Anna got up and approached Stephanie Knox and said she had forgiven her. The two women hugged.

Because we had previously filed a Civil Remedy Notice, we were allowed to file a new suit against Nationwide alleging their bad faith and outlining the facts of the case. Jeffrey Liggio helped me with the bad faith case. At mediation in the bad faith case, the entire remaining case settled for $750,000, plus the attorney's fees paid to Mr. Liggio for his work. This case was a homerun.

Epilogue

Anna and her daughter ultimately sold their home in Port St. Lucie and relocated to the West Palm Beach area near where Anna worked. Anna would come to my Christmas party on many occasions and would occasionally come by the office with gifts for the paralegals, who she had a great deal of affinity for. She continued to work at JFK Hospital, but because of her injury, she was no longer able to jog after work. She said she had taken up walking, but it was a poor substitute. Anna still looked to be in fairly good physical condition.

About four years after the case was concluded, the Nationwide adjuster who had tried to settle the case for only $25,000 came to our office with a relatively minor case. She volunteered that she knew the case was worth at least the $50,000 limit, but her bosses had nixed that idea. This lady was no longer working for Nationwide.

Book 20

One I Should Have Lost

Chapter 54

Any lawyer who tells you that he has never lost a case hasn't tried very many. Over my forty-five-year career, I've had well over one hundred trials to a verdict, and I've won more than 90 percent of them. I've been most fortunate.

I remember the ones that I lost, and especially those two or three that I was certain I would win. The jury system works very well a great percentage of the time. At times, it seems broken, but it is the best system we have for obtaining justice in these cases.

There was one case I tried which certainly should have been lost but turned out to be a victory. John Polumbo (not his real name) was a guy who worked in various jobs. He was a jack-of-all-trades but a master of none. He was married but had no children. Mr. Polumbo lived down in Port Salerno, just south of Stuart.

John Polumbo and his wife came into my office to discuss a potential case.

It seems that Mr. Polumbo was rear-ended in a collision with a cable television installer. As a result of that collision, he had had back surgery and incurred medical bills which, after adjustments, were still in the tens of thousands of dollars. This was a clear liability case with a rear-end collision.

When they were first in my office, I had at least an hour discussion with my client and his wife about his medical history and his litigation history, if any. He assured me that he had never had an injured back before in his entire life. He was not taking any prescription medications when I first saw him as he was recovering from surgery and had stopped taking the pain medication. His back was still a little bit sore, and he had restricted range of motion. He told me he had never seen an orthopedic surgeon or even a chiropractor before this crash.

Unfortunately, the cable installer only had a $100,000 insurance policy, but the cable company was substantial, and I expected we could collect monies beyond the $100,000. The initial offer from the insurance company was quite low. To lock in the possibility of bad faith verdict, we offered to take the $100,000 and settle the claim for that amount. We didn't think they would pay. The insurance company refused to settle, and we filed suit.

I had gone through painstaking discovery in this case. The defense had hired an out-of-town radiologist. His reputation with the plaintiffs' bar was that he would kneel down in front of the jury box while showing them the x-rays or MRIs or whatever it was he was talking about. He was reputed to be a terror in the courtroom.

Prior to that deposition, I talked to my friend and fellow AFTL member, Attorney Dorothy Clay Simms, who, at that time, had an office in Ocala. Dorothy was a master of taking these kinds of depositions and a master of cutting through the bull hockey of medical jargon in any case. Dorothy's husband was a surgeon. I got some excellent pointers from her. She helped me with the deposition, which took place in Orlando. I thought we had damaged the ability of this doctor to hurt us in this case. Later, Dorothy published a two-volume treatise entitled *Exposing Deceptive Defense Doctors*. I have those volumes in my office and refer to them regularly. She sends updated volumes every year or two.

All depositions of our treating physicians had been completed as well as the depositions of the defense compulsory medical examiner. We had MRI evidence of the herniated disc in his lower back and had subpoenaed the neuroradiologist to appear at trial.

Approximately two weeks before trial, the defense dropped a bomb on us. They filed a motion to dismiss, accusing my client of committing fraud on the court. It seems that Mr. Polumbo had seen an orthopedic doctor for a prior lower back injury. He had lied about that on his answers to interrogatories in the case and had lied about it when he gave his deposition, both times, under oath. He also lied to me from the beginning.

Before believing the allegations contained in the motion, I had my clients come into the office, and I discussed it with them. Mr. Polumbo explained to me that he was shocked that they had found the evidence. He indicated that his prior injury happened four years before and was caused when he was working moving some car stops in an orthopedic surgeon's parking lot down in Stuart, Florida. His wife had worked for that doctor at the time.

Mr. Polumbo indicated that the treating doctor had been retired for quite some time, and he thought that that doctor was now dead (it turns out that he was). Mr. Polumbo had indicated the MRI company where the MRI from the first injury was done was closed and out of business.

The defense had gotten some records recently from the company that took over that doctor's practice. The records were sketchy but indicated that Mr. Polumbo had been in the doctor's office twice. The first time when he came in the doctor's office directly from the parking lot where the injury occurred. The doctor had given him a prescription for an anti-inflammatory, Butalizydine. He had also referred him for an MRI. We had the read report on the MRI but did not have the MRI films. The second visit to the doctor was when the doctor discussed the MRI result with Mr. Polumbo. The MRI report wasn't that bad.

I had a large amount of money invested in this case, and I thought we still had a chance of winning. The judge who handled the case was Marc Cianca, a senior judge who had come back from retirement to help clear up some case backlog on the docket. Because he did not have his own courtroom assignment, they assigned him to the courthouse annex which had a beautiful large courtroom. That annex was in a short walk from my office in Port St. Lucie. I wish all my trials could be there.

After the hearing, on the defense motion, the judge indicated that all the facts of this case were nice fodder for cross-examination by the defense but very possibly were explainable by total forgetfulness on behalf of Mr. Polumbo or something else. Judge Cianca ruled the case was set to go forward for trial. There was case law supporting Judge Cianca's ruling, but it was still at the judge's discretion.

It turns out that the defense had learned of Polumbo's lies by doing a records request to every pharmacy in Martin County. The pharmacy who had filled the prescription for the anti-inflammatory had provided them with a copy of the prescription which had been signed by the deceased doctor. That doctor was a known orthopedic surgeon, and the defense assumed correctly it was a back injury.

As soon as we received the motion, I went into discovery overdrive. We ran down all the information possible on the MRI company and learned that all of its assets had been purchased by another company in Orlando, Florida. I contacted that company and was shocked to learn that they still had a copy of the read and the films. I obtained them. We gave a copy of the reads and the films to the defense, and I provided them to John's neuroradiologist to read. Dr. Walker assured me that the first MRI was not bad, and it should help us because it proved Polumbo's complaints now were from a "new injury." That still did not explain away why Polumbo had lied.

In this particular case, early on, I had hired a jury consultant as I was thinking we would get maybe $250,000 on the case, even though my client was difficult for me to like even early in the case. I should have recognized it when he had hedged the truth, but I did not. The top offer from the defense in this case never got over $10,000.

I hired Dr. Melissa Pigott with a PhD in psychology, an excellent jury consultant who I had worked with successfully on one other occasion. She was very good at her craft. I decided to spend the money and have her present for the jury selection process. She helped me prepare the voir dire questions, and she was taking notes feverishly in the audience as we were questioning the jury panel.

We wound up with what I thought was a pretty good plaintiff's jury but was unsure. You never know how jurors will react to testimony that was proven false.

Before the start of the trial, the insurance company withdrew the $10,000 offer and changed it to a zero. Therefore, we had nothing to lose except court costs by going to trial.

The trial started all right for us. Polumbo's treating physician, who had performed the surgery, did an adequate job. Our neuroradiologist, Andrew Walker, indicated that he reviewed both sets of MRI films, and the first accident did not cause the injury which caused the surgery. The damage to the back from the first injury was not a herniated disc. In fact, the existence of that film proved this was a new injury.

I finally had to put my client on the stand. He turned out to be a terrible witness. I asked him, under oath, about his previous statement that he had not had a prior injury, and he said that he had "forgotten it and that he had no longer had any symptoms from it." He apologized for messing up his interrogatories and sworn deposition testimony. John did not seem that believable.

I stopped my direct testimony as soon as I brought home the facts about the crash and about the surgery. My direct of Mr. Polumbo was only about thirty minutes.

The defense attorney was from an insurance defense firm in Stuart, Florida. He stood up and began haranguing Mr. Polumbo. His cross-examination lasted the rest of that day and about half of the next day. He must have used the words *lie* or *liar* a hundred times. The first time he used it, I objected, and the court overruled my objection. When he asked the same question the second time to Mr. Polumbo, I would ordinarily be able to make an objection that the question was "asked and answered." However, I noticed, even on the first question, that several of the jurors looked troubled and were staring horrible looks at defense counsel. I thought they were siding with the witness. By the end of the cross-examination, most of the jurors were sitting as far back in their seats as possible and had their arms crossed and a frown on their faces. After Mr. Polumbo was on the stand, I placed his wife on the stand, and she made a pretty good witness, and the defense didn't really shake her testimony.

I was certain that we were going to lose the case. Despite that, I made a decent stab at my closing argument. I said that if Mr. Polumbo did, in fact, knowingly not tell the truth about the injury, the testimony was that that first accident did not cause the surgery. The injury had been caused by this severe collision between a work van and a small car.

Defense counsel got up and did his closing argument and once again used the word *liar* over and over again. The jurors' body language was not receptive to that.

The jury went into deliberation. My clients and I went out to the courtyard and sat in a gazebo to get out of the sun. It was a pleasant day outside. I looked at the clock on the wall as soon as we left the courtroom.

The deliberation went on and on. I can tell you that if a jury verdict is rendered in less than thirty minutes, it is usually a defense verdict in a personal injury case. If the verdict is rendered between one and a half and three hours, it is a good sign for the plaintiffs, and the majority of those are plaintiff victories. If, however, the deliberation lasts more than four hours, the very real chance for a hung jury and a mistrial exists. When the jury exceeded the four-hour time limit in Polumbo, I explained to my clients that there was a very real chance that we had a hung jury. I also told them that it was my desire that Judge Cianca read the jury a "dynamite charge."

Over the years, I have witnessed several dynamite charges being given to juries. The first and best one was in Fort Pierce with Judge Rupert Jason Smith back in the mid eighties. In that case, my client was injured by a drunk driver and had some minor surgery as a result thereof.

There was a major flaw in the case. My client was in his late thirties and was driving his wife's automobile at the time of the crash. Unfortunately, the young lady sitting next to him on the front seat was not his wife. I was afraid we might get an extremely religious person on the jury, and I tried to avoid that, but apparently, I failed.

When the jury broke for deliberations, Judge Smith summoned myself and Dewey Varner, defense counsel, into judge's chambers "for a cup of coffee." Once in chambers, the judge took off his robe and said, "Gentlemen, what do you think the verdict will be in this case?"

I responded that I believed it would be around $40,000. Mr. Varner indicated that he felt that the maximum the jury would give us would be $5,000.

Judge Smith looked at him and said, "Sir, you are wrong. This jury will come back much nearer Mr. Messer's number than yours. Now how long do you think the jury will be out?" We both agreed that it was a fairly straightforward case, and we expected a verdict in an hour or less. Judge Smith agreed.

In that case, the jury was three and a half hours into deliberating when Judge Smith called them into the courtroom and asked them if they were close to entering a verdict or should they break for lunch. A small gray-haired man stood up at the end of the jury box (where he was all alone) and stated, "It's eat or fight."

The person who I assumed would be the foreman of the jury stood and said, "Your Honor, I think I speak for five of us, and it's best if we broke for lunch."

The group came back from lunch and deliberated a couple more hours before sending a note to the judge that said they were "hopelessly deadlocked."

Judge Smith talked to me and defense counsel, Dewey Varner, and said, "I'm not going to let them get away with this." He called the jury into the courtroom and stated, "Ladies and gentlemen, you see this lady here in the courtroom. She's the court clerk, and she's done a wonderful job during this one-week-long trial. The other lady across the room here is the court reporter, and she likewise has done a good job. The attorneys in this case have presented a very clear and cogent case to you. Even I have been extremely attentive in this trial. The only people in this room who have not done their job are you. I had planned on playing golf this afternoon as I did not believe it would take that long to reach a verdict. When you broke for lunch,

I called my golfing partner and told him I would not be able to play today.

"I intend to keep you here today until around five thirty. Tomorrow, this courtroom will be open especially for you, and you will be allowed to work all day Saturday from nine a.m. until five p.m. with a short break for lunch. I believe that no one should work on Sunday, and therefore, I'm giving you Sunday off. I do not have a trial scheduled to begin until Tuesday of the next week. On Monday, I have hearings. However, the jury deliberation room will be open, and you will be there. At around five p.m. on Monday, I will entertain the idea that you are hopelessly deadlocked. Now get back to work."

The jury returned a verdict of $35,000 approximately thirty minutes later.

The verdict which we got in the Polumbo case surprised me a great deal. The jury awarded Mr. Polumbo the sum of $312,000. To say that I was ecstatic is an understatement. I was shocked because my client was such a slug. State Farm paid this, plus the costs, without an appeal.

Sometimes you lose when you should win, and sometimes you win when you should lose. This is an unfortunate truth.

Book 21

Brain Injury

Chapter 55

On Thanksgiving Day 2008, Tommie Bowes was driving north on US Highway One north of Fort Pierce, Florida, on the way to his sister's house for Thanksgiving dinner. Seated beside him in his automobile was his longtime girlfriend, Robin. They were traveling at approximately the fifty-five-mile per hour speed limit when, out of the blue, a teenager named Ian Landis, from Vero Beach, Florida, turned left across oncoming traffic and caused a T-bone collision.

Airbags exploded in the Bowes vehicle, and they were both jostled around quite a bit. Robin, who had not been paying attention to oncoming traffic, asked Tommie, "Hey, what just happened?"

Tommie replied, "We were hit." Tommie proceeded to open the door on his car, and when he stood up on the street, he suddenly passed out cold. He was on the highway asphalt for approximately ten minutes.

A nurse witnessed this and ran across to Tommie and put his head in her lap. As it often is in St. Lucie County in the fall, it was still quite warm, and the asphalt was hot to the touch.

The EMTs arrived about ten minutes after the collision occurred. At that time, Tommie was coming to. They asked him where he was and what day it was. Tommie knew those answers. They asked him his name, and he could not remember it. They asked him repeatedly.

As a result of the fact that Tommie was not cognizant of his identity, the emergency worker wrote on the report that Tommie has a Glasgow coma score of 13.

Glasgow coma scale (GCS) is a rather inexact tool which has been used for years by emergency personnel and hospital emergency room personnel. It is a statement regarding the state of consciousness of an individual at a point in time. Fifteen is a perfect score on GCS. It does not mean the person does not have brain damage. The GCS score only indicates that the person is "oriented times 3." The three things a person needs to be able to state are his name, the date, and where he is.

Robin received less serious injuries, but both of them were transported to Lawnwood Regional Medical Center by the same ambulance. On the way to the hospital, the EMTs kept repeatedly asking Tommie his name. About two minutes after leaving the scene, Tommie suddenly said in a very mild voice, "Hi, my name is Tommie Bowes. I am the head groundskeeper for the New York Mets. Would you like tickets to tomorrow's game?" This was said in a very sing-song manner. About every fifteen or twenty seconds, that entire narrative would be repeated by Tommie until about the time he got to the hospital.

Because he had regained knowledge of who he was, the hospital emergency room indicated that Tommie's GCS was 15—normal.

At the hospital, they discovered that Tommie had a significant break in his nose. It was swollen to one side and was rather grotesque looking. The hospital noted that Mr. Bowes had a concussion. Because he was post-concussive, the hospital required him to stay there about six hours so they could make sure that it was not life-threatening. They performed a CT scan of his head and confirmed there was no subdural hematoma. The head CAT scan does not rule out brain damage. It only shows large bleeds into the brain which, if they are not rapidly dealt with, can result in death. Therefore, the CT scan should always be done on concussion victims.

Robin accompanied Tommie from the hospital and was taken home by taxi. She was told to watch him for three days and look out for nausea, vomiting, severe headache, and other symptoms which would indicate that there might be mild traumatic brain injury involved. She was referred to take Tommie to an ear, nose, and throat specialist in Fort Pierce, Dr. Richard Allen. This was to address the broken nose. She was not to take him until the swelling had been reduced some. She had to place ice on the nose to help with the pain and swelling. They gave Tommie prescriptions for painkillers while he was at the hospital.

Approximately seven days later, after she had obtained a substitute vehicle, Robin drove Tommie to see Dr. Allen. Dr. Allen diagnosed the fractured septum in Tommie's nose. He also noted in his first record that Tommie was complaining of severe headaches, tinnitus (ringing in the ears), and some vertigo problems. Initially, Dr. Allen only scheduled the surgery to fix Tommie's nose.

On the way back from Dr. Allen's office, Robin drove Tommie to my office in the St. Lucie West portion of Port St. Lucie. She knew me because a few years earlier, I had represented Robin in an accident with two drunk drivers. She had been hit at an intersection on US One in Port St. Lucie by a drunk driver. The police came. She was shaken from the first accident and was sitting in her car talking to the police through the window. Suddenly, another drunk driver came on the scene. The police officer barely escaped being hit, but Robin's car was pummeled once more. We had assisted Robin in receiving a relatively modest recovery in that case given the fact that most drunk drivers do not have coverage. These had low levels of coverage and no assets other than that. Unfortunately, at the time of that accident, Robin did not have any uninsured motorist coverage.

Tommie's nose looked terrible. He was in pain with his neck and head as well.

Anyway, when Robin and Tommie came into my office, they brought with them the initial medical records from Dr. Allen's office. I read it and was concerned that Tommie might have a mild traumatic brain injury.

Tommie had to leave my office fairly early since he was to check in with his job with the New York Mets. The Mets spring training complex and minor league headquarters complex is located in the St. Lucie West area less than one mile from my office. As Tommie got up from the chair, he reached in his pocket and said, "Oh my god, I lost my keys." Robin stayed behind. Tommie was going downstairs to check out his car to see if the keys had been left in the car.

About three minutes after he left, Robin saw the keys lying on the edge of the chair, and she said, "Tommie is forgetting everything nowadays. This is just an example." She took the keys and went outside. I looked in the parking lot, and I could see Tommie bent over, trying to find the keys underneath his driver's side seat of the automobile.

Eight months before this, I was attending an Academy of Florida Trial Lawyers Workhorse Seminar in Orlando, Florida. One of the speakers was Dr. Andrew Walker, a board-certified neuroradiologist from Stuart, Martin County, Florida (just south of us). Dr. Walker was speaking regarding the latest brain imaging MRIs that were available to diagnose and treat mild traumatic brain injury. I wondered why Tommie had not been referred for a brain MRI.

I knew Dr. Richard Allen. He had been my ENT for several years, and we seemed to like each other. I picked up the phone with Tommie here in the office and called Dr. Allen. The conversation went something like this: "Hello, Dr. Allen. This is Roger Messer, but I'm calling regarding my client, Mr. Tommie Bowes. I noted that you are scheduling surgery to fix his broken nose. I also noted from the record that Tommie was experiencing nausea, vertigo, tinnitus as well as splitting headache. What do you believe that is caused by?"

Dr. Allen said, "Tommie has some sort of injury to his brain." I asked him why he had not referred him for an MRI to confirm there was brain damage. Dr. Allen replied, "Roger, there's nothing I can do to help Mr. Bowes with that."

I responded "Well, I can, I think."

The doctor then said, "Well, maybe I should call Dr. Walker. Andy Walker is doing some amazing things with brain MRIs at his facility down in Port St. Lucie." I encouraged Dr. Allen to follow-up with that idea.

Tommie Bowes, according to the medical records, continued to have severe tinnitus (unending ringing in the ears) and migraine headaches. He also had occasional bouts of vertigo, which was often accompanied by nausea and vomiting. All these symptoms are signs of a traumatic brain injury.

Taking us back to what happened at the crash scene, according to Robin, the at-fault party was a young man who had talked to the police but was hopping around and talking to no one else. Mr. Landis appeared to not have alcohol on his breath, and the police simply ticketed him with causing the accident. When we got the police report, we learned that young Mr. Landis had refused all medical treatment at the scene. Instead, he called his father, Dr. Ian Landis, from Vero Beach, Florida, who came and picked him up in an automobile. Both cars were totaled and were towed to the police impound yard.

Three days after the Landis vehicle was impounded by the police, the records custodian of the police decided that they might want to take an inventory of what was in the trunk. When the trunk was popped, the police were surprised to find illicit drugs and drug paraphernalia. They considered bringing charges against Mr. Landis but realized they had a problem with proving the "chain of custody with regard to this evidence." Therefore, young Mr. Landis was not charged with any drug violations.

When I saw that, I thought, *Just what is a nineteen-year-old boy from Vero Beach, Florida, doing on Highway One near north Fort Pierce?* I wondered if Mr. Landis was heading to the area around Avenue D in Fort Pierce which, at that time, was a notorious neighborhood known for illicit drugs and prostitution. The old joke was "The only reason that out-of-town White boys go to Avenue D in Fort Pierce involves two possible reasons, and both of them are illegal."

Although I could not prove that Mr. Landis was under the influence of drugs at the time of the crash, it certainly would explain his surprised turn across oncoming traffic.

A week or so after Tommie was in my office and signing my contract, Tommie went to Beaches MRI and had a regular MRI of the brain taken which Dr. Walker read as being "abnormal." MRI-DTI is routinely not given to brain injury patients for approximately six months after a collision. This is because the brain will try internally to reroute message areas and try to compensate for any injury which has been received. The rapid changes in the brain made the possibility of false negatives or positives possible. After six months, this possibility is no longer in existence.

After the initial MRI, Tommie came under the care of local neurologist, Tagrid Adili. Dr. Adili was an excellent neurologist. However, she had very little experience in the court system. She was a reluctant witness, but she would do well on deposition and at trial.

Approximately seven months after the collision, Dr. Walker performed an MRI-DTI. We had ordered a copy of the MRI read as well as a copy of the films. I was surprised when Dr. Walker called me into his office and explained exactly what DTI was. DTI (diffusion tensor imaging) is an image of the brain which shows movement of the messages in the brain from the gray matter to the white matter. The gray matter of the brain is where all thought processes and senses are located. All the gray matter is connected together with axons which are white in color and therefore called "white matter." The most vulnerable area for injury of the axon is at the gray/white junction area of the brain. Surprisingly, Dr. Walker did not charge me for the conference. He said he wanted to make sure I was cognizant of the process as he fully expected to have to go into court and defend it.

DTI works by tracking ionized and nonionized water molecules as they move through the axons. Water is the best conductor for electrical sensation in the body. Dr. Walker explained to me that a standard brain MRI was very much like a satellite picture looking down at automobiles traveling down I-95. He said that a satellite that takes only one photograph would show you the automobiles and trucks on the highway. It would not show the speeds that they we retraveling, nor the directions that they were traveling. This could be accomplished by taking many pictures in rapid succession, like a moving picture. With MRI-DTI, the speed and the direction can be quantified, and the computer produces a picture which shows the exact location of any damage. While MRI-DTI misses positive brain damage cases over 70 percent of the time, if the MRI-DTI comes out as positive, it is absolutely certain that this person has sustained a traumatic brain injury.

The significant finding in Tommie's MRI-DTI stated:

> 1. DTI shows abnormal decreased white matter FA (Factional Anisotropy) within the left anterior corona radiata region. In addition, the white matter FA is at the lower limits of normal within the superior corticospinal tracts bilaterally. Abnormal decreased white matter FA on DTI has been shown in multiple studies to proportionately correlate with cognitive deficits with poor clinical outcome in TBI patients.

We were not successful in settling with the insurance company. We filed suit in the case when it was confirmed that Tommie had a brain injury. If I had settled the case whenever he only had a provable broken septum, the case would have been worth a lot less. I'm always reluctant to settle these cases too early. Oftentimes, it takes six months to a year to determine what really is wrong with an injured person. We are particularly concerned with chronic injuries.

Chapter 56

I sued Blake Hunter Landis and his father, Dr. Ian Landis, in the circuit court in St. Lucie County, Florida. The case was assigned to Judge Burton Connor. We obtained service of process. It turns out that Dr. Landis had substantial insurance, enough to cover any result we might obtain. The owner of the car, Dr. Ian Landis, was also listed as a defendant. In Florida, the owner is responsible with the driver for the driver's acts of negligence.

Approximately twenty days after obtaining service of process, the defense filed an answer and affirmative defenses, which denied many of the allegations in the complaint and further raised affirmative defenses including, among other things, the false allegation by the defense that Tommie Bowes had not used an available and operational seat belt, which failure would have greatly reduced any recovery he was entitled to. In addition, the affirmative defenses stated that the accident was caused by Tommie Bowes or by "some other third party out of the control of the defendants." There were a total of twelve affirmative defenses, and there were no surprises among them as this is routinely done by defense firms early on in the case.

We took a number of depositions, including that of Blake Hunter Landis. I asked Mr. Landis what he was doing driving toward

Fort Pierce on Thanksgiving Day. His reply was that he was going to visit a "friend" named "Willy." Mr. Landis claimed to not know Willy's address but indicated it was somewhere near Avenue D in Fort Pierce. He did not know Willy's last name.

I was looking forward to reading the deposition to the jury in the case since almost everyone in St. Lucie County understood the drug and prostitution reputation of that area of town. Thankfully, in the fifteen years since this accident occurred, the reputation of that community has been greatly improved.

We were engaged in settlement negotiations with the defense in this case. They were stuck on the number $30,000 for a long time. We believed that the case was worth somewhere between $300,000 and $500,000.

A major problem with our case was that Tommie Bowes did not miss a day of work. When he asked the EMTs if they wanted tickets to tomorrow's game, he obviously was out of it, because neither the major league Mets spring training nor the Mets minor league program started until February each year. Tommie had the rest of November, December, January, and half of February to more or less straighten out his life. Tommie went back to work with the Mets.

It turns out that Tommie's job with the Mets was supervisory in nature. He, at various times, oversaw the work of a crew of from twelve to sixteen individuals, depending on the task that needed to be done. I had seen Tommie once in a while when I was able to attend a spring training game for the Mets. I was not a Mets fan, but I always tried to be there when they were playing against my favorite team, the Cardinals. Tommie was very recognizable. He was very tall (perhaps six six) and weighed around 225 pounds. He always wore a smile and had a head full of absolutely white hair. You would see him at every game once the field was immaculately prepared, glad-handing with the patrons and being a good ambassador for the Mets.

I learned that not only did Tommie hold down his job, but he and Robin had also been voluntary bartenders for the local American Legion post for many years. Tommie was a veteran of the armed services.

The police officer who was in charge of the accident scene was a specialist in the Florida Highway Patrol in the specific area of documenting the accident scene and, in some ways, reconstructing the accident. We wanted this highway patrolman to appear for trial but were surprised when he was removed from the local troop and sent to the FHP school in Tallahassee to teach other highway patrolman how to do his craft. I did get him to come down to the trial. He showed the jury the photographs the highway patrolman took at the scene, which were impressive. He also explained in detail the evidence at the scene which showed how the accident occurred. I felt that this presentation was much better, and very much less expensive, than hiring an accident reconstructionist.

Prior to trial, our office put together demonstrative exhibits for use at trial. These included, but were not limited to, an outline of the total medical bills and a graphic display which was prepared by a company known as Medical Visions Inc. out of the Atlanta area. This exhibit began with a photograph of Tommie's facial condition pre-surgery. This was obviously taken after the swelling had gone down in the nose, but still was rather grotesque. The exhibit also showed the deviated (fractured) septum. The surgery also required an incision into the gums to fix a problem on the inside of his mouth, which was caused by the collision. In addition, while doing the surgery, they had to fix "out fractures" of the left and right hypertrophic inferior turbinid to help clear the airway. I was familiar with that particular surgery because Dr. Allen had performed the same on me several years before.

I always try to have these attractive colored depictions of any medical procedure for use at trial.

Oftentimes in traumatic brain injury cases, the most important witness, as far as the jury is concerned, is a before and after witness. In this case, I wanted to get someone, other than Robin, who could testify to the changes at Tommie's workplace. Robin was excellent at discussing the changes in their day-to-day life, his loss of memory, etc. I talked with Tommie, and he had first suggested some of the men that worked in his crew. I felt that might work, but I would prefer to have somebody else in the Mets organization that is either a supervisor of his or, better still, someone with a similar level position of supervising other folks.

I contacted an individual that Tommie told me about who was an excellent witness. I went over and talked to this gentleman at the Mets complex. Their complex is less than a mile from my office. He explained that first of all, the Mets absolutely love Tommie Bowes. He explained that Tommie had been with them for many years. Tommie worked not only on the Port St. Lucie property but also had been sent by the Mets to college to learn all about turf science and the growing of grass. Tommie's fields at the complex were absolutely gorgeous. The Mets had also sent him to their school down in the Dominican Republic to straighten out the problem with the grass in the fields there. He also visited many of the minor league stadiums around the country where he also fixed problems.

The gentleman said that he was part of the management team that worked for the Mets at the local offices. He explained that his position was about an equal one of importance to that of Tommie Bowes. He recalled an amazing change in Tommie after the accident. He explained that when Tommie returned to his duties in February of 2009, they noticed changes in Tommie. The witness said that before that date, if something needed to be done around the complex and it was brought up in the meeting, nine times out of ten, Tommie had already fixed the problem. He did not need a list. He would attend the meetings in the morning and would be told about specific assignments that he needed to get accomplished during the day. The witness indicated that Tommie always accomplished the work that was assigned and more. He described Tommie as a "brilliant self-starter."

After Tommie returned to work, there was a meeting where a large number of things were proposed to prepare the facility for spring training. A decision had been made to put a plastic cap on the top of all chain-link fences where a customer might come into contact. Tommie was to see to the installation of this plastic cover, which only fit over the top few inches of the fence in question. Later at the end of the day, that matter had not been completed, and it turns out that Tommie had totally forgotten that task. The witness said that if any rookie groundskeeper had made that mistake, he would have been out of a job, but Tommie was a favored employee of the Mets organization. It was decided that Tommie needed an assistant. In all the years before this accident, Tommie never needed an assistant. The existence of this assistant was resented somewhat by Tommie because he was afraid the assistant was trying to take his job.

In addition, but more importantly, the Mets officials said that one solution to Tommie's forgetfulness was something called "Tommie Boards." Tommie Boards were whiteboards which, every morning, were marked with erasable magic marker with a list of assigned tasks for the groundskeeper. These boards were placed all around the Mets facility where the workers would see them and Tommie would see them. Tommie indicated that it was an embarrassment for him to see them. Tommie's memory was that bad.

Neuropsychology

Chapter 57

Brain injuries are typically treated by a neurologist. While the clinical outlook for traumatic brain injury is not particularly good, oftentimes, the doctors will suggest ways in which to ameliorate memory loss problems. There's no real treatment for the tinnitus that many brain injury patients endure.

Tommie's neurologist, in this case, referred Tommie for a neuropsychological examination with Dr. Lawrence Salmansohn. Dr. Salmansohn was a highly respected neuropsychologist whose office was down in Boca Raton, Florida. I had researched him to make sure that he was above board. I had never before seen Dr. Salmansohn as a witness.

Neuropsychology is a very "soft science." It has been around about seventy-five years, so it predated MRIs by thirty-five years, at least. The original purpose of neuropsychology was to determine whether or not a person had suffered a traumatic brain injury. This was accomplished by a battery of tests given by a neuropsychologist. These include a test of long-term and short-term memory, as well as the ability to do simple and complex tasks requiring manual dexterity. There were several other psychological tests that had to be taken. The neuropsychologist has a huge number of tests to choose from in deciding how to go about examining the patient. The most widely used test among neuropsychologists is the Minnesota Multiphasic Personality Index II (MMPI-II), which had as its lead author, Dr. Lawrence Butcher, a professor at the University of Minnesota.

Nowadays, the neuropsychologist's report is an adjunct to the objective results from the brain MRI. A properly administered neuropsychologist test can determine many things. It can measure premorbid (before accident) IQ as well as post-morbid IQ. It could detect whether or not the memory problem was a long-term or a short-term problem or a combination of the two. It could determine whether or not the test taker was being honest in his presentation or was he fibbing. The test takes several hours, and the test results themselves are a closely guarded item.

Dr. Salmansohn found that Tommie had long-term and short-term memory problems, especially short-term memory problems. He determined that Tommie was being straightforward in his answers. The MMPI-II has over five hundred questions in it. There are imbedded questions which tend to determine whether or not a person is being honest and straightforward. A test taker does not realize that these subtests are included.

The neuropsychological test can also determine with some specificity what areas of the brain function are disrupted.

The neuropsychological test can also assist other treating doctors in determining whether or not the patient has sustained post-traumatic stress disorder (PTSD).

Dr. Salmansohn, after the conclusion of his test, determined that Tommie Bowes was being completely honest during the test. He determined that he had lost perhaps five points of IQ as a result of the crash. He further determined that Tommie suffered from short-term and long-term memory loss. The test accurately indicated the areas of the brain which had been damaged. This was correlated by the neurologist with the brain MRI findings.

As they were entitled to do, the defense sent Tommie for a compulsory examination with a neuropsychologist of their choice. As I indicated, this is a "soft science." Typically, the defense hires one of a handful of neuropsychologists whose purpose is not to help the patient.

But instead, their purpose is to show that somehow, the patient was not forthright in his answers so that the validity of the entire exam is called into question. In this case, the defense brought in a Palm Beach neuropsychologist named David Bush, PhD. Dr. Bush administered his own battery of tests, which included many tests not given by Dr. Salmansohn. As most neuropsychologists do, the MMPI-II was administered by Dr. Bush. However, he also administered several other tests including, most importantly, Green's Word Memory Test.

Using a controversial subtest called the Fake Bad Scale (FBS), Dr. Bush determined that Mr. Bowes was perhaps malingering and was not forthright in his answers. He also indicated that Green's Word Memory Test did not show a significant problem with Tommie's memory.

I took my copy of Dr. Bush's report down to Dr. Salmansohn and talked to him about it. Dr. Salmansohn told me that the FBS was not generally accepted in the neuropsychological community. In fact, it was quite controversial. The lead author of the MMPI-II had written extensively regarding the holes in the FBS test. Some years before, another neuropsychologist had successfully embedded in the MMPI-II a series of perhaps thirty-five to fifty questions. These typically dealt with physical symptoms a person might have.

If a person admitted that they were having any of those symptoms, one such symptom would count as one point toward malingering. This test was extremely unfair for individuals like Tommie, who had multiple traumatic injuries and lots of symptoms. For instance, when Tommie would indicate truthfully that he suffered from tinnitus, it counted a point against him. When he indicated he had neck pain, likewise, that would count against him. Migraine headaches would count against him. You get the gist.

After discussions with Dr. Salmansohn, I decided to challenge the right of Dr. Bush to testify in this case, pursuant to old law from the United States Supreme Court called *Frye vs. United States*, 293 F.20313 (DC Cir. 1923). Frye indicated that:

> While courts go a long way to admitting expert testimony deduced from a well recognized

> scientific principal or discovery, the thing from which the deduction is made must be sufficiently established to have gained general acceptance in that particular field in which it belongs.

Under the Frye standard, we were required to come forward with proof regarding the fallacy of the science behind Dr. Bush's opinion. We needed to find an expert witness in that area.

I decided to retain the services of Dr. James Butcher who, at the time was, a professor emeritus at the University of Minnesota but was still very active in monitoring the MMPI-II Program. Dr. Butcher had written extensively in the past regarding the failures of the FBS, which he said had been improperly inserted into his test. He indicated that this test was not generally accepted in the field of neuropsychology.

While still visiting Dr. Salmansohn, I asked him about Green's Word Memory Test. I asked DR. Salmansohn why he had not used that test. He told me, "It's not a very good test. You will note that Dr. Bush only administered six of the seven tests called for in the Green's Word Memory Test booklet." He said that the reason for that was that Tommie was showing significant problems with memory in the fifth test and in the sixth test, and the seventh test would really hammer that home, in Dr. Salmansohn's mind.

After doing some research, I filed a Motion in Limine to prevent Dr. Bush from testifying regarding the FBS or regarding any question of Tommie malingering or having lack of forthrightness. This was done pursuant to the standard outlined in *Frye.*

By this time, Judge Connor had been elevated to the Fourth District Court of Appeals, and the judge handling the case now was Judge Dwight Geiger, who was a no-nonsense kind of judge.

Defense counsel in this case was my old friend from the second grade, Richard Gaunt. Back when I was at Lynnhaven Elementary School in the second grade, the shorter and thinner kid who sat in the next seat from me was Richard Gaunt. He and I became good friends over that year, which was the only year I'd seen him until I got to law school. When I started at Stetson Law School, the first day, I went into the cafeteria for coffee. I took a seat at a table, having asked whether anyone was taking that seat. Sitting directly across from me at the table was Richard Gaunt, who was a year ahead of me in law school. We immediately recognized each other. We had quite a conversation. After graduation, Richard eventually began working for a defense firm in Palm Beach, which was run by another friend of mine from Stetson, Kent Pratt.

Mr. Gaunt attended the depositions of Dr. Bush and Dr. Salmansohn. We had scheduled the deposition of Dr. Butcher for Minneapolis in late October, when it is cold in the twin cities. I was sure I did not have enough winter clothing, so I bought a new coat.

We had already scheduled the hearing with Judge Geiger to determine the admissibility of this testimony as we were getting very close to trial.

On the day before we were to take off for Minneapolis, Mr. Gaunt filed an agreed order deleting from all of Dr. Bush's testimony, any mention of FBS, and any mention of any possibility of Tommie malingering or not being straightforward. We did not have to go forward with that deposition of Dr. Butcher, nor the hearing before Judge Geiger, for which I was thankful.

Early on in the case, the defense attempted to settle this case for $30,000. We thought the case was worth something between $300,000 and $500,000, at least. On behalf of Mr. Bowes, we filed a proposal for settlement against the defense in the amount of $350,000. In the event that we went to trial and exceeded that amount by 25 percent, we would be entitled to attorney's fees against the other side.

In reply to our PFS, the defense filed one of their own in the amount of $60,000. Under the law, we were required to obtain a result of at least $45,000 to at least avoid Mr. Bowes being responsible for the defense attorney' fees and costs. We were fairly certain that we would have no problem meeting that standard.

Chapter 58

The trial began in November 2011. On the first morning of trial, as I entered the courthouse lobby, I could see Tommie Bowes standing with a group of sheriff's bailiffs and other police officers near the main door. They were vociferously encouraging Tommie and telling him that they wished him the very best. It seems that Tommie was in charge of dealing with all the police officers who are admitted, free of charge, to Mets spring training games to provide security. It was a very "cushy" job for a police officer, and the benefits of such were distributed by Tommie between the sheriff's department, the Port St. Lucie Police Department, and the Fort Pierce Police Department. Tommie had established a relationship with these police officers over the years.

I noticed that many potential jurors were coming in the front door of the courthouse and turning left to go to the jury assembly room. They passed right by this group of police officers and Tommie. Tommie was extremely tall and had a beautiful head of solid white hair. He was quite distinctive looking. I thought that if any of the jurors had seen this, they might be slightly more inclined to give Tommie the benefit of the doubt.

In any event, I believed that the voir dire in this case went well for us. We did not have to use all our peremptory challenges, while the defense ran out of theirs in fairly quick order. Opening statement was a rather bland discussion of what the facts would show in this case. One cannot be particularly emotional during an opening statement, or there's a risk of a mistrial.

Testimony from the plaintiff's witnesses could not have gone any better. Robin Tucker came on and testified to Tommie's condition, both before and after the collision. She also testified regarding the EMTs questioning of Tommie about his name, which took place on the ambulance from the scene of the crash to Lawnwood Regional Medical Center. Robin had driven Tommie home after the six-hour stay at the emergency room and had been told to watch after him because he was a concussion patient. She was told to watch for such things as vomiting, tinnitus, and migraine headache. If Tommie's condition worsened, she was to take him back to the hospital.

I put on the stand Blake Hunter Landis. Prior to his testimony, the defense successfully filed a motion in limine to prevent me from discussing any charges which were made against that reckless driver and preventing me from discussing the fact that there were drugs and drug paraphernalia found in his trunk three days after the crash. I did establish from Mr. Landis that he was on his way to visit a "friend" on Avenue D in Fort Pierce, Florida, on that Thanksgiving Day. He said he was just going there to "hang out." Even in 2011, probably 80 percent of the people in St. Lucie County understood the illicit items that were available in the Avenue D area of Fort Pierce. Mr. Landis had no explanation as to why he veered to the left to cross oncoming traffic.

Dr. Richard Allen testified to his treatment of Tommie's broken nose. We had ordered a demonstrative exhibit prepared by Medical Visions outlining the surgery on Tommie's nose. This was blown up and was extremely effective in explaining the surgery performed by Dr. Allen.

The defense made a big mistake in cross-examining Dr. Allen. They asked him why he had referred Tommie for a brain MRI since he was only an ENT. Dr. Allen said, "Because I am a medical doctor and am concerned with all injuries to my patient."

Dr. Andrew Walker, a local neuroradiologist who was trained at Yale and Harvard and operated Beaches MRI, testified regarding the MRIs to Tommie's brain, particularly the MRI-DTI. He indicated that the injury to Tommie's brain was a "sheer" entry to the axons and that the location of these injuries (and they were numerous) was the gray-white junction of the brain. He explained just how the injury occurred.

He had a very interesting way to show the jury what the damage meant to a person like Tommie. Dr. Walker used a laptop computer which was hooked up to a large-screen television by my videographer, Jim Young. On the screen of his laptop, he drew an approximately one square inch square for the right frontal lobe of Tommie's brain. The picture on the MRI glowed with various colors. Some were blue, some were red, some were yellow, some were white, etc. These glowing spots appeared to be just like the end of a freshly cut coaxial cable. It showed what looked to be a very fine wires bundled together. When Dr. Walker dragged his cursor over the one square inch section, on the screen appeared certain speeds in parenthesis, which Dr. Walker explained showed how fast the messages were being transmitted from the gray matter. It also showed which direction the messages were being sent. The numbers that were printed out were all in the 1.0 range for speed. Some of them were as high as 1.2, and some were as low as .97.

Dr. Walker then drew the same square over the left (injured) frontal lobe which Dr. Walker had indicated was shown to have the injury through MRI-DTI. The numbers which the machine spit out over that area were in the range of .5 or less. Dr. Walker explained that the messages in that particular area were traveling approximately one half the speed of normal. He also explained that many of the messages were going in the wrong direction. Dr. Walker had a way of explaining very technical scientific matters to jurors, who, if they had a high school education, could totally understand what he was talking about.

Tommie got on the stand and told his life story and explained how things had gone after the accident happened. During his testimony, the courtroom was packed with police officers who were obviously there in support of Tommie. The jury noticed that they were there but didn't know why.

Tommie came off as a very nice person who engendered a lot of sympathy from the jury.

My last witness was the representative of the Mets. He told the story about Tommie being a great employee before the accident. He also explained about the fact that the Mets were not going to get rid of Tommie because they loved him. He explained that an accommodation was made as a result of Tommie's injury. The Mets had hired an assistant head groundskeeper. They had also brought in the system of the "Tommie Boards," which were particularly offensive to Tommie. They were, however, necessary for him to continue doing his job.

With that, I sat down and let the defense go forward. The defense put on a radiologist expert from Fort Lauderdale, Dr. Kagan. Dr. Kagan had a reputation of working extensively for the defense. He was not board-certified in neuroradiology, but his board certification was in something called nuclear medicine, a field Dr. Walker assured me was not the same thing as neuroradiology. Dr. Kagan had previously issued a report with some interesting findings in it. He had indicated that the MRI-DTI was "totally experimental." He said it could not be used for early diagnosis or treatment of traumatic brain injury. He also indicated in his report that the machine used by Dr. Walker (a 2.5 Tesla Seimon's machine) was not sufficiently strong to enable the computer to understand the data it was taking in on MRI-DTI.

A couple of months before the trial happened, I journeyed down to Fort Lauderdale to take Dr. Kagan's deposition. I had been reading extensively about MRI-DTI and was pleasantly surprised to find an article in the *New England Journal of Medicine*. This article discussed a study which was originated and paid for by the US Army, US Marines, and Veterans Administration.

At the time the study began, the United States was involved in military action both in Iraq and in Afghanistan. Many soldiers and Marines had been injured from bombs (IEDs) which had been placed next to the roadway. The injuries often involved the brain. Under the study, the injured soldiers were first examined, in theater, to determine whether or not they exhibited signs of traumatic brain injury. They then were flown to Ramstein Air Force Hospital in Germany, where they were first put through an MRI-DTI regimen. Of the ninety soldiers and Marines who were examined at Ramstein, sixty of those had positive MRI-DTI results showing brain damage. It was noted that MRI-DTI only picks up about 25 percent of the truly brain damaged individuals. Most of the other 75 percent of concussion victims might have brain damage, or not.

After leaving Ramstein, these patients were flown to Walter Reed Hospital in Washington, DC, where they underwent another test with the same Model 2.5 Tesla Siemens machine which had been used in Germany. These tests which were performed several months after the German test verified almost exactly the findings from the prior MRI-DTI. Then, as a further control, all the soldiers were sent to Washington University Hospital in Missouri, which was the premier neurological hospital in the country at the time. There, the patients were once again evaluated with a Siemens 2.5 Tesla machine. This was done more than three months after the Walter Reed test. This test also confirmed the findings from the first two locations. In addition, a few more of the ninety people tested showed positive signs of brain damage along the way.

The article in the *New England Journal of Medicine* indicated several things which were helpful to us. The article pointed out that the Siemens 2.5 machine was the "gold standard" in MRI-DTI. It explained that lower powered machines were not sufficient and that higher powered machines such as 3.0 Tesla created so much artifact as to call into question the accuracy of the test.

The authors of the study also stated that the MRI-DTI was a useful tool in the early detection and treatment of traumatic brain injury. This article, from the most trusted peer review medical journal in the country, tore apart the opinions of Dr. Kagan.

After I read this study, I went down to Fort Lauderdale to take Dr. Kagan's deposition. I had in my briefcase a copy of the study from the *New England Journal of Medicine*. I printed it off the internet.

When I got to Dr. Kagan's office, the secretary indicated to me that I could go back to his office where the videographer was setting up. She said that Dr. Kagan would be with us in fifteen or twenty minutes.

When I went into Dr. Kagan's office, I was surprised. There was one item on the corner of Dr. Kagan's desk. The desk was otherwise empty. That item was the actual June 2011 *New England Journal of Medicine* which contained the McDonald study in it.

In the deposition, I first asked Dr. Kagan if he considered the *New England Journal of Medicine* to be authoritative. He said he did. I asked him had he ever written an article for the journal. He explained that when he graduated from medical school in the early 1970s, he had done a study and was extremely pleased that his study was accepted by the *New England Journal of Medicine* for publication. That fact could easily be determined from Dr. Kagan's curriculum vitae, which I had read. However, I wanted to establish that he believed in the *New England Journal of Medicine*. Then I asked him if he had seen the article about MRI-DTI, which was in the June issue of the *New England Journal of Medicine*. He answered, "You mean the McDonald article?"

I said, "Yes." I pulled out my copy from my briefcase. The doctor said that copy is only from the internet. The actual journal is much better. "Would you like to have a copy?" I said I certainly would.

The secretary quickly prepared a xerox of the entire article. From that article, I cross-examined Dr. Kagan regarding his opinion that the 2.5 machine was not powerful enough to handle MRI-DTI. He responded that his own MRI machine, which was in his facility, was a 3.0 machine, and it was his opinion that that was a much better machine for handling this type of test. He also testified that the test should "never" be used for diagnosis and treatment of patients. He said that insurance would not pay for the test. He said that the test was experimental and was only used for research purposes, which was why there were so few machines in the state of Florida at that time doing MRI-DTI.

It is true that every university teaching hospital in Florida had such a machine, and several doctors around the state, including Dr. Walker, had such a machine. One reason they are not more widely used is that the machines typically cost well over $1 million each. Dr. Walker was so well regarded when he opened Beaches MRI that Siemans gave him his machine because they wanted their machine to be used by the best. We could not tell the jury that.

I pointed out to Dr. Kagan that his opinions were the opposite of those contained in the McDonald article. He said, "Well, the McDonald study had been recently criticized by certain individuals, but not in a peer reviewed article." At trial, Dr. Kagan projected pictures on the wall of the MRI-DTI studies. He made a very cursory discussion about how the system worked. He repeated that the Siemans machine was not sufficiently strong to perform MRI-DTIs. He also repeated his statement that the test was completely experimental and was under research. When I brought up on cross-examination the McDonald study and his prior deposition, the jury literally laughed Dr. Kagan out of the courtroom.

The defense then put on Dr. Bush, who repeated his statement that he did not believe that Tommie had any measurable brain injury as a result of the accident in question. I questioned on cross-examination Dr. Bush about the fact that the MMPI-II exam he gave had embedded in it several specific tests to determine the validity of the answers. I quoted those particular test results and asked Dr. Bush if they, in fact, showed that Tommie was giving a full effort. He had to admit that he did.

I then questioned Dr. Bush about the Green's Word Memory Test. I had blown up demonstrative exhibits of the computer printout generated by Green's. The Green's test was typically given in seven parts. The first parts of the test were essentially validity tests to determine whether or not the patient was being honest and straightforward. Tommie scored almost a perfect score for being honest on the test.

The fourth, fifth, sixth, and seventh tests all measured memory problems. The computer would print out a statement as to what the tests meant. I asked Dr. Bush why he only administered six of the seven tests. He explained that it was his choice to do that and that neuropsychologists are not required to give all seven tests. I then pointed out to the computer read regarding test number six. Tommie was fifty-five years old at the time the test was given. The computer indicated that while that was true, Tommie's brain age was that of a sixty-five-year-old. As we get older, our brains deteriorate. Hopefully, we make up for this deterioration by experience.

In Tommie's case, the printout confirmed that he had a brain injury, in my mind, and apparently in the mind of the jury.

The defense also showed surveillance tape they had taken of Tommie which showed him opening the gate at the Mets minor league facility. It showed him coming out of a bagel shop in the morning with a bagel and a schmeer on his way to work. I thought that the surveillance was a waste of time and money by the defense, and I did not challenge it.

The defense rested, and I decided to do something which I do not usually do in trial. I decided to call rebuttal witnesses. I called Dr. Salmansohn, who testified to a critique of the Green's Word Memory Test. He also said that had Tommie taken the seventh test, it would have shown even greater damage. I asked Dr. Salmansohn why he did not use Green's in this or other studies he had done with other patients. He said it was his opinion that the test was "not a good test."

I then put Dr. Walker back on the stand. He proceeded to shoot holes in the testimony of Dr. Kagan.

Closing argument was set for the next day. When the closing argument started, there must have been twelve or fifteen sheriff's deputies and police officers in uniform in the room to listen to the argument. We went over the testimony in detail, and I felt that the presentation went well.

The defense did not have much to work with, in my mind. Mr. Gaunt did indicate that Tommie had not missed a day of work. Gaunt said that if he hadn't missed any work, his memory problem was obviously not that bad.

After about two hours, the jury came back with a very nice verdict. They determined that Tommie Bowes had been injured as a result of the negligence of Blake Hunter Landis and by virtue of the Dangerous Instrumentality Rule, by the negligence of his father, Dr. Ian Landis. The jury returned a verdict in the exact amount of $557,726.90.

When the jury was dismissed, a large number of law enforcement personnel came into the well of the court and shook Tommie's hand and congratulated him and me on the result.

It should be noted that we had filed a Proposal for Settlement in the amount of $350,000. Our verdict was well in excess of 25 percent over that PFS. We would be entitled to attorney's fees from the day our PFS was filed forward.

With attorney's fees and costs combined with the amount of the verdict, the total judgment in that case was approximately $750,000. This was a huge victory.

Epilogue

In the more than ten years since the Bowes verdict, there seems to have been an explosion of traumatic brain injury cases throughout the country. An important and well-publicized study was done by the NFL in conjunction with several Ivy League schools which determined that repeated concussion could cause debilitating, even fatal brain injury and result in changing personality, memory, etc. These studies were discussed on television, in shows like *60 Minutes*, as well as on ESPN. There were protocols implemented in high school and college, as well as pro football, to prevent players from continuing to play after repeat concussions.

Verdicts in this area have continued to rise so that a half million-dollar verdict would not draw that much attention at this time. It was very nice for 2011. However, the result in this case was gratifying to me and my client.

In 2019, the Florida Supreme Court retreated from its position on *Frye vs. US* and decided that Florida would follow the federal standard in this area of the law outlined in *Daubert vs. Merrill-Dow Pharmaceuticals Inc.*, 509 US 579 (1993). This test, in my opinion, would have also prevented Dr. Bush from testifying to the FBS test results. Under Daubert, the standard for excision of certain expert testimony is changed. Daubert indicates:

> A witness who is qualified as an expert by knowledge, skill, experience, training, or educa-

tion may testify in the form of opinion or otherwise if:

(a) the expert's scientific technical or other specialized knowledge will help the trier of fact understand the evidence or to determine a fact in issue;
(b) the testimony is based on sufficient facts or data;
(c) the testimony is apprised of reliable principals and methods; and
(d) the expert has reliably applied the principals and methods to the facts of the case.

The Daubert standard requires an evidentiary hearing, which was allowed, but not required, under the Frye standard. Nowadays, the Daubert hearing has become a separate little trial which one has to endure on the way to obtaining justice.

In June of 2022, I was shopping for a new pair of shoes, as my old ones had worn out. As I sat down in the shoe store to try on a pair, Tommie Bowes walked up and sat in the chair next to me to try on a pair of shoes for himself. I was shocked and surprised to see him there as I had not talked to him in some time. We had a nice conversation. Tommie indicated to me that he had retired from the Mets the year before. He said that he and Robin were still together, but both of them were afraid of getting married because they had been through difficult divorces in the past. He thanked me for helping him and said that the result of the case enabled him to have a comfortable retirement. Tommie was still experiencing occasional problems with tinnitus and with memory. The migraine headaches were being effectively treated and appeared to be under control.

BOOK 22

Actionable Sexual Assault

Chapter 59

Late in the school year 2015, Joanna Sweet (not her real name) was a student in a high school in St. Lucie County, Florida. She was enrolled in a program for "exceptional" children. Joanna's IQ was only 56, but she was a young woman who had certainly reached puberty. She was virginal and had no clue what sex was about. Her favorite activities consisted of talking with her few friends or listening to her music through earphones in the phone that she always brought with her.

Hers was a tiny classroom with only seven students. Six of those students were there because of their severe developmental disabilities. One of them was there because he had been a problem student since he was first sent to school as a young child.

The school obtained permission from all the parents or guardians to take these kids on a field trip. They had arranged for a tour of the local Walmart Supercenter where it was thought that some of these kids, when they obtained adulthood, might seek employment in the most menial jobs that were there, including cleaning crews, shopping cart corral technicians, greeter, or perhaps stock boy or stock girl. It was doubtful any of these children could ever become cashiers.

The trip to Walmart went well, and none of the children got in trouble while in the store. They had a guided tour of the facility, and they had discussion regarding all the jobs that the employees of Walmart were performing. Everyone had a soda before getting back on the bus.

There was a bus driver and three adult chaperones on the bus, one of whom was a teacher. The other two were also employees of the school system.

On the way back to the school from the field trip, Joanna was raped. The other children had been sitting far apart in the back of this large bus. Video showed that each of the kids were nodding and had earbuds in their ears while they were listening to music or whatever they were listening to. The bus driver was looking forward. The three adults were sitting in the front row of the bus and were having an animated conversation between themselves. There were lots of smiles and perhaps loud talking going on, although the video did not have sound.

Joanna was sitting in the next to last row of the bus, and there had been no children sitting within four or five rows of where she was. Each child was sitting separately.

The problem child on the bus, Tyrone (not his real name), was age sixteen and was a muscular Black boy. Tyrone got up from his seat and quietly walked to the back of the bus. He then proceeded to rape fifteen-year-old Joanna in her seat. Because of her limited mental ability, Joanna did not even understand what was happening. When this attack was over, Tyrone zipped up his pants and walked back to his seat on the bus. No adult in the front row noticed what was going on, and all the other children were oblivious to it.

When they got back to the school, all the students went back into class, and Joanna did not tell her teacher what had happened, nor did she tell her parents what happened.

The next day, someone at the school viewed the videotape of the bus ride, and the stuff hit the fan.

A school resource deputy from the sheriff's department, accompanied by another deputy, went to Tyrone's home and were greeted by Tyrone's grandfather. Tyrone's grandfather had guardianship over the boy. They began to explain why they were there, and the grandfather called Tyrone into the room. In front of the sheriff's deputies, the grandfather asked Tyrone, "What is this all about?"

Tyrone's response was rather chilling. "It's the same stuff I got in trouble for last year."

Tyrone was arrested and was initially placed in juvenile hall. The juvenile justice system is no justice at all. Usually, a horrible perpetrator is released in a couple of weeks with no real follow-up, although technically, he has to visit with probation officers after release. Tyrone would not be so lucky. The state's attorney decided to try Tyrone as an adult and keep him in jail with a high bond. Tyrone already had a rape case hanging over his head from a year before.

The school contacted Joanna's parents and told them what happened. They contacted our office.

Joanna's father was a local minister. Her mother was an LPN, and both of them were of normal intelligence. They were quite upset at what had happened to their daughter. They had had her examined by a physician, who confirmed that she had been molested and had lost her virginity. Thankfully, he also confirmed that she was not pregnant.

I went over various options with the parents and explained that this was a case involving so-called "sovereign immunity." At English common law, no one could sue the king or any of the king's ministers or officials that were carrying out their duties.

In the United States, many jurisdictions, including Florida, passed specific laws allowing a lawsuit to be filed against a government agency. In Florida at that time, the law included a provision that said the maximum recovery in a case such as that was $200,000. The statute also capped plaintiff's attorney's fees at 25 percent of any award.

Under the law, we were required to file a notice with the school board and send a copy to the state. There was a mandatory six-month delay before a lawsuit could be filed.

Theoretically, this delay was built in to encourage people to settle their claims with the agency short of litigation. In our office, we had gone through this process several cases before Joanna's case. In practice, the way a delay worked was an unwarranted extension of time to the agency. Rarely had we been successful in settling a case against the government without at least filing suit.

Six months after the notice was sent to the school board, we were able to file suit and did so. We received some shocking records on Tyrone. When he was twelve, he had raped a young boy in a wheelchair in the handicapped stall of the bathroom. He was caught and held at juvenile hall for a short time. There was an alleged investigation, and the person in charge of the exceptional student education (ESE) department of the school board had decided to assign Tyrone to a different school. The only person at that school that had been advised of Tyrone's problem was the principal. Tyrone did not stay in that school long until he was assigned to a different school because he was so disruptive. We feared that other sexual attacks had occurred before our victim was attacked. We later learned that when the police opened their investigation of Joanna's case, they discovered that Tyrone had raped another little girl in the class after he followed her into the bathroom. They learned this by talking to each student in the class. The little girl in the class who had been violated earlier was very ashamed and was not able to discuss the rape with her teacher or with her parents.

The evening after I had filed the necessary notice with the school board under the statute, I attended a meeting of the Treasure Coast Justice Association. The Treasure Coast Justice Association is a volunteer organization of plaintiffs' civil trial lawyers in the Treasure Coast of Florida which includes four counties—St. Lucie, Martin, Indian River, and Okeechobee. One of the services of our organization was that the "gray hairs" in the organization would act as mentors for any young attorney in the thirty minutes before the meeting began. Under the agreement, none of the mentors could profit by trying to take over the case of the younger attorney. Often, if we only had one or two young attorneys with a problem, the three of us would discuss the matter with them together. Most plaintiff's trial lawyers are quite collegial. The Treasure Coast Justice Association members were all members of the Florida Justice Association. Being in the FJA was like being in the largest law firm in Florida. If you had a problem, someone in the group had an answer and could provide help if you needed it. Over the years, I have used that help many times with attorneys scattered all over the state.

On this particular evening, I was one of three experienced litigators who were on the panel. One of the other litigators was a talented and pleasant female attorney from Stuart, Florida, named Gloria Seidule. Gloria opened the conversation with a "Hi, Roger, have you been doing anything interesting lately?" Without divulging my client's name (which I'm not in this particular case as all names have been changed in this case except those of the attorneys), I explained that I had a very interesting case that had just walked into my office regarding a rape which happened on school property. Surprisingly, Gloria said she had a similar case ongoing in her office. She explained that her young girl had been raped on the school grounds at a different school than the one Joanna was attending. In Gloria's case, one teacher was supervising perhaps a hundred kids on a large playground, and the rape occurred without the teacher noticing it. That attack occurred at a middle school with an eighth-grade ESE student as the victim.

I told Gloria about what occurred at the grandfather's home, and she said, "Oh my god, my perpetrator's name was Tyrone as well." I feared that we had a serial sexual predator in the school system, and Gloria said she bet it was the same guy.

Gloria said that Tyrone's criminal case in her incident was still pending. There had been a lot of delays. She had sent the required notice a year ago and had filed suit. I asked her to see her pleadings, and she kindly emailed them to me the next day.

After the attack on Gloria's client, an individual educational plan was prepared by the school for this particular child, Tyrone. This plan indicated that "Tyrone, while on school property, should never be more than an arm's length away from an adult." Unfortunately, this had not been explained to any of the people on the bus in question, and it appears that it was also not explained to the classroom teacher. It was unclear whether or not the principal at the school was even aware of the history of this serial sexual predator. Apparently, the IEP (Individual Educational Plan) was not forwarded from the middle school to the high school Tyrone was attending.

We wrote the risk management specialist as well as the school board's attorney and asked them for records of this perpetrator, and they were not, initially, forthcoming. Apparently, there are rules regarding divulging information about individual students. It would take court action on our part to get these records.

The school board's attorney and risk management officer contacted our office and wanted to have a settlement conference to be attended by myself as well as both parents of Joanna. The risk management officer and other officials from the school board, along with their attorney, would also be present.

I had a very long conversation with Joanna's parents. They very emphatically indicated that they did not want to put their daughter through a trial on this matter. They said she was already feeling ashamed. She was upset when she had to go to school, and she now hated it. Before the attack occurred, she enjoyed the interaction with the other kids.

I told them that whatever settlement we could reach would have a requirement that the money was protected, and Joanna would have access to needed support later in her life. Her parents were both about forty years old when Joanna was born. Joanna was their first child, and given her situation, the parents decided to never have another child. After the attack, Joanna's out-of-the-home activities had been reduced to attending church where her father preached on Sunday, going to Sunday school at that church before the services, and going to prayer meeting on Wednesday nights.

Finally, the day for the mediation conference came around.

In a conference that only lasted a couple of hours, we were able to cobble together an agreement which was accepted by all parties. Joanna would receive a structured settlement in an amount I cannot disclose. This money would be invested in a special needs trust and would provide funds in the future to help with things that Medicare or Medicaid would not pay for. The way this "special needs" trust was set up, Joanna's entitlement to Medicaid or any welfare type of benefit would not be affected.

I took a fee which was slightly reduced from the 25 percent I could have legally charged for handling this matter. The only goal that we did not obtain through the settlement that we very much wanted was to have the director of the ESE Program removed from office. He had screwed up with Tyrone's cases for years and apparently did not learn from any of them.

That gentleman just retired this year from the school system. Joanna's parents were thankful for the help I gave them. We had set up a guardianship for Joanna with her parents as guardians. We did not charge a fee for that service. Once a year, they will sign the necessary legal documents to continue that status, and we will file it with the court.

Under the terms of the settlement, everything was confidential, and therefore, I have deleted everyone's name, except for mine and Gloria's, and substituted names for the individuals involved. I also changed the date of the attack and a few other identifying facts. This case and the result thereof was never divulged in any Bar journal or other publication relative to the practice of law.

Tyrone was a predator who needed to be in jail, not in school. The prosecutor had Tyrone removed to the county jail from juvenile hall, where he was placed in an area without adults in his cell. A decision had been made to try Tyrone as an adult.

Ultimately, Tyrone pled guilty and was sentenced to a short period of prison time and an extensive period of supervised parole. At least he is no longer in the school system.

BOOK 23

Medical Malpractice

Chapter 60

Bill Majewski died on January 12, 2016, as a result of horrible medical negligence. At the time of his death, Bill was, hands down, my best friend. Before I get into the details of medical negligence and Bill's death, I need to tell you a few things about him.

As I indicated before, when I opened my office in Port St. Lucie, I already knew and liked Bill Majewski. I had met him somewhere around 1980 when I was in Vero Beach, Florida, taking a full day to do three separate depositions. All the witnesses had been subpoenaed. I showed up before the appointed time for the deposition and met the court reporter, who turned out to be Bill Majewski. I had an instant dislike for him. Bill spoke with a Bronx accent, and I had an accent which was distinctively Southern but not totally redneck. It occurred to me that Bill had a very sarcastic sense of humor. We had a long conversation about each of our families and what we planned for our lives as the first witness was late getting to the deposition. The first deposition ended long before the second one was to start. We continued our discussions as we were around the same age. We both had families. At the time, Bill's son was graduating from high school and had been accepted at the University of Florida up in Gainesville. Bill and Suzanne Majewski were about to be officially empty nesters.

I, on the other hand, in 1990, still had two youngsters living in my house. I learned that Bill was an avid bowler. At the time, I was an avid golfer. I thought bowling was a stupid game, and Bill thought that golf was even more stupid, hitting a little white ball and then chasing it down the fairway to hit the thing again. I wasn't an excellent golfer. Many of my swings was followed by a mild curse word. The old joke is "Why did they name it golf?" The answer is "Because all other four-letter words were taken." I had never been a very good bowler, but Bill was extremely competitive and was carrying an average in the 260s, if memory served. He was active in several local leagues.

By the time the second deposition ended, it was lunchtime, and we still had quite a bit of time until the third deposition was to take place in the afternoon. We decided to go to lunch together. We went to Two Jay's Deli in Vero Beach. Of course, we chatted more. By the end of the third deposition, I had become a friend of Bill Majewski, and Betsey and I had been invited by him to go to dinner with him and his wife, Suzanne, at a later date. The friendship would continue from there.

By the time I decided to take the leap of faith and move my office to Port St. Lucie, Bill, by then, had opened Atlantic Reporting as an owner. I used Bill's court reporting firm, exclusively whenever possible, for depositions and trial testimony. I found all his employees to be very capable and efficient and was pleased with the competitive prices that they charged me for their services.

One day in approximately 1986, Bill cajoled me into taking up bowling. I became a league bowler, and although I was not particularly skilled at it (an average of about 170), I still contributed to our team, of which Bill was the captain. His average was in the 260s.

I had an accident with a herniated disc within two weeks of opening my office in Port St. Lucie. As a result of that accident, I had to drop out of bowling because it put too much strain on my neck.

Once I opened my own office, it became apparent after six months of the first year that I was going to have problems with the cost of the practice. Bill understood this, and he told me that he would carry my accounts payable for a while. He said that I could pay him the entire bill once I could afford it. He had taken depositions in the Petroski case and understood that it was a very good case and should result in a nice attorney's fee for my office.

We had scheduled a lunch together in Port St. Lucie after my office opened there. Bill and his wife already lived in Port St. Lucie, and Betsey and I were looking to relocate to that community. At lunch, Bill told me that "Suzanne and I have decided to adopt a little girl."

I replied, "Are you sure you guys want to take on that responsibility?"

He said, "Yes." He also said that there were complications. The little girl they wanted to adopt was named Barbara. Barbara was a child who had cerebral palsy and mental retardation problems and had been abandoned at an early age. They saw Barbara in the hospital and were told by the staff that she was failing to thrive and might have a very short life expectancy. She was extremely in need of love. Bill told me, "If we did not agree to take her, nobody would." They adopted the little girl.

I think I may have helped Bill and Suzanne with their adoption procedure, but I no longer have those files, and I'm not certain. It sounds like something I would have done.

They brought Barbara home near Christmastime. Her health had improved. The little girl could not believe what a Christmas tree looked like, nor did she accept the fact that many of the presents under the tree belonged to her. Bill very soon became a "Daddy" again and would be forever joined in a loving relationship with Barbara. She seemed closer to Bill than to her mom, Suzanne.

When it came time for Atlantic Reporting's Christmas party that year, Bill asked me if I would agree to be Santa Claus for Barbara and all the other children of the court reporters. I was not offended, even though it was an obvious reference to my chubby condition. I said I would be proud to. Bill bought a Santa suit and had me rigged up with it, including a pillow on my belly. I must have had ten children, including Barbara, take turns on my lap. The oldest was perhaps eight years old, and the youngest was maybe two. Bill's employees, who were almost all women, were very pleased at the party and thanked me for my Santa role. I recognized several of them from work they had done for me.

In 2000, my best friend in the world was Ron Martin. When Ron died, his wife, Bonnie, asked me to do the eulogy. Ron was not a particularly devout Christian, although he professed to be of the Christian faith. He did not belong to or attend church. The funeral had been scheduled at Haisley-Hobbs Funeral Home in Fort Pierce, Florida. Ron and I had been active in the Fort Pierce Lions Club as well as in the Florida Lions Foundation for the Blind, an organization in which I was general counsel (pro bono) from 1983 until now. Ron was president of that organization from 1999 to 2000. Ron had previously served as district governor for our District 35D in Florida. He and I had attended every foundation meeting for about seven years before Ron's death. Some of the meetings were in Pensacola, some were in Miami, some were in Fort Myers Beach on the west coast. Many were in Orlando, and some were in Tallahassee. I figured that over the years, Ron and I had logged together over fifty thousand miles on either his vehicle or mine.

When I showed up on the day of the funeral, I had prepared a eulogy for Ron. However, when I met with Rick Haisley, the funeral director, he said, "You ought to see the funeral booklet which they pass out to every attendee at the funeral." I opened the booklet, and it had listed as "Clergy in Charge—Roger Messer." I was shocked. I was certainly no clergyman, though my brother was an ordained Methodist minister. Ron was also a past Grand Puba (or whatever they called it) of the local Elks Club (an organization I did not join). The funeral chapel was filled to capacity, as was the viewing room across the hall, which had a big screen. Lions from all over the state of Florida were in attendance. In addition, Ron's stepchildren and stepgrandchildren were there as well as his wife and many friends of their family.

Bill Majewski, who also knew Ron, was also in attendance. In part of my eulogy, I described Ron Martin as "my best friend." At the end of the service, I met with Bonnie, and she asked me if she could receive a copy of the eulogy I had written. I was only glad to give it to her.

The next person I talked to was Bill Majewski, and he said, "Roger, I'm disappointed. I thought I was your best friend."

My reply was "Well, Bill, you are now."

Deputy Sheriff Bill Hardman was also standing there and heard the conversation. He broke out in a huge guffaw of laughter. Bill was indeed my best friend at that time. In 1995, when Ron Martin was the district governor, he asked me and another member of the Fort Pierce Lions Club who lived in St. Lucie West to open a St. Lucie West Lions Club. We did organize that club and chartered with thirty-nine members. Bill Majewski was one of the first people to volunteer to join the club, along with his wife. Bill had refused to join the Fort Pierce Lions Club because the travel was not convenient to him. By that time, I had talked Bill into taking up the game of golf, and he became a golf crazy. He was forever changing drivers, putters, and other clubs to meet the newest fad. He was a good, but not great, golfer, and we often played in a scramble tournament with my son, who was an awesome golfer, and with another member from the community. We won a lot of tournaments. Many times, when just the two of us were playing, Barbara would ride along in Bill's cart while I was alone in mine.

In 2017, both of us were living in Port St. Lucie, and both of us were beyond the age of sixty-five but still went to work every day. We were still very close friends, and we had, in fact, traveled with Bill and Suzanne and Barbara to the Bahamas as well as to Las Vegas and other trips. We had enjoyed meals with them on a fairly regular basis, including meals at their house and meals at our house as well as at restaurants.

Chapter 61

Bill's death was sudden and shocking and was totally preventable. Bill had gone to work at his office down in Stuart, Florida, that morning, and before lunch, he had begun to feel bad. His stomach hurt tremendously to the point that he didn't think he could continue working that day. Sometimes he would go home for lunch in Port St. Lucie to be with his wife and child. On this particular day, he called Suzanne and said he was coming home for lunch at approximately 1:00 p.m. but did not feel well. Bill came home and refused to eat anything. Suzanne noticed that Bill's stomach, where most of his pain was emanating, was slightly distended. Suzanne was a registered nurse herself who was out of work on disability at the time. She took Bill's pulse, which was normal, and his breathing rate, which initially had been normal. His condition deteriorated, and his breathing was irregular. Bill told Suzanne that he needed to go by ambulance to the hospital.

The EMTs were there quickly. Suzanne did not ride in the ambulance to the hospital with Bill. She had to arrange with friends to watch Barbara. She also called Bill's son, Matthew, and advised him that his dad was going to the hospital. However, once Suzanne got to the hospital, she stayed with Bill until very late in the evening, at which point she was told to go home and rest. If the hospital had fully informed the EMTs of their equipment problem, Bill would never have been taken to Martin Memorial Hospital at Tradition. It seems that the CT scanner for the hospital was broken.

Bill arrived at the emergency room at approximately 4:00 p.m. Bill was seen by the ER physician, who ordered that a CT scan of the torso be taken "*Stat.*" *Stat* means "right now." Bill found himself on a gurney in the hall of the emergency room. All twenty-five emergency room beds were filled, and there were thirteen patients, including Bill, on gurneys against the wall in the hall. Suzanne was there with her husband and was extremely concerned that he was not being properly cared for. His breathing became difficult, and his stomach became much more distended. Bill had a very strange color to him. He was in pain.

Around 9:30 p.m., someone at the hospital got around to transporting Bill by their ambulance to another hospital facility owned by Martin Memorial. If only the EMTs had taken Bill to any other hospital in the three-county area, and if a competent radiologist read the film, Bill's life could have been saved at that point.

By the time Bill got back to the Tradition location, the in-house radiologist had gone home for the night from the hospital. But never fear, the hospital's plan was to send copies of the CT scan films by the cloud to a doctor's service out in California called Night Hawk. Unfortunately, the Night Hawk radiologist only made a cursory examination of the scans. There were three hundred scans. That doctor sent back a report less than eight minutes after he got the film and gave an opinion that all scans were clear.

When there is free gas or air in the abdominal area, it will appear on a CT scan as a black blob. If there are any such black blobs in the CT scan, it would be considered abnormal and would be a sign of a severe internal injury. When our expert reviewed these films, he showed us numerous instances of the gas which was caused by perhaps a perforated bowel.

When Bill got back to the hospital around 10:00 p.m., the computer system at the hospital called a "sepsis alert" on Bill's case. The sepsis alert system had been designed for the computer to warn hospital staff if sepsis was imminent in a patient. Apparently, staff ignored this warning, not only this time but several times during the evening. Meanwhile, Bill developed tachycardia, which is a very rapid heartbeat. He was panting for breath, and his color was awful. He developed a temperature, though hospital staff did not regularly monitor it. Suzanne Majewski commented to the nurse when she saw it.

The hospital, its doctors, and staff ignored Bill Majewski to death.

Finally, around 11:00 p.m., there was a change in shift, and a new doctor came by and saw Bill and gave her opinion that he needed to have exploratory laparoscopic surgery done on his abdomen to see what the problem was. The hospital called the specialist who did this kind of surgery for them to come into the hospital to perform the surgery. He didn't arrive before 6:00 a.m.

Unfortunately, around midnight, one of the doctors decided to change Bill's medications and, unfortunately, cut off the pain relief medication which Bill was on. All night long, Bill was in excruciating pain and was wailing. Had the exploratory surgery been done by midnight that night, Bill would have had an excellent chance of recovery, although it was not certain. If the surgery had been done by 9:00 p.m., there was about a 100 percent chance of recovery.

The surgery was done the next morning at around 7:30 a.m., and when the doctor opened Bill's lower thorax, he was overcome by the smell emanating therefrom. It was obvious that Bill's colon had ruptured, spilling deadly fecal matter into the body cavity where the toxic mix attacked the other organs. The doctor basically drained the abdomen and copiously washed it with saline solution and did his best to undo the damage, but he was not successful.

An extremely exhausted Suzanne Majewski was with Bill until after midnight. She had harangued the local staff that her husband was in tachycardia and was having difficulty breathing, but they were apparently too busy to get around to him. Suzanne had to go home to take care of Barbara. Meanwhile, overnight, the computer kept issuing warnings to the hospital staff that there was a sepsis alert. The machine was monitoring the telemetry of the leads hooked up to Bill, and numerous factors go into the telemetry. These are more than just temperature, heart rate, and blood oxygenation. When enough problems come together to raise a concern of a current or impending sepsis, the machine will send on the computer to all the terminals in the emergency room the words *Sepsis Alert*.

Suzanne had gone home and got to sleep around 3:00 a.m., but around 7:00 a.m., she was awakened by the phone call from the hospital. She was told that "Mr. Majewski's condition has worsened, and it is grave." She was told that Bill was in surgery, and not much would be known until the surgery was over. She was asked to come back to the hospital, which she promptly did, accompanied by her son.

Bill's final twenty-four hours of his life were absolute hell.

I learned of Bill's passing within minutes of it occurring. I was not even aware that Bill was in the hospital when Suzanne called me and told me that he had passed suddenly and asked if she could come into my office to discuss this with me in a day or two. I told her that I would certainly see her. She also told me that she wanted me to attend Bill's celebration of life when it was scheduled and do a eulogy on behalf of my friend. I said, of course, I would do that.

In the office, Suzanne told me what happened to the best of her ability. Suzanne was so distraught she could barely communicate. She only told me what she observed, and I was shocked. I explained to Suzanne that I was no longer handling medical malpractice cases by myself, as I was getting "long in the tooth," but I would get her with the best, or one of the best, medical malpractice lawyers in the state, and I would be working with him.

Chapter 62

For the Bill Majewski case, I chose to bring in a Jacksonville attorney who was one of the top malpractice attorneys in the state. His name was Fred "Catfish" Abbott. His real middle name is Catfish. Why did I choose him? I met Catfish Abbot (his friends call him Catfish or Fish) at an Academy of Florida Trial Lawyers (now FJA) Workhorse Seminar, where he was one of the presenters. It was an evening presentation and in a small group setting. Toward the end of the seminar, Mr. Abbott asked the question, "Who in the room thinks they had the shortest mediation?" I raised my hand, and he said, "Did you beat five minutes, which was my personal record?"

I said, "Yes, I did. My mediation lasted one minute."

He said, "You've got to tell us the story." I told him the story about the mediation in the case which is discussed earlier in this book.

After the seminar was over, Mr. Abbott came up and shook my hand and noted on my name tag that I was from St. Lucie County, Florida. He asked that I go have a beverage with him for a few minutes. I think I had a Diet Pepsi, while he had a beer. Catfish explained to me that he needed to find an attorney who would not rip him off to handle a probate for a large medical malpractice death case that he was pursuing in St. Lucie County. He asked me if I knew if such a person existed. I told him I did. I also volunteered that my office had a full-time probate paralegal, and we handled such matters in addition to my doing litigation. I quoted him a very reasonable price, and he said, "You're hired."

That was a case of medical malpractice against a local HCA hospital, St Lucie Medical Center.

As that case progressed, Catfish used my office in Port St. Lucie to hold depositions and also let me do some work on the case. That case was about the hospital giving the wrong blood to an eighty-year-old lady on a one unit of blood transfusion after hip surgery. The hospital gave her the wrong blood and essentially killed her.

Shortly after the decedent's family had hired Mr. Abbott (the personal representative resided in Jacksonville), he had a call from a volunteer whistleblower. That volunteer had resigned from the hospital about the same time as this incident had occurred. She was the one person that refused to cheat on a test. She was so furious that she made a xerox of the questions and answers the blood lab had placed with the computer when the test was taken. The whistleblower came into my office, and we videotaped her sworn statement. She gave us a copy of her evidence.

That nice whistleblower was afraid. She was now retired, as was her husband, and her intention was to get far away so that the hospital could not find her. They were going on an extended motor home trip, but she gave us her cell phone number so we could be in contact with her, if it was necessary for her to come back and testify. Catfish Abbott prepared his trap for the unsuspecting boss of the blood lab.

I was present in the room when Catfish took the deposition of the supervisor of the blood unit at the hospital. He asked her extensive questions about the requirement for continuing education for blood technicians. The witness explained that this duty was farmed out to a firm that does nothing but such continuing education training. That firm would periodically send a test to each of the registered phlebotomists at the hospital. The phlebotomist was to sit at a computer and answer the questions on the test. If the blood technician scored 90 or above, they were not required to go through the special training regimen for that particular field.

Catfish asked this lady if the hospital ever gave the answers to these blood technicians before they took the test. The witness emphatically said, "No. That would be dangerous and unethical." Catfish then stood up and flipped over a page on a flip chart which showed questions and answers from the test, which had the appropriate answers filled in. The witness said, "Where did you get that?" She turned ashen.

Apparently, when the test came in for that subject, the hospital had their smartest blood tech take the test, and she had scored a 95. The hospital had corrected that answer so that they had all the correct answers on the page. When a subsequent tech was supposed to take the test, they would sit at the same computer, open the desk drawer, and pull out the answers. Therefore, they all scored 100 on the test and did not have to go through the training necessary to be knowledgeable in that subject.

After the deposition of the blood lab supervisor, Catfish fashioned together a motion for punitive damages and filed it with the court. Punitive damages are rarely given, and it takes extremely egregious conduct to warrant punitive damages. They are rarely granted in malpractice cases. The case had been assigned to Judge Dwight Geiger, who had just recently turned seventy years old and was about to retire. In fact, the hearing on this case took place on the last day Judge Geiger was handling hearings. Judge Geiger had always been a fair jurist, and the attorneys appearing before him had a hard time finding any bias in him. However, on this last day of hearings, I had several hearings in front of the judge and was pleased to watch hearings conducted by other attorneys in various cases. Out of the six or seven cases I viewed before Catfish's case got called, the plaintiffs won every motion. When Catfish did his presentation, I had no doubt that the court would grant our motion. After the judge entered an order allowing punitive damages to be claimed, a settlement was reached in the amount $3.5 million. The only survivor under the statute, at the time of this lady's death, was her eighty-three-year-old husband. This was an amazing result for an octogenarian to obtain.

Over the years, I would associate with Mr. Abbott on approximately four large cases. Three of the four came in at over $1 million. The fourth was almost at that level. Needless to say, I felt good about bringing Catfish into the mix in the Bill Majewski case.

Catfish was an interesting guy. He is, unfortunately, in the University of Florida Hall of Fame for football. I went to Florida State, the archrival of the University of Florida. I remember going to the games during the four years of my college career at Florida State and seeing Catfish Abbott's Gators beat up on us every time. Mr. Abbott was a middle linebacker and always accounted for numerous tackles. He made one of the all-SEC teams and went on to have a two- or three-year career in the pros. After that, he studied at Oxford in England for a year and then came back to the United States and attended University of Florida Law School, where he graduated near the top of his class. He had become a personal injury attorney almost immediately upon graduation. He had developed a reputation as a top-shelf medical malpractice lawyer.

As I indicated, Mr. Abbott and I became close friends despite our animus that occurred on the one day of the year when our two college teams played each other. I would be invited to Catfish's vacation home in Cedar Key, Florida, to fish inshore for redfish and offshore for red snapper, grouper, mackerel, etc. Fishing in Cedar Key was always great. The only bad part of going up there to fish was that I had to stay in Catfish's home, which should be considered beautiful in most instances. It's built on stilts, as are most homes are in Cedar Key. I thought the home was particularly ugly because the stairwell up the front of the building has alternating orange and blue steps. In addition, the interior or the home is completely done in Gator regalia. The room where I am forced to sleep has a very nice soft bed, but on the wall is the head of an alligator, which is absolutely huge and scary if you wake up at night and open your eyes.

The only revenge I get against Catfish is that when he comes to St. Lucie County, I make him ride in my garnet pickup truck.

Chapter 63

Why did I stop doing medical malpractice cases by myself? The last medical malpractice case I handled alone was in the late eighties. This was a case of clear-cut negligence, also against Martin Memorial Hospital. My client's husband had been in an auto crash with a light pole. He suffered a fractured hip and had a stomachache when he got to the hospital. The hospital very quickly sent Robert Pereia to an orthopedic surgeon for immediate surgery on the hip, which was performed successfully. While he was still in the emergency room, there was a decision made to do an abdominal tap to see if they could figure out what was wrong with his stomach. At that time, the routine procedure for abdominal taps was to inject into the abdominal cavity a sterile saline solution. That solution would be withdrawn through a trocar and would be analyzed. The only record of that medical procedure which existed was a nurse's note which stated, "Abdominal tap slightly bloody." The doctor's notes did not mention this. In that case, the patient developed sepsis while being ignored by his assigned doctor. His temperature went up, the patient went gray, and his stomach was more and more distended. He had come into the hospital in the early evening.

The next day, the surgeon thought it might be prudent, duh, to do an exploratory laparotomy and just see what the problem was with that gentleman's abdomen. When the exploratory laparotomy was done, it was discovered that the patient had a fractured pancreas. Pancreatic fluid had flowed into the body cavity and had essentially destroyed other organs. This was a result which could have totally been avoided had the exploratory laparotomy been done in the "golden hour" which is, in fact, the first few hours after admission to the hospital.

After the exploratory laparotomy was completed, the doctor spoke with the wife of the victim and told her that her husband had suffered an injured pancreas and that in the future, he would have to take insulin. The doctor did not explain the fact that her husband was in extremis. Robert Pereia (not his name) died later that day. This was a rather straightforward instance of malpractice. At that time, malpractice cases were easier to handle. One major problem for plaintiffs' attorneys was that it was hard to find a local (Florida) expert in the field who would testify against another Florida doctor. The other side always had a stable of experts who wanted to come forward and help their brother doctor.

I had finally found a physician who was the head of the trauma unit at Georgetown University Hospital. I hired him to examine the records and testify for us in the case. Before the case was too far along, this doctor changed positions and took a similar job at University Hospital in Jacksonville, Florida. I now had a Florida expert!

I had filed the suit early, and there were many delays in the suit. Four different judges had sat in on this case. One had died, and the case had been reassigned. The next judge did not complete the case before his term in office expired. The next circuit judge who was assigned wound up having a stroke.

When the first judge had the case, the defense filed a motion to dismiss challenging the sufficiency of the pleadings and whether or not there was a cause of action for medical malpractice. The first judge had ruled in our favor. When the second judge came on the bench, the defense filed what was, essentially, the same motion, and the second judge rejected their claim and told us we could go forward with the case. When the third judge showed up, the defense filed essentially the same motion. The motion was once again denied. With the fourth judge, we were on the upcoming trial docket, although we were quite a way down the list of cases to be tried. The other side had filed their usual motion to dismiss and had also filed something called a Motion to Bifurcate, which would have us try the case on liability to one jury and on the amount of damages to another.

The judge scheduled the hearing for the Thursday before the docket would begin on Monday. I went down to Stuart, in Martin County, to appear before Judge Jack Finley, who was an attorney I knew before he was elevated to the bench a couple of years before. I liked Jack as a person, although he was extremely conservative. When the hearing started, defense counsel said, "We're here on our Motion to Dismiss."

He was then cut off by the judge, who said, "Sir, if I hear you mention this particular motion again, you better have your toothbrush with you because you're going to be held in contempt of court. You have filed this same motion three other times, and it's been denied every time. That motion is denied." Now Judge Finley said that he would take up the Motion to Bifurcate and stated, "This Motion to Bifurcate has become a darling of the defense bar. I can tell you that the same jury that hears the liability portion of the case will decide the damages. Your trial is to start on Monday morning, and I'm moving you to the top of the list."

As we walked out from the courthouse, defense counsel asked me, "Mr. Messer, what did you say you would settle this case for?"

We settled the case for a reasonable amount, which was confidential. I noticed that when the case was completed, I had over $50,000 invested costs in the lawsuit. At that time, my entire annual budget for all my costs on all my cases was approximately $75,000 a year. I determined that I could not afford to lose a case such as Pereia, or it could bankrupt the firm. I decided that I would, in the future, refer all medical malpractice cases out to lawyers who did almost nothing but that, and I would participate as co-counsel at a tremendously reduced fee. That is a decision I followed since that time.

Because of changes enacted by the legislature, malpractice cases had become a lot more expensive to handle than the last case I handled in the eighties. There were many hoops you had to jump through before you were even allowed to file suit. You had to find an expert in the same field or fields as the persons you were suing. They had to review all the medical records and give you an opinion as to whether or not there was a violation of the standard of care for that particular doctor. Catfish would scour the country and find the absolute best expert regardless of where they resided. He tended to favor doctors from the Ivy League but would still find the experts wherever appropriate.

Chapter 64

Suit was filed against Martin Memorial Hospital and against the local radiologists who were not there to read the CT scan. Several of the doctors who neglected Bill were named as defendants. One of the most important defendants in the case was the radiologist from California who worked for Night Hawk. He had received three hundred slides from Bill Majewski's CAT scan. He claimed to have read these scans and sent back a report in exactly eight minutes to the hospital in Port St. Lucie claiming that there was no problem with the CT scan. Even Ray Charles could see the obvious signs of free air or gas in the abdomen which was apparent from the CT scans. Catfish went to California and took the deposition of this doctor. He discovered that the doctor had been admonished in the past for the same things. He had been barred from practice in New Hampshire and moved to California and continued with his practice. The deposition of that doctor was devastating for the defense.

I was particularly happy that we were also suing the Martin Memorial radiologists. One of those doctors had routinely appeared for the defense as an expert on radiology and neuroradiology over the years and almost never found anything wrong with an MRI read that someone else had done. He would ignore obvious herniated discs and was very careful never to use the word *herniated* in his testimony, both on deposition and in trial. I absolutely hated the guy. I got revenge on this doctor in 2019. I had his curriculum vitae as well as his report in this case claiming that our first class neuroradiologist was wrong in his reading of the MRI films. I had talked to our local neuroradiologist, Dr. Andrew Walker, who was extremely qualified (trained at Yale and Harvard and later did a teaching fellowship at Yale). I asked him what you had to go through for certification, and he explained the rather harsh process that a person needs to go through to be able to hold himself out to be a board-certified neuroradiologist. He also said they had to do a full recertification every ten years, and they had to go to continuing education regularly and take a mini test once a year to maintain their certification.

I contacted the American Board, which handles the certifications, and asked for information regarding Dr. Pfeiffer, the defense doctor. I discovered that while he had become board-certified in 1990, he had not bothered to recertify since that time. Despite that fact, he advertised that he was board-certified in neuroradiology and, in fact, testified that he was a board-certified neuroradiologist. When this doctor was going on vacation the week of that trial, his testimony would be by video to be shown to the jury at the trial. I let him dig a hole through his direct testimony and had very few objections. On cross-examination, I asked him whether he was sure he was board-certified in neuroradiology. He said that he was. I pulled out and entered into evidence a sealed certificate from the American Board which certifies neuroradiologists. It was signed by the president of the governing board and indicated that Dr. Pfeiffer was not board-certified. The doctor stammered his reply and said, "Well, I had been board-certified, and therefore I was not being untruthful when I says I was." At the trial, the jury laughed at his testimony, and we obtained a good result for our client in a case involving a herniated disc surgery to a patient's neck.

In Bill Majewski's case, I attended all the hearings and depositions in the case and was involved at the mediation in the matter.

For the mediation, we had an excellent mediator, Joaquin Fraxedas from Orlando. Suzanne Majewski and her son attended.

Bill's son, Matthew, was personal representative of his father's estate, so he was the nominal client. Barbara was staying at a friend's house.

Sometime after the mediation was over, the case settled for a confidential, but substantial amount. The beneficiaries of this settlement were Barbara and her mom, Suzanne. Barbara's money was put in a special needs trust.

Epilogue

Within a few months of the settlement, Suzanne Majewski decided that she could no longer stand living in the house that she and Bill had built together and had enjoyed so many happy years. She and Barbara sold the home and moved into a much smaller home in a development less than a quarter of a mile from my office. Bill Majewski and his wife, Suzanne, had been members of my Lions Club, and Suzanne continued in that status. In addition, Barbara joined. I would see them at the club meeting a couple of times a month and on other occasions when they dropped by my office. My wife and I get along very well with the Majewski family.

Over the years, it has become extremely hard to do medical malpractice lawsuits in Florida. The doctors have a great lobby, and the legislature listens to them. The statute of limitations for medical malpractice is only two years. Other tort cases have a four-year statute of limitations. All kinds of legal obstacles are in place in an attempt to thwart these cases. I am happy to allow the medical malpractice attorney experts handle these cases.

BOOK 24

Golf Cart Negligence

Chapter 65

In 2016, Adrian Moreno (not his real name) was enjoying, as best he could, his retirement. Mr. Moreno was a retired school principal from New York City who lived in Toms River on the lower New Jersey shore. He was seventy-two years old and in wonderful physical condition. He had been running New York marathons until he was sixty-five. To say he was an avid golfer is an understatement.

He had been married to his wife for almost fifty years. Unfortunately, she was a multiple sclerosis victim and was wheelchair bound most of the time. She could not stand the cold in the dead of winter in New Jersey. They kept their home in New Jersey because it was near their children and grandchildren.

Every winter, Adrian would bring his wife to Port St. Lucie, Florida, where they would stay in a vacation complex. The pool there had a Hoyer lift which enabled Mrs. Moreno (not her real name) to get in and out of the pool. She found that she had some movement and was able to walk if she was submerged in water, so she used that for purposes of exercise as well as relaxation. She used a similar heated community pool up in New Jersey. Every day, Adrian would take her down to the poolside along with a good book. At least five days a week, Adrian would leave her for three or four hours and go golf with friends from Florida or vacationing friends from New York and New Jersey.

Mr. Moreno was extremely fit for his age. He was also an excellent golfer. He had not yet "shot his age," but he was confident that he would one day.

Adrian had been down here for a month or so when he had reservations to play at Gator Trace Golf Course in Fort Pierce. He teed off with his foursome, and they had played a few holes when tragedy struck. Mr. Moreno had completed putting out (he made a par), and he walked around to the back of his golf cart. He was putting away his putter in the golf bag when another golf cart driver, James Blackburn (not his real name), who was not paying attention, struck him.

The driver, Blackburn, had indicated later that he was talking to his fellow rider in his cart and wasn't particularly paying attention. He said when he looked up and saw that he had someone standing in front of him, he slammed on the brake but missed it and hit the accelerator instead. He slammed into both of Adrian's legs, with devastating effects. The tibias and fibulas on both sides were broken, and these were compound comminuted fractures. It was extremely bloody. The people at the golf course took the name of the at-fault party who was driving a golf cart loaned from the golf course.

St. Lucie County Fire Rescue showed up and placed Adrian in the ambulance and were closely administering to him along the way to the hospital. He was close to being in shock. He found himself praying to God that he wouldn't die so that he could continue taking care of his wife. He was able to get out his cell phone and called his best friend, who, unfortunately, was not playing golf with him that day. He explained that he was on the way to the hospital and was afraid if he called his wife, she might have a heart attack with the news. Adrian's friend, Bobbie, said he would come to the hospital to be with him. The EMTs transported Adrian to Lawnwood Regional Medical Center's Trauma Unit, which is the only level 1 trauma center here on the Treasure Coast.

Bobbie went to see his friend in the hospital, and together, they decided to wait until Adrian should have completed his round of golf to call Mrs. Moreno and sugarcoat the facts. Bobbie told Adrian, "You really need a lawyer to help you on this."

Adrian said, "Do you know any good ones?"

Bobbie replied, "No, but we have friends here in Port St. Lucie who play golf with us who know attorneys very well." Bobbie indicated he was going to immediately send out an email to all their golf buddies and would get back with a reply to Adrian as soon as he had someone lined up. Adrian went into surgery, where they may have saved his life. He was in a great deal of pain, but they stopped the bleeding and stabilized him.

When he got out of the surgery, his friend Bobbie was there and told him that one of their golf buddies had called him. It turns out that I had represented that individual fifteen or twenty years before in an injury case and had done very well for him. They decided to give me a call after speaking to Adrian's wife.

It was the day after the collision when I got the call from Mr. Moreno, asking if I "could go to the hospital to visit with him."

I said, "Of course. I will be there in about thirty minutes."

I made sure my tie was on straight, and I hurriedly got in my car and drove the twelve miles or so from my office in Port St. Lucie to Lawnwood Regional Medical Center in Fort Pierce. I went to Adrian's room, and he was there with his friend. Adrian explained to me how the accident happened and said he understood that he needed legal representation. He asked if I was able to handle the case, and I told him I was and that I would be honored to represent him.

Despite his age (seventy-two), Adrian had been in excellent health before the injury. As I indicated, he exercised and played golf on a regular basis. He had run the New York City Marathon more than once. Adrian was a natural athlete. He was approximately six six tall. In talking with him, I learned that Adrian had played basketball in college at St. John's in New York and had played for Lou Carnesecca on some of his excellent teams. Adrian had a basketball scholarship. Adrian told me that Carnesecca told him that he was the "tallest Puerto Rican he had ever seen in his life." Adrian was of Puerto Rican decent. However, he spoke with nothing but a New York accent.

I told Mr. Moreno that I would bring back a contract for his signature. I left him a Statement of Client's Rights explaining the rights the clients have in these cases and made an appointment to see him the next day.

On the way back from the hospital, I swung by Gator Trace, where the accident happened. I knew the pro there, Lannie Hughes. I had played in tournaments there with my son and my friends on more than one occasion. It was a nice tight golf course. Lannie was a good guy. I talked to Lannie and asked him if he had any information regarding the injury. He said yes. He had gone to the accident scene shortly after it occurred and had the name, address, and other information regarding the perpetrator. The man that hit Adrian was a tourist from Connecticut. Lannie showed me the golf registration Mr. Blackburn had signed.

I promptly did some research and discovered that, to my surprise, "Florida's Dangerous Instrumentality Rule" also applied to golf carts. The owner of a golf cart is responsible, along with the driver, for any negligent acts and all damages that flow therefrom. So I knew we were going to have ample coverage, even if the perpetrator were a pauper.

I ran a property search for the township where Mr. Blackburn lived and was rewarded with a nice picture of a home and all the information on the home. It was a spacious house which had been appraised at $750,000. I realized that the owner of such a home must have a very ample homeowner's policy. Even if Blackburn had no homeowner's insurance, we could still attach his house to satisfy any judgment. Unlike Florida, Connecticut does not exempt homestead from attachment by creditors.

I sent notices to the golf course and to Mr. Blackburn and let them know of my representation. I asked Mr. Blackburn to send me all information regarding all insurance policies he owned. Mr. Blackburn was very apologetic for what he had caused. He promptly sent back the name of his homeowner's insurance company and their contact information. He also provided us with a copy of his automobile insurance policy, which was a large policy and had a provision that it also covered him while driving other vehicles. We now had three sources of potential recovery.

In the meantime, Adrian was having a very difficult recovery. I met Mrs. Moreno, and she was an absolute sweetheart. Except for being in a wheelchair, she was quite good-looking for her age. She obviously adored her husband and told me they had been sweethearts since college.

Adrian was eventually transferred to a rehabilitation hospital. His son, an accountant from New Jersey, came to Florida to assist his father. The rental was expiring on the facility the Morenos ordinarily stayed in on vacation, and it was impossible for them to extend the rental as the property was already leased to the next customer. The son flew home with his mom. On such flights, they were required to sit in the front row of the plane so that the son could lift his mother and take her to the restroom, if necessary. Adrian had told me that they had, for years, followed the same procedure when he and his wife were flying together before this accident happened. The son took the mother back to her home to New Jersey and then came back to Florida to help his father. The Morenos' daughter would make sure her mom was okay living alone. A nurse also came in to help in the way Adrian had before his injury.

Adrian had a very difficult time at the rehab hospital. His heart briefly stopped working, and he was rushed back to Lawnwood Regional Medical Center for further treatment. Adrian had no history of any heart disease. He had other surgeries performed. He was in the hospital in Florida for about four months after the accident occurred. He was progressing slowly. Adrian wanted to go back to New Jersey and pursue medical treatment there. However, the doctors indicated that Adrian could not fly, nor could he drive home. His legs couldn't handle it. A decision was made by the son and father to take the train. Adrian's Florida doctor said that was okay. They had a wheeled stretcher which rolled Adrian onto the train, and the two of them rode from the train station in Florida all the way to their hometown in southern New Jersey.

While on the train, Adrian became extremely sick. It turns out that either at the trauma hospital or at the rehab hospital, Adrian had contracted MERSA, which is a very dangerous infection. Many MERSA patients do not recover. As soon as he got to New Jersey, Adrian was rushed to the hospital there, where he remained for another five months.

Chapter 66

I had filed suit against Mr. Blackburn, as well as against Gator Trace Golf Course. An attorney for both the auto insurance carrier and the homeowner's carrier were defending Blackburn. Gator Trace's insurance company hired their own lawyer, so we had two attorneys on the other side. We obtained service of process upon all the defendants, and twenty days later, we got answers from both of them. With those answers were a large number of questions called "interrogatories," which a client must answer and swear under oath and return them. There were also interrogatories for Mrs. Moreno. All interrogatory answers were sworn to under penalty of perjury.

I decided to go to New Jersey to go over those questions with Adrian and his wife so there was no doubt as to the truthful answer. Some of the questions were quite technical, and we routinely help all clients when they're answering these questions in writing. Oftentimes, the most difficult questions in the interrogatories are ones where the defense asks the injured party to list all physicians or chiropractors he has seen in ten years before the accident. Adrian's memory of this matter was excellent, as was that of his wife.

While in New Jersey for the first trip, I met their son, who spent some time grilling me to try to determine if I knew what I was doing.

He very much wanted to testify at trial, if necessary, about everything his father had been through and what he had done to help his dad. I told him that could be arranged, but the trial would eventually happen in Florida, and he would have to come down to Florida with Adrian and his mom for the trial. He said he was going to do that.

On this visit, Adrian was wheelchair bound. He rolled up his pants legs and showed me the mess that was his lower legs. One of them, because of the MERSA and the loss of tissue, had to have a skin graft taken from Adrian's back. The wounds looked rather grotesque.

Adrian told the story of his love affair with his wife and the battles that they had had because of her MS. He explained that they regularly came down to Florida during the cold months up north. He explained that when they fly down, they would always reserve the front row of the airplane so that Adrian could physically lift his wife up and carry her to the restroom and help her onto the toilet seat. There is more space in the front row, and it is closer to the bathroom. Adrian would then wait until she was finished and would take her back to the front seat. He told a story of one trip when the airline representative came to them and told them they were going to have to bump them from those seats to another location.

Adrian said, "Okay, but when things get messy because my wife can't get out of the seat, it's your responsibility." The airline decided they would not force the Morenos to change locations.

While visiting Toms River, I was impressed at how nice it looked in the summer months when it is brutally hot here in Florida. Adrian and his wife lived in an upscale gated community with access to the community pool. There were nearby golf courses which Adrian had frequented whenever possible before his injury. Adrian had an impressive golf average score for a man of his age.

I spent the better part of the day answering those interrogatories and obtaining materials that the Morenos had in response to a Request to Produce from the defense. Many of the items requested included medical records and bills which we had acquired at our office in Port St. Lucie, but also other materials that the defense thought might be relevant. I also went over with the Morenos how their health was progressing.

I was told that the MERSA was in remission. While his symptoms had passed, the virus remains in the body and can become active again, especially if there is another trauma.

It is a truism that in practicing law that "You don't ever win cases at deposition. You could lose them at deposition." As the deposition for Adrian was scheduled, I had to fly back up to Toms River, which was located perhaps thirty miles from the Atlantic City Airport. I had gone over Adrian's testimony, and I was amazed at his memory and was amazed at the life story he could tell. We had decided to videotape the deposition, even though the defense was holding the deposition. Adrian was an awesome storyteller.

In deposition, Adrian was extremely pleasant and polite, and he told a story that was a page-turner. There's one anecdote he discussed that occurred while he was in the ambulance when Adrian was riding to Lawnwood Regional Medical Center. The EMT asked Adrian what he was praying about. Adrian told him that he was thanking the Lord for sparing his life so that he could continue helping his wife. He had assumed he was going to recover.

Adrian talked about his almost one year being sent from one hospital to the other and going through the near-death experience at the rehab hospital plus the excruciating bout with MERSA. He went over the medical procedures he had been through. He rolled up his pants leg and showed the horrible disfigurement of his legs to the video camera. Adrian also outlined his life story.

The deposition itself lasted less than an hour, and it was a major home run. I thought if I could copy that testimony word for word for trial, we were looking at a huge verdict. I had discussed with Adrian what I thought a reasonable result would be. He thought that $1 million would be enough. I assured him it was not. Finally, he settled on $2 million that would satisfy him. Of course, I was intending to ask for $5 million at the jury trial.

I had sent interrogatories to both defendants, who truthfully provided me information which made the case easier for a trial.

The trial was scheduled in St. Lucie County, Florida, and the court ordered a mediation before the trial took place. Because Adrian and his wife were flying down, the mediation was to take place shortly before the trial was to happen. The mediation took place in March when the weather in St. Lucie County is awesome. The New York Mets train in Port St. Lucie, and the town is always filled with baseball fans as well as baseball players. The Mets entire minor league program is here year-round and in the spring, and the major leaguers also show up. Hotels are at a premium.

We helped get Adrian and his wife lined up for the local hotel with conference facilities. We also booked the conference room, which we used for mediation. The mediator we had insisted on was the man I would consider to be the very best mediator in the entire state of Florida, Joaquin Fraxedas. I met Jay when he arrived, and he came by my office before he went to the mediation location. We had mediated cases before, and I really respected the man, who not only was a skilled attorney but also a published author. Jay had practiced medical malpractice defense before becoming a mediator.

Jay asked me, "Roger, just what number are you looking for in this case?" I told him the client would accept $2 million. We went over the facts of the case with the mediator, and I showed him an edited version of the film of the deposition which I intended to play at trial. I asked Jay if he minded me playing that video for the defense team that was there. Only the two attorneys for the two defendants were present at the deposition. However, there were three different insurance adjusters who had not seen Adrian's performance. I told him before the mediation opened that I had provided the defense with copies of all the medical bills and records. Some of the records were recent. Most of the bills had been paid by Medicare, which had a lien for a major portion of their money back when the case is settled. Thankfully, Medicare negotiates a fairly low price from the hospitals and medical providers. I then told the defense attorneys and adjusters that I was not qualified to tell them Adrian's story. I said, "Instead, I want to show you a clip from when his deposition was taken, which I think tells it very succinctly." We then showed the approximate twelve-minute edited version of the video, and the adjusters in the room were paying rapt attention

After both sides had completed their presentations, the defense team, which was quite large, remained in the conference room, and we relocated to an area with a few chairs which had a table near the entrance to that part of the hotel complex. We were sitting there and having a cold drink when two tall athletic-looking gentlemen came by, and Adrian, who was a Mets fan, said, "Roger, those are the two best pitchers in the Mets Organization." I was not a Mets fan but had seen and heard of one of the players, Jacob LaGrone. Alex said that my choice of hotels was excellent, as seeing those guys made his day.

Four hours after the mediation started, Jay Fraxedas made Adrian's day by coming out and saying, "Roger, we're going to get you the $2 million which you said your client would accept." Adrian and his wife were extremely pleased. I had agreed, to help them, to reduce my fee from the maximum 40 percent I could have earned under the law down to 35 percent. I thought that was the least I could do. Five percent of $2 million is still a princely sum, but I thought I could afford it, and Adrian's happiness was worth a lot.

After the settlement was reached, I proceeded to negotiate with the Medicare Claims Office. We were able to get their lien down to a mild roar, and it was settled.

Adrian and his wife netted right at $1 million, which I was assured would be appropriately invested. Adrian told me he was continuing to rehabilitate the legs and promised he would one day play golf again. He was already puttering around the putting green.

My office generally got a Christmas card from Adrian and his wife. Those stopped a couple of years ago, and I wonder whether one or both of them has passed. They were fine people who deserved a better hand than life dealt them in the end.

Book 25

Tragic Death

Chapter 67

On February 7, 2018, Stewart Feketa came into my office to see me an hour after he called the office. I had not met the man before that time. He explained to me that his beautiful eighteen-year-old daughter had been killed the night before in a horrible head-on collision. Before I got into the details of the accident, I asked him how he got my name, which is a question I ask all new clients as I do not advertise on television or radio. Stewart said, "I got your name three ways. The first person I asked to be head pallbearer for my daughter's funeral was a dear friend of our family, Steve Jungjohan." The only Jungjohan family that I heard of was Steve's family. I represented that family in a very serious injury case involving their young daughter. The Jungjohans' daughter had suffered a head injury when her school bus made a turn in front of a semi-tractor trailer, essentially causing the collision. She was unconscious at the scene. The eight-year-old girl had been airlifted from the accident scene to St. Mary's Medical Center Pediatric Neurology Unit down in West Palm Beach. A small boy was killed, and sixteen children, aged eight or nine, were all maimed in the collision. We had settled the case and had done very well on behalf of the Jungjohan family, and they appreciated it.

Next, Mr. Feketa said that he wanted to get more than one source for finding an attorney. According to him, his accountant, Chris Fogal, knows everyone in the county and would probably steer him in the right direction. It turns out that Mr. Feketa and I shared the same accountant (Chris Fogal), who gave a glowing report about me. After speaking to Mr. Fogal, Stewart had gone home to discuss it with his wife, who told him that her best friend was a lady named Jeannie Errickson. It turns out that I had settled Ms. Errickson's case just two weeks before the horrendous crash happened. Mrs. Errickson had told Marcie Feketa what a good job I did on her case. Stewart told me, "You're my lawyer."

I have never seen a case in my entire career which had better liability against a defendant than the Feketa case. The vehicle that hit Santia head on was a dark-colored Prevost motor home, the biggest one they ever made, very much like a large Greyhound bus. Its driver, Walter Roney from Michigan, was ninety-nine years old. He had only recently regained his license as it had been suspended for a mental problem he had the year before. He was driving down the wrong side of a divided highway with all lights extinguished at the time of the crash.

Stewart indicated to me that he ran a rather large landscaping business, including a sod farm, and had about fifty employees. He said that he had to meet with all the men at around four or four thirty each morning, and therefore, he usually went to bed around 8:00 p.m. On the night of the crash, he was in bed sleeping when, at approximately 9:30 p.m., the highway patrolman knocked on his door with the news of Santia's death. He could not believe what the highway patrolman told him.

Stewart had immediately told the highway patrolman that he was going to the scene. Stewart's wife and son got up and went with him, and they stopped to pick up Santia's maternal grandfather. When they got there, the police tape and cordon of police officers was several hundred feet from the crash scene. Stewart saw the vehicle (by then, the bodies had been thankfully covered). He ran through the police line and made it a few feet beyond that when he was tackled by

St. Lucie County sheriff's deputies. Stewart told me that he fought them off and hit a couple of deputies before they calmed him down.

Stewart told me that he was a regular volunteer at the sheriff's department where he taught recovery to prisoners who had a drug problem. Stewart had experienced serious drug dependency several years before. Stewart did a little time in the county jail because of crimes committed at that time under the influence of prescription drugs. He has been clean of illicit drugs for over fourteen years. Stewart had developed dependency after a very painful injury to his back and leg. When the prescription ran out, he had self-medicated himself with street drugs. He had struggled with addiction before "finally overcoming the problem through counseling and through Jesus" (Stewart's words).

Stewart stayed at the scene for quite a long time, but he decided that he needed to speak with Santia's mother, who lived in Jensen Beach, Florida. He did not want to give this message by phone. If Highway 70 was not blocked at the accident scene, it would have been a relatively short trip, but because of the closing of the road, it was quite a distance to circle around to come toward Jensen Beach from the south. It took perhaps forty-five minutes to an hour for him to get to Stacy West's neighborhood. He parked his vehicle and got out of the truck. Before he could get to the door, a neighbor's security light came on, and the neighbor came through the front door of his house with a shotgun. Stewart says, "It's okay. I'm coming to tell something serious to Santia's mother." The shotgun was lowered.

At that time, Stacy and her older daughter, Sierra, were living together. Sierra and her mother came out the door and saw Stewart on the front porch. Sierra already had a fear that something had happened as she had seen a news report that there was a bad crash out on Highway 70 west of Fort Pierce. She said she had a premonition. When Stewart confirmed their worst nightmare, Stacy, in particular, wobbled and had to be caught to be kept from falling to the ground. Everyone had a good cry.

The day after the collision, Stewart went to the sheriff's department and apologized to the officers who he had hit. He had known them from before. They told him, "Sir, no one hit us, including you. We feel so upset at your loss, and our heart goes out to you."

At the time of the collision, Santia Feketa was driving her father's F-350 pickup truck (the largest pickup truck that Ford makes). Stewart let her drive the truck because it was "safe." Sitting beside her was her best friend, Britney, who was seventeen years old. According to the GPS device in the truck, both girls died one second after Santia lifted her foot off the accelerator. Before she took her foot off the accelerator, the girls were proceeding at sixty-three miles an hour in a sixty-five-mile-per-hour zone. The vehicle that hit Santa in the opposite direction was going about sixty miles an hour and was huge compared to the F-350. Death was, thankfully, instantaneous.

Stewart explained to me that Santia was to be buried in the family plot and that his daughter and her best friend, Britney, were to have a combined funeral on Saturday in a large Christian church located in Port St. Lucie. He asked me if I would attend with him, and I said I would.

Stewart asked me if it was possible for me to also represent the family of the other deceased girl, as the two girls were best friends. I explained that it would be a conflict of interest for me since the two families might be competing for the same potential recovery. I told Stewart I was hopeful that they would hire a competent attorney I could work with and perhaps save some cost money by working together on certain matters.

The case was complicated somewhat in that Stewart was divorced from the mother of Santia, and he had remarried and now had a son of his own, along with the two daughters he shared with his first wife, Stacy. As the attorney for Santia's estate, I needed to represent both of these individuals. One thing that made it difficult was that Stewart and Stacy did not see eye to eye on certain issues, including an issue as to whether they should hire me. Thankfully, we were able to work that out. We named Stacy as the personal representative of the estate, who was the person required by law to proceed with the wrongful death action.

Stewart and Stacy divorced when Santia was a young toddler. Stewart blamed the divorce on his drug abuse. Santia kept a close relationship with her father and her mother but lived with her mother for the first few years after the divorce. When she was nine, she decided, and the parties both agreed, that she would principally live at her father's house/ranch as she enjoyed the horses, cows, and other animals that were on the farm. From that point forward, she not only rode the horses but also mucked the stables and was quite a country girl. Santia had maintained her excellent relationship with her mom as well.

I obtained the initial accident report, and I learned who the insurance company was for the at-fault party, Mr. Walter Roney. I immediately contacted this particular insurance company and let them know of my representation of the estate of Santia Feketa. I had requested permission to go into the salvage yard and take pictures and investigate everything possible. I was told that the police would not allow that yet as there was a criminal investigation ongoing, and the highway patrol was actively researching the situation. I was told that I would be cleared to make my visit in two to three weeks.

Two days after signing the case up with the Feketa family, I drove myself out to the accident scene. On the way, I stopped by a roadside fruit stand which is owned by a friend of mine, retired captain Mike Monahan of the St. Lucie County Sheriff's Department. I bought some fresh temple oranges from Mike, and he asked me what I was doing out in that area. I told him I was going to the accident scene. He said yes, that was a horrible thing that happened. He said, "The two girls were dear friends of both of my sons, and they are taking it pretty hard."

I proceeded on to the accident scene and was surprised when I got there that approximately fifteen people had stopped at the scene and were praying. Over half of those people standing there were under the age of twenty. At the scene, I could see massive evidence of the crash in the highway's asphalt. From the scene, I determined that right before the collision occurred, Santia was driving her F-350 around a curve which swung to the right. As soon as she cleared the curve, she met the Prevost motor home and therefore had no opportunity to even see a glint of reflection off the vehicle before the crash happened.

Three weeks post-crash, the other family hired the Searcy, Denney, Scarola, Barnhardt & Shipley Firm out of West Palm Beach to represent them. I had known and respected Chris Searcy since I started my practice here back in 1978. I had attended seminars that he presented on trial tactics. We were both members of the academy and had seen each other there and talked numerous times before this happened. On more than one occasion. he had pointed me toward an expert I needed for a case. My small law office had two attorneys and two full-time paralegals. His was a very large personal injury firm, including twenty-five or thirty attorneys, and they had an excellent reputation. I contacted them and got an agreement we would work together and split costs as it related to liability in this case.

I finally obtained permission to go into the Co-Part Salvage lot to view the damage and to have our accident reconstructionist do all his studies. We were also told we could take pictures of anything present but could not take anything away from the vehicles.

Our appointed day finally arrived, and I met with our accident reconstructionist, Martin Garcia, and his team. Mr. Garcia's firm had been jointly hired by me and the Searcy firm. I was the only attorney present. We also met with an investigator from the Searcy firm who came equipped with a very nice Nikon camera and loads of film. The defense had their accident reconstructionist there but did not send an attorney or an investigator at that time.

Co-Part was a huge facility just north of Fort Pierce which had row upon row of smashed vehicles. Apparently, all the insurance companies use this facility to store their crashed vehicles until they have been released by the owner and the insurance company to be sold for salvage. We first drove to the allotted space for the Feketa F-350 pickup truck, or what was left of it. The vehicle was literally demolished. The top of the cab was sitting in what was left of the bed of the pickup truck. The axles were broken, and the tires were all flat. The interior was open, and when I looked down into the vehicle, the smell of death hit me in the face. There was obvious blood adhered to some of the surfaces inside the truck. I promptly went over to the side and threw up as it was sickening. The investigator took several pictures, and the accident reconstructionist took 3D pictures of the truck, along with pictures of such things as the odometer.

Mr. Garcia attempted to pull the black box from the vehicle, but it had been taken by the highway patrol and was in their possession. Later model vehicles typically have a black box system in the passenger compartment of the vehicle. It is a small computer device which has a plethora of information, including all the actions by the driver such as braking, turning, and speed regarding the last few minutes before a crash. We would have to wait for the highway patrol to finish its investigation before we could get our accident reconstructionist access to that box.

The accident reconstructionist carefully documented every bit of evidence that he could at the site of the pickup truck. We then drove, perhaps a quarter of a mile, around the facility to find the row of larger damaged vehicles which included our subject Prevost motor home. I was shocked by the size of this older Prevost. It was the size of a very large Greyhound bus. In fact, Prevost built many of the Greyhound buses which are on the highway. These Prevost coaches are considered a luxury item, and new ones can set you back about half a million dollars.

This particular Prevost had seen better times as the front end of it was smashed, and where the Prevost rode over the F-350, the front axle on the bus was broken and pushed back underneath the bus. Mr. Garcia and his crew began to set up to take their 3D pictures outside, and the Searcy investigator and I decided to see what was inside the Prevost.

I opened the side door to the motor home and was suddenly hit by a very unpleasant smell. Debris was on the floor of the motor home, almost knee-deep. There were scattered open and closed bottles of alcohol all over the floor. Apparently, the liquor cabinet in the Prevost had opened during the collision and scattered Mr. Roney's alcohol all over. Some of the bottles were broken. There was lots of glass and metal and wood thrown about. The main feature inside was the amount of paper and notebooks scattered throughout the Prevost. I said to Jim Leonard, the investigator, "I wish I had a Hazmat suit."

He said, "Well, we've got to start somewhere."

I immediately saw that there was a blue spiral binding tablet lying on top of the pile. I picked it up to see what was inside. I was shocked to find basically Mr. Roney's daily list of activities dating quite a ways back from the accident. Roney kept a meticulous list of everything he did. The last entry on the tablet had the date of the collision written in at the top of the page, February 6, 2018. This document was essentially a statement that they were going to get the Prevost repaired, and there was a two-page list of repairs that needed to be done. The only thing on the list that was all caps was "REPLACE HEADLIGHTS." There were other recent notes where Mr. Roney was directing the operation of his trust where most of his money back in Michigan resided. We took pictures of every page and put this back where it came from. Our pictures turned out to be crucial. We found other evidence around the motor home, but none as damning as the list. Mr. Roney was driving down the highway, at night, when he knew there were faulty headlights.

Upon returning to my office, we sent a letter to the insurance company advising them of the fact the Prevost was open and had some exposure to the elements. We asked them to preserve all written materials in the wreckage, as we would be requesting them.

My accident reconstructionist told me that the only way to tell for sure if the headlights were on or off was that in the unlikely event that one of the headlights survived the crash, they could do a "shock test" to determine whether it was illuminated or not at the time of the collision. One headlight was still attached to the Prevost, but it had been smashed. so the shock test could not be performed on it. The other headlight was missing. Mr. Garcia did, however, check every exterior light around the motor home, including the brake lights, taillights, and all individual running lights. There must have been twelve or fifteen of those on this particular bus. He performed a shock test on those and determined that none of them was operating at the time of the collision. It took us a half day to complete the inspection at Co-Part.

I attended the funeral for the girls the weekend after the crash and entered the huge sanctuary with Steve Jungjohan and Chris Fogal. The sanctuary was crowded, and there was a line to get in. We found some seats which had been added late to the back of the hall. There was a huge number of people in attendance. Many people had to stand outside the church and view the service on a big-screen television. It was a two-casket ceremony. Of course, there was no open casket because of the severe injuries of the two girls.

Really, the event was more of a celebration of life rather than a funeral. I learned a tremendous amount of facts relative to the kind of person that Santia Feketa was by attending the event and listening to what others discussed regarding her life. There was also an excellent slideshow of photographs of Santia's life. I made sure I got a copy of that from the funeral director, Rick Haisley.

Santia was eighteen years old and already a college junior. She was a very bright girl who, in high school, had taken advanced placement courses in a dual enrollment program with Indian River State College (our local state college). Santia was an A student throughout high school and college. Santia's older sister is an accountant with an accounting degree. Intelligence runs in the family.

As a college junior at the time of her death, Santia had been studying the become a special needs teacher. There were so many people at the funeral, young and old, both from her schools, her church, and friends of the family, as well as friends of Britney's family. There were several Down syndrome kids there with their families.

I learned that Santia essentially ran the Special Olympics Equestrian Program in St. Lucie County for several years. She was an accomplished horsewoman and competed at barrel racing at the huge county fair. As I could see from the pictures on the screen, Santia was a beautiful young lady (as was the other teenager who was with her at the time of their death).

From the accident report, I learned that the defendant driver was Walter Roney of the Detroit area in Michigan. Unfortunately, Mr. Roney died four days after the accident happened from the injuries he received in the accident. Mr. Roney had lost his wife a couple of years before and was, in fact, a widower. At the time of the collision, there was a passenger in his motor home, who I derisively referred to in private as a "gold digger." She was more or less a nice-looking lady of seventy-five years. This woman, Kay Bruns, had some injuries in the collision but was, in fact, the only survivor of it. I was looking forward to taking her deposition.

There was a tremendous delay in receiving the traffic homicide report. From reading the initial accident report, I recognized a few names of the first responders who were present the night of the crash. I noted that the head of the Traffic Homicide Division was present at the scene. I had met Sergeant Stuhr before, and I liked him.

The Searcy firm and I were both working hard to obtain evidence of just what happened in the case. Fairly soon after they became involved, we discovered a witness who had passed the Prevost motor home as it was stopped at a stop sign at the intersection of Midway Road and divided Highway 70. The witness said that the Prevost looked strange and that it was dark. The witness saw no interior or exterior lights on in the vehicle. Apparently, after this witness passed the Prevost, Mr. Roney decided to go on with no lights, and it turned left (which was westbound) on the eastbound side of the road. This was a somewhat confusing intersection where a few people have been killed over the years at the intersection itself. Steven Jungjohan's daughter was severely injured at this intersection. The Feketa crash occurred a quarter of a mile from the intersection.

We filed our lawsuit as soon as possible against the estate of Walter Roney. The Searcy firm filed on behalf of their client the same day, a few minutes before I filed mine. Upon the motion of the defense, the court consolidated the two death cases together as they arose out of the same set of facts. We had filed the case in the United States District Court for the Southern District of Florida because the amount in controversy was greater than $75,000.00, and there was a diversity of citizenship between the two girls and the at-fault party, Walter Roney.

Eventually, a traffic homicide report was filed, and we received a copy. We also received numerous photographs from the Highway Patrol as well as photographs from the medical examiner's office which were too gruesome to describe. I made sure my clients did not see the pictures. We also did not show them pictures of the scene, which showed their daughter lying partially out of the remains of the vehicle, obviously dead at the scene. The pictures were too shocking.

I noted with surprise that the individual patrolman who signed the traffic homicide report was not Sergeant Stuhr but was, in fact, a rookie in the department. I thought that rather strange. Since the traffic homicide report had been released and there were no criminal charges pending because of the death of Mr. Roney, the Highway Patrolman indicated that we could meet with them to have our investigator examine the black box. I called and asked Sergeant Stuhr to meet us there at an appropriate time. I wanted to talk to him. I also coordinated with the Searcy firm so that they had a representative at the meeting.

When we got to the meeting in North Fort Pierce, I was greeted by Sergeant Stuhr. I had a lengthy chat with him, and I asked him how long he had been involved in the Traffic Homicide Department. He told me, "Fifteen years." I asked him how many death cases he had investigated during that time, and he told me, "Approximately ninety." I asked if he had remembered this particular case, and he said, "More than all the others put together." He said that "this case had a profound effect on me and on every other first responder who was at the scene." I asked him why he did not sign the traffic homicide report, and he told me that it was so that the rookie could get some experience. Sergeant Stuhr had approved the rookie's preparation of the report. I also asked him about pictures the Highway Patrol had taken at the scene. I noted on one of the pictures that there was a headlight lying in the highway, and the headlight was not broken. It was the one missing headlight from the Prevost. I asked Sergeant Stuhr if he had the headlight. He said he did and showed it to me. I also asked him if he had done a shock test on the headlight, and he said he did and that it showed there was no illumination in the headlight at the time of the collision. My accident reconstructionist was looking on, and he performed his own test and confirmed that the lights were off when the crash occurred.

I asked Sergeant Stuhr what he did when he first came on the crash scene. He indicated, "I was the second or third officer on the scene and was the first person there from the Highway Patrol. The other responders there were from the St. Lucie County Sheriff's Department. As I pulled into the scene, my first statement out the window at these police officers was 'Who the hell let that civilian into our crash scene?'" There was a man standing just a few feet away from the remains of the pickup truck. It was the father of Santia's friend, Britney. He was literally less than ten feet away from his daughter and her friend, Santia. This man lived about a half mile from the scene and was in his yard working that evening and noticed flashing lights from Highway 70, and he got into his vehicle and drove there to investigate what was happening. He was devastated by what he saw and still showed signs of that devastation at trial.

Then we obtained the black box. Portions of it had already been downloaded by the Highway Patrol, and our investigator downloaded it to his computer at the meeting and compared his findings with those of the Highway Patrol, and they matched. The printout showed that Santia had been traveling sixty-three miles an hour in a sixty-five-mile-per-hour zone until one second before her untimely death. It was estimated that the Prevost was traveling approximately sixty miles per hour at the time of the collision. It was an earlier model Prevost, and therefore, there was no black box on the Prevost to prove exactly how fast it was going.

Mr. Roney's passenger, Mrs. Bruns, got out of the hospital after a short stay and went to San Diego, California, to be with her son during her recuperation.

By that time, I was principally working with Attorney Karen Terry and several other of their associates of the Searcy firm on this particular case. Karen was a very smart litigator and was an accomplished attorney in her own right.

We agreed to take the deposition of Mrs. Bruns in San Diego. Karen could not be there, and another associate in their firm, Matt Schwencke, attended the deposition on behalf of the Searcy firm. The trip to California turned out to be time well spent.

We discovered at the deposition that Mrs. Bruns had been dating Mr. Roney for a little over a year, and they spent quite a bit of time together. Mrs. Bruns was a widow who had buried, I believe, a couple of husbands over the years. I got the feeling that she had thought there might be another marriage in her future, this one to a ninety-nine-year-old with some money. She denied that was anyone's plans.

We established that Mrs. Bruns had accompanied Walter on his trip south from Detroit and was accompanied by one of Mr. Roney's sons, who helped them drive along the way. Mrs. Bruns indicated that she only drove in the daytime and hopefully when there was not much traffic on the road. She indicated they arrived in Melbourne Beach, Florida, a couple of days before the collision happened. She also indicated that it was their intent to drive the Prevost across Florida to Punta Gorda, Florida, where Mr. Roney knew a good mechanic who he trusted to fix his large toy.

We had previously filed a Request to Produce to the defense, asking them to give us copies of all documents in the motor home. They sent us lots of pictures. Surprisingly, they had not given us the list which we had pictures of. We had just learned of that a day or two before the deposition.

At the deposition, I asked Mrs. Bruns if she recalled Mr. Roney and his son making a list of things wrong with the motor home that they intended to have repaired. She said, "Yes, a list was prepared after they did a walk-around of the motor home." She said that she understood that the list had been lost in the crash. During the deposition, when we showed her the list, she and her attorney almost had a cow.

I established that on the way to Melbourne Beach from Michigan, the Prevost experienced quite a few electrical problems, including problems with the interior lighting and with the heater. It was cold as they were traveling through the Smokey Mountains, and they decided that even though it was late, they would drive on and share the driving between Mr. Roney's son and him. Mrs. Bruns only trusted herself to drive the motor home during the daytime.

Bruns indicated that they were planning on going to Punta Gorda beginning at 3:00 p.m., February 6, 2018, when Mr. Roney's son was leaving to go to the airport to fly back to Michigan. Unfortunately, when the son left, Mr. Roney was taking a nap, and she wouldn't wake him up until around 5:00 p.m. or 5:30 p.m. Mrs. Bruns indicated that she helped drive the motor home from

Melbourne Beach, Florida, to Fort Pierce, Florida. She claims to have not noticed any problems with the lights during her drive. Of course, she drove during the daytime.

Ms. Bruns indicated when she got to Fort Pierce, it was getting dark. She decided to not drive anymore, and she handed the keys to Walter Roney. This handoff took place approximately seven miles from the crash scene. Mrs. Bruns testified she never saw the truck that they hit.

We decided to amend our complaint to also sue Mrs. Bruns as an alleged "co-driver" of the motor home and as the navigator for the mobile home. She had testified that she had a GPS device and had indicated to Mr. Roney shortly before the accident that they were a couple of hours out from Punta Gorda. There was not much legal precedent for this type of lawsuit against a passenger, but we thought we had nothing to lose in going forward with it. Mrs. Bruns had a million-dollar policy, and we asked the company to pay it, and we would give her a release. They absolutely rejected that offer and offered zero dollars on that part of the claim.

Mr. Roney was underinsured for the total amount of damage that he caused. He had an insurance policy for $2,400,000. Also, from reviewing the notes I had taken from the motor home regarding the trust, we knew that Mr. Roney had assets in a trust which he controlled. No one in the plaintiffs' firms were trust lawyers, but all of us had taken trusts in law school and realized that if a person setting up the trust retains total control of the trust, that it is not necessarily irrevocable, and therefore, there might be a chance to get the assets from the trust.

The suit was filed in the Southern District of Florida and assigned to Judge Rosenberg, who kept offices at the Fort Pierce Courthouse and at the courthouse in Palm Beach County. Because St. Lucie was a smaller jurisdiction, she was the only federal judge in St. Lucie County, though she split her time with Palm Beach.

We had been asked by the court to prepare a pretrial plan of when we were to do everything in the case, including required mediation, time for cutoffs of discovery, and a proposed trial date. We told the court that we felt it would take two weeks to try these two cases since the court was requiring us to try them together as one. I conferred with the Searcy firm. Mr. Searcy had recently completed a trial with Judge Rosenberg, and he said that she allowed in that trial the parties to do voir dire of the jury. One of the things which I hate about federal court (and there are many) is that the judge retains the right to perform voir dire herself, though in certain rare instances, some of these judges will allow the attorneys for both sides to ask jurors questions. I consider the most important part of a trial to be the voir dire.

In addition to the California deposition, there was also discovery taken in the State of Florida as well as in the State of Michigan. I personally attended those, along with Karen Terry from the Searcy firm, as well as defense lawyers for Mrs. Bruns and the insurance company and for the Roney estate's insurance company. The Roney estate and trust had its own attorney in Detroit, Mr. Camargo.

In Michigan, we discovered that the decedent, Mr. Roney, had lost his license the year before the accident because of health and mental problems. We discovered that he had eight children, and I suspected from viewing the trust information contained in the paperwork we obtained from the motor home that it appeared Mr. Roney was playing the eight adult children against each other to get attention or respect from them. Two of the adult children, particularly, had in the past been more or less estranged from the other children, and their relationship with their father also seemed to be strained.

These two adult children went out of their way to help Mr. Roney obtain, once more, his license. Mr. Roney's daughter worked for the hospital where Mr. Roney had to go and prove he was competent mentally to drive a vehicle. Although we could not prove any collusion, it is amazing that this department at the hospital passed this individual. We took the deposition of the person who had given the test, and he had the test results which indicated that Mr. Roney could only properly identify 25 percent of the road signs in the test. We learned that the son, who was helping his father relearn to drive, would take his dad out into a huge parking lot with a family car and attempt to show him how to drive. This lasted several weeks. Eventually, there came a time for Mr. Roney's driving skills to be tested by the same official from the hospital who had passed him mentally to drive. This was a road test, and shockingly, the official allowed the son to ride along in the back seat during the test. It's important the test was only performed in a passenger automobile.

The only limitation that the hospital made on the reissuance of the license was that Mr. Roney was not to drive any motorcycles or any recreational vehicles or other vehicles except a passenger car.

The daughter of Mr. Roney had prepared an affidavit for her father's signature that was filed which also indicated that he was not going to drive any long distances, but he was only go to go across town to visit his girlfriend, Mrs. Bruns. Mr. Roney was issued a license exactly twenty-three days before he killed Santia Feketa.

The first thing that Mr. Roney did after getting his license was to go with his son to the storage facility which contained the motor home and add air to the tires. It turns out this motor home had been used by various Roney children over the years.

Another deposition disclosed that a different daughter and her family took the motor home out on a short day trip in the summer of 2017. The trip was in daylight hours. That daughter testified that on the way back from the trip, the motor home was experiencing electrical problems, including the interior lights and other problems. She was happy when they locked the motor home up at the end of their drive.

Immediately upon obtaining his license, Mr. Roney began planning a lengthy trip or vacation to Florida with his girlfriend. The son who helped him get his license volunteered to help him drive the motor home down to Florida. He and Mrs. Bruns and Mr. Roney shared driving all the way from Detroit to Melbourne Beach. The testimony was that they were planning on spending some time in Tennessee on the way down, but through emails we found, Mr. Roney and his son had notified the other remaining children that he was having electrical problems with the vehicle and that the heater was not working in the vehicle and it was getting cold. They decided to press on through the night, and they shared the driving. For a while, Mr. Roney and his girlfriend were sleeping in the bedroom in the back of the Prevost while the son, Daniel Roney, was driving.

We took Daniel Roney's deposition. He said that when they arrived in Melbourne Beach, he had spent the night with his father and Mrs. Bruns. The next morning, he did a check of the motor-home with his dad, and it was decided that Mr. Roney should have it repaired. The two of them made the list. Mr. Roney had a mechanic who had worked on this vehicle up in Michigan in the past, and that mechanic had moved to Punta Gorda, Florida. Walter Roney was not familiar with the route to Punta Gorda but had Mrs. Bruns with him to assist with the directions, using her GPS device.

The intention was that they were to leave the Melbourne Beach location in the early afternoon, but they were waiting for the son to leave. They wanted to say goodbye to him. The son was waiting to see a rocket launch from Cape Kennedy and was meeting with friends that he knew so they could watch it together. Apparently, the launch was delayed from its planned 1:00 p.m. launch until later in the afternoon. After the launch, the son took off for the Orlando Airport (being driven by his friends), and according to Mrs. Bruns's testimony, Mr. Roney took a nap, preparatory to making the trip across the state. He woke about around 5:00 p.m. and proceeded south.

We learned that Mrs. Bruns drove the motor home from Melbourne Beach to Fort Pierce, Florida, when it got too dark for her to see how to drive. She did not trust herself driving at night. She handed the keys over to Mr. Roney, and approximately seven miles later down the highway, tragedy struck. Five miles from the crash scene, there was a surveillance camera on an FP&L roadside facility that showed the Prevost driving by with headlights on. Less than a half mile from the scene of the crash, a witness had seen the Prevost stopped on the side of the road with no lights visible.

As required by the court, we met for a mediation a couple of weeks before the time the trial was set to go forward. Stewart Feketa and his wife, Marcie, were there. Santia's mother, Stacy West, was there, along with Sierra Feketa, the other daughter. In addition, the personal representative of Mr. Roney's estate, Mr. Zacharzewski, was present in Florida, while one of the Roney children was present by Zoom, as was Mrs. Bruns present by Zoom.

During the presentation, unfortunately, the Searcy firm showed some of the pictures from the scene which Stacy and Sierra had not seen, particularly the picture taken by the Highway Patrol which showed Santia partially out of the vehicle and lying dead on the pavement. This was taken before the bodies were covered with tarps. Stacy and Sierra both practically collapsed and were extremely upset. Thankfully, those pictures were removed very quickly from the PowerPoint, and we proceeded with mediation.

Until that date, the offer from Mrs. Bruns's insurance company had been zero. One of our goals at the mediation was to convince Mrs. Bruns that we were likely to get an excess verdict against her individually greater than the amount of her insurance coverage, which was $1 million. We hoped to show much of the evidence we were going to show at trial and spell out specifically why we thought Mrs. Bruns was responsible. The mediation did not settle the case.

Seven days after the mediation, Bruns's insurance company sent a check to my office for half a million dollars and one check to Mr. Searcy's office for the other half million dollars to settle with our clients. We were quite happy to do that. Even though Mrs. Bruns had substantial assets to respond in damages, there was rumblings out of the Eleventh Circuit Court of Appeals in Atlanta, which had turned very conservative with all its Trump appointees. We felt that it was doubtful that the claim against the co-driver/navigator would necessarily stand up on appeal. We were, therefore, happy to accept their limits and allow her out of the case.

We also made some offers to the defense in excess of their coverage limits. Some of those involved raiding a part of the trust, which we indicated was not irrevocable.

Shortly after the mediation, Judge Rosenberg called us to her office as a final pretrial meeting. Her office was in West Palm Beach. The meeting served several purposes. First of all, the judge indicated that we were not going to have two weeks to try this case. She expected the case to be tried in "three to four days." She said we were going to start every day earlier than usual during the trial. There would be very few breaks in each day during the trial.

She also indicated that we had a new federal courthouse in Fort Pierce which would ordinarily be the location for the trial. She said she also had her very nice courtroom across the hall from her offices in West Palm Beach, and she volunteered to have us look in and see what the accommodations that were there, which were very nice. She said that she would be happy to try the case for her convenience in West Palm but would also be happy to go to Fort Pierce to try the case, if all the parties did not agree to the West Palm Beach location.

Judge Rosenberg also said she would handle voir dire. She was only going to ask fifteen questions, and she gave the printed questions to us. She did, however, say that she was going to allow the defense to fashion four questions of their own, and she would review those to determine if they were proper. She also said the plaintiffs can (combined) submit four questions which she would likewise consider before giving them to the jury.

After this hearing was over, I proceeded to the Searcy Law Firm, which was there in West Palm Beach, and met with Chris Searcy, Karen Terry, and two other attorneys from their office. Chris immediately spoke up and said that there was a tremendous advantage to us having the trial in West Palm Beach. In addition to it being convenient for his office, it was also convenient to defense counsel, who were from Fort Lauderdale, which is a close neighbor to West Palm to the south. He said the biggest advantage of the West Palm location was that the entire jury panel would be drawn from Palm Beach County, which was a fairly liberal stronghold in Florida and was notorious for having good plaintiffs' jurors. On the other hand, were the case decided at trial in Fort Pierce, the jury panel would be drawn from all the counties in the district north of Palm Beach County. Those included some extremely conservative places, such as Martin County (Stuart), Indian River County (Vero Beach), Okeechobee County (Okeechobee City), and Highlands County (Sebring), as well as the slightly less conservative St. Lucie County (Fort Pierce). The panel we would get there would, of necessity, be much tighter with money and more difficult to deal with than a jury we could pick in Palm Beach County. Chris Searcy had indicated that he was immediately intending to indicate his preference for West Palm Beach as the trial location. The defense had not yet spoken, and I had not spoken on behalf of the Feketa family. Chris asked that I contact defense counsel and indicate that my clients were somewhat hesitant to change to West Palm Beach as we had many witnesses who were from St. Lucie County. He said, "But don't tell the court what your decision is at that point." Mr. Searcy was pretty sure that defense counsel would, for their convenience, agree to having the trial in West Palm. In fact, they made that decision and filed their notice with the court agreeing to West Palm Beach. After consulting with my client, we also agreed to West Palm Beach.

I scheduled a time for me to come down to West Pam Beach for me to help cobble together four questions for the plaintiffs' portion of the voir dire.

I drove down a couple of days later, and we spent the greater part of the day working on those questions. Karen Terry and Jack Hill and other attorneys from the Searcy firm were helping with that project. Jack is also an accomplished trial lawyer. We submitted our questions to the court, as did the defense, and both sides received copies of the other's proposed questions.

We made sure that all the expected witnesses were subpoenaed to appear in federal court in West Palm Beach and were preparing for the rapidly approaching trial.

The trial, in this case, was to start on Monday morning. Even though at normal hours, I could make the drive from my home in Port St. Lucie down to the West Palm Courthouse in about an hour, I gave myself a couple of hours to get down there because of rush hour traffic and because I wanted to meet my clients early before the trial at the courthouse.

The trial started promptly at eight thirty in the morning. There were thirty potential jurors in the courtroom. Judge Rosenberg started the trial by doing her voir dire. She asked her fifteen questions. Then she asked the four questions that the defense submitted, and she said, "Have I forgotten something?"

I raised my hand and stood up and said, "Yes, Your Honor. You didn't ask any of our questions, and they were not similar to any questions that have already been asked." We asked that we at least be allowed to go through those questions with the jury.

The judge shrugged her shoulders, looked sad, and said, "Well, I'm going to give the plaintiffs a total of ten minutes between the two of them to voir dire the panel."

As I indicated, there were thirty jurors, and that was an extremely short period to do an adequate voir dire. That would be particularly if I had to split my time with the other plaintiff's firm.

Jack Hill, from the Searcy firm, was there and had a lot of expertise in voir dire. I said, "Jack, you handle it, and I'll take notes." I couldn't clear my throat in ten minutes.

Jack asked four questions (which were mostly on the subject of tort reform), and during his brief voir dire, he was able to uncover three jurors who would have been on the first row of the jury who were poison for us. The judge agreed to remove them for cause, which saved us some peremptory challenges. We were happy with our final eight jurors. Judge Rosenberg explained that the first six jurors and the two alternates would participate in the deliberation. I had never seen that done before. Usually, all alternate jurors are excused at the end of testimony and not allowed in the jury room during deliberations.

The way the trial was set up, the first person who could speak in opening statement was Karen Terry, who was acting as lead counsel at trial for the Searcy firm. Once she had completed her presentation, I gave my opening statement next. In opening statements, you really should not dwell on emotions. I felt the facts of the case were message enough and basically recited a major portion of what the evidence was going to show.

After I spoke, the defense attorneys stood up and gave their presentation, which was fairly brief. We then proceeded to call witnesses to the stand. Once the trial started, plaintiffs' counsel would ask questions first, and then the defense would do cross-examination. We were alternating which plaintiffs should go next. I called my first witness for our side, and it was Stewart Feketa. Stewart is an excellent speaker, and in fact, in the past, he has been a pastor of a church. He spoke of his checkered past and the difficult time around his divorce.

It sounded like the salvation in his life for Stewart was when his nine-year-old daughter, Santia, decided to come live with him and Santia's mother agreed. Stewart described the relationship that Santia had with himself, his new wife, and his son.

He also talked about just who Santia was. He went into great detail regarding her work with the horses and the fact that she was the face of the St. Lucie County Special Olympics Equestrian Program. She took time to teach Down syndrome children and guide them through their paces. She had also done some work with autistic children. He explained that she was studying to be a special needs teacher and that she was a junior at Indian River State College and was in pursuit of that degree. He talked about her relationship with her best friend, who had lived a few miles away from them. That friend was with her the night they both died. Stewart explained that he had given the truck to his daughter to drive because it was about the safest vehicle on the road for its size. His presentation was powerful, but there was no crying or sobs that might be construed by the jury as being contrived.

As I indicated, after I finished with the witness and the defense completed cross-examination, Karen Terry would call their next witness.

The most important witness who I believe I called in the trial was Sergeant Stuhr. The defense had not taken the deposition of Sergeant Stuhr. Instead, they took the deposition of the rookie who had signed the traffic homicide report. Sergeant Stuhr repeated what he told me about his experiences. and this particular case had upset him so much. He indicated that every first responder who was there, he believes, had gone through some counseling to try to get over the shock. He testified that the headlights on the Prevost motor home were absolutely out at the time of the crash. He showed the picture taken by the Highway Patrol of one of those lights on the pavement, which had survived the crash without being broken. In the crash, it had been disengaged from the Prevost motor home. He explained what the shock test was and said it proved conclusively that the lights were not working at the time of the crash.

Mr. Roney's son, Daniel Roney, had indicated in his testimony by deposition that the headlights were, in fact, working when he examined them, although he said they were "frosty" on the inside, which tended to make them burn less brightly. Of course, he was not there at the accident scene. We were able to show that many of the statements he made regarding the trip down from Michigan were refuted by emails which he and Ms. Bruns were sending back to the other seven children who were up in Michigan.

I put Stacy West on the stand and thought she did a pretty good job. She was obviously tremendously shaken by the loss of her daughter. Although she did not audibly cry, there were tears in her eyes as she was telling the story of her life with Santia. She showed pictures of an event that she and Santia participated in every year for several years. It was called Night to Shine, which was a charity founded by the former University of Florida quarterback and Heisman trophy winner, Tim Tebow. The purpose of this charity was to provide a promlike event for young disabled adults, particularly those who had Down syndrome. Every year, Stacy and Santia would dress in their finest ball outfits and get their hair specially set. They would help outfit their assigned client for the evening, and they would accompany her to the ball. The pictures were impressive. Santia and Stacy were smiling together.

Stacy talked extensively about her continuing relationship with Santia. She said that she and Mr. Feketa still got along well and had shared parental responsibility for Santia from the time the divorce occurred. She said that her daughter was so enamored with being a horsewoman that Stacy would not stand in her way of living on the farm. Stacy knew Stewart had changed his lifestyle. She made sure that Santia would be a regular visitor at her house, including dinner on some weeknights and often on weekends. She talked about the relationship that Santia had with her sister, Sierra.

As I indicated, Karen Terry and I were alternating putting on evidence. We got to the part of the trial where each of us had discussed putting on our before and after witnesses. The plan was to have Karen put on all her listed three such witnesses who could testify to the life of her client. I was then going to put on our three individuals who I had subpoenaed to be there on our behalf. I had previously discussed this matter with St. Lucie County Sheriff Ken Mascara, who was a close friend of the family and had known Santia a long time, and he had volunteered to be one of those witnesses.

When Karen Terry put on her first before and after witness, it was the aunt of Britney. At the time of Britney's death, Britney's mom, Yvonne, was visiting her sister in the state of New Hampshire. Yvonne learned of the death of her daughter through a call from her husband, and the aunt really brought home to the jury what happened to Yvonne after she got that news. She and her husband helped Yvonne get back to Florida and were with her at the funeral. The aunt explained what a wonderful child Britney was. I cannot describe how powerful the aunt's testimony was, and the jury was sitting on the edge of their seats. The defense had very few questions to ask.

As soon as she had finished with her witness, Karen came over to my counsel table and said, "Roger, I'm going to really upset you. This witness was so good for us, I'm going to rest. I know that you don't necessarily have all your witnesses lined up to be here, but you need to move on this."

Well, I did have the first witness I wanted to speak to because I thought her testimony would be good. I had counseled Sierra Feketa about her testimony. I called Sierra to the stand and, to use a baseball term, "she knocked it out of the park." Her testimony was gripping and personal, and the jury seemed to really understand what the case was about from listening to her. I decided then and there that I did not need Sheriff Mascara or the other witness to testify regarding their knowledge of the family's life. I wanted to end on a high note. I rested.

Closing argument was a bit of an adventure. Ms. Terry got up and very factually went through the liability in the case. She had photographs, including photographs I had shielded my clients from, that she showed the jury. This was particularly upsetting to Stacy. I felt that Karen's presentation, while it was excellent, did not have enough passion. I decided to throw away the remarks I had previously prepared and make mine a somewhat more emotional rehash of the evidence. I had no problem in explaining Santia's fine relationship with her father. I had some anecdotes that had been testified to in trial to bring those home. I felt I did not need to go into the liability of the case since Karen had handled it so well.

My one concern as I was writing my original argument, and also as I stood up to talk, was how I could tell the jury properly what Stacy's relationship was with Santia. Early in my closing argument, it came to me. I got the photographs from the Night to Shine from the year before, showing the mother and daughter together on the Night to Shine with their outfits and hairdos and Down syndrome consorts at the event. I put the photos on an Elmo device which projected them on a screen for the jury to see. Everyone in the pictures seemed to be having a good time. I explained to the jury that the testimony in this case showed that the last day and evening that Stacy spent with her daughter was the Thursday night before the crash. She explained that they went over their outfits and plans, bouquets, etc. for the event and basically did all their final preparation for the Night to Shine. Stacy was planning to attend the event, which had been scheduled for Friday of the next week. I told the jury at the end of my closing that Stacy had a special relationship with her daughter, and I went through the testimony once more about their last day and night together. I said to the jury that Stacy was extremely excited about the Night to Shine events to help these disabled adults. However, I told them that Stacy could not go to the event which occurred on Friday of that week since she had to attend the funeral. I saw some tears in the eyes of most of the jurors, and I decided to shut up and sit down. As I turned and looked at the judge, I saw a tear running down her face as well, and I was shocked. I asked for $10 million dollars in my closing argument for the family. This was a similar amount that Karen had requested for Britney's family.

The defense, in their closing argument, stood up and told the jury that that was a very large amount of money and that $1 million for each of these girls' families would be appropriate.

The jury received final instructions from the judge and retired to the jury room. Immediately thereafter, Judge Rosenberg addressed everyone present in the courtroom and said that she also was a mother and understood what these two families had gone through. She said her heart goes out to them.

As the jury went out, I said a silent prayer that I had done well enough to receive as big a verdict as the Searcy firm received. When the jury came back a couple of hours later, we were extremely pleased. Mr. Searcy's clients received a verdict in an amount of slightly more than $5 million. My verdict was a little bit more than that, and I was over the moon. My verdict was not substantially more than Karen's, however.

The combined verdict, plus the settlement from Mrs., Bruns was over $11 million.

My son, Steven, had finally made it to the courthouse in time for the closing arguments. He had been out all week with a family emergency, or he would have been at counsel table with me.

He came into the well of the court and shook my hand and said, "Dad, that was the best argument I ever saw you do. Just when did you make the decision to put that part in about Stacy missing the Night to Shine to attend her daughter's funeral?" I told him about three minutes before I made the statement. He said, "It was wonderful!"

While the jury was out, my clients, Stewart and Stacy, both asked me not to give a statement to the press, which was present in the courtroom during closing arguments. They said they wanted to have closure.

After the verdict was read, hugs were had all around at our table. Defense counsel said what a tremendous job Karen and I both did, and we congratulated them on a very fairly fought trial. The trial ended late in the day on the third day of the trial, which was an amazing rocket docket performance of two major death cases. The verdicts that we received exceeded the underlying insurance coverage.

Karen and her group exited out to the lobby of the court. When Stewart, Stacy, and I came through the door, we noticed that Karen and the Searcy group were giving a press conference about the big victory. A reporter shoved a mic in my face and asked me, "Did the Feketas have any comments?"

I told him our family was not commenting on anything. That we were headed out the door and I appreciated their privacy. I certainly didn't care whether I had my face on the evening news or not, and my client felt the same way.

We know that the Searcy Firm forwarded pictures of the crash to the *Palm Beach Post*. That evening on their electronic news, the *Post* showed the very offensive picture of my client's daughter lying on the ground outside the crashed truck. My clients were appalled and called the *Palm Beach Post* and discovered that lots of other people called asking them to take those photos down, which the paper did. Thankfully, those photographs did not appear in the next morning's *Palm Beach Post*, although a story about the case did.

Chapter 68

A month or so after the trial ended, a final judgment had been entered for each of the cases. The insurance company sent us a check for half of the coverage, plus costs, and sent Ms. Terry's office the other half. I talked to Mr. Searcy and Karen Terry about pursuing the Roney estate for the balance. The Roney children had insisted that the Roney trust had become irrevocable at the time of Walter Roney's passing. We were pretty sure that was not the case, but we had to go to Michigan to prove it. We hired as Michigan counsel an excellent lawyer named Virginia Cardwell, from Ann Arbor, Michigan. Both Chris Searcy's office and I had spoken with this nice lady and retained her to help us. Her specialty was trusts. We didn't know how much money was in the trust, but my clients' goal was that the money should not go to the adult Roney children. Stacy and Stewart both indicated that a large part of this money would go to a scholarship fund in the name of their daughter to assist needy students who were studying to be special needs teachers.

The Roney children hired a couple of Michigan lawyers to represent them. These lawyers would not be present at the final hearing as they had been, apparently, discharged. I was happy about that.

Before being discharged, these lawyers were nasty to deal with during the depositions in Michigan.

We sued the estate and sued the trust. The trustee was also the personal representative of the estate, and it was Mr. Zacharzewski (I will refer to him as Mr. Z from now on). Mr. Z was at the trial as an observer and was also present for the mediation and understood the facts of the case. We got a copy of the trust, which was interesting. The second paragraph of the trust made a statement that "I direct that all my just debts be paid before any distribution is made." Notwithstanding that provision, the children were insistent that we were stealing from their father's trust and that they were entitled to the money. Unfortunately, the case was assigned to a judge from a neighboring small-town suburb from Detroit. This was because Mr. Z lived in that county. That county was very White, conservative, and Republican. Wayne County (Detroit) was the opposite.

I made an interesting trip up to Michigan for the scheduled final hearing in the Oakland Hills area of Michigan. Stewart Feketa indicated he wanted to go, and he wanted me to accompany him. We flew up to Detroit and stayed in the same hotel I had stayed in when I was up there for discovery in the underlying case. We had contacted the judge's office and indicated we were going to attend as interested parties. Our attorney from Michigan was also going to be there and confirmed that with the court. The morning of the scheduled hearing, as we were about the leave the hotel, Stewart Feketa, on his cell phone, received a message from the court indicating that the case was being postponed and that it would be scheduled "at a later date." We called the airline and adjusted our tickets so we could go home later that day and flew back to Florida. I believe it was on a Thursday night.

On Friday, we were notified by the judge's office that she decided to have the hearing on Monday morning. So Stewart and I got back on the airplane and flew back to Detroit. We drove up the hearing site, which was less than an hour from our hotel. We entered the courtroom with our Ann Arbor attorney and sat on the petitioner's side. Mr. Z was represented by counsel from Michigan, Nicholas Camargo, and all eight of the Roney children were present, but none of them sat in a group larger than two. They appeared to be staring daggers at each other across the courtroom. They no longer had representation.

Stewart had done research regarding this judge and believed that she was ethically challenged. Several of the Roney children lived in her jurisdiction, and Stewart was concerned that undue influence might be placed upon her to rule in their favor. We had a court reporter present.

The hearing was supposed to start at 9:00 a.m. At 9:05 a.m., the court's clerk came in and took a roll call of everyone there saying that the judge wanted to know who was present before the hearing started. He said that the hearing would start shortly. He went back to the judge's chambers and seemed to be back there forever. It was actually fifteen or twenty minutes later that the judge came on the bench. She said that it was her belief that the proper venue of this case was in Detroit, and she signed off on the case. She would not enter a final order. We had initially tried to file the case in Detroit but were told the proper venue was the neighboring county. We were nonplused that the hearing hadn't concluded the issue but fairly happy that it was not in this judge's hands.

As we were walking out of the courthouse, we approached a corner of the hall where Mr. Roney's son, Daniel Roney, was standing and looked to be fuming. Britney's mother, who was also present, said to Stewart Feketa, "Who is that guy?"

Stewart said, "He's Roney's child who helped kill our daughters."

Mr. Roney heard this statement and balled up his fist and started to come at Stewart. I took Stewart by both shoulders and held him back. Stewart is a large person who is in good physical condition and would have probably pummeled that guy. Fortunately, a court bailiff stepped between them, and cooler heads prevailed. I told Stewart on the way back from Detroit that I had saved him a trip to jail, and he thanked me. We flew back to Florida.

The case was reassigned to Wayne County, which is the home of Detroit. Our counsel in Michigan, Virginia Cardwell, told us that the judge it was assigned to was excellent for us and that she had had a good relationship with him. We had reached an agreement with

Mr. Z's attorney, Camargo, on behalf of the trustee, to settle the case with 90 percent of the funds in the trust being paid to the two plaintiff families and the remaining percentage being used for trust administration expenses. The new judge was to determine whether such a settlement was proper. At the hearing, Mr. Roney's eldest son spoke against the agreement on behalf of the beneficiaries of the trust. Stewart went up to a hearing before that judge, but I could not go. He told me that the judge looked "just like Barrack Obama." He also said that he seemed friendly and nice and intelligent. The judge indicated that he was going to take the case under advisement and enter his opinion on this case in a week or two.

Please understand that this first hearing that Stewart went to took place in early March of 2020. COVID came knocking before the judge entered his order, and all the courts in Michigan were shut down by the governor.

When the suspension order was finally rescinded approximately a year later, after vaccines became available, the judge rescheduled the entire hearing apparently to refresh his memory as to just what the agreement he was supposed to rule on was. Here again, Stewart went to that hearing along with Attorney Virginia Cardwell, and the judge, while sitting there, ruled in our favor and approved our settlement. The Roney children still opposed the agreement and were at the hearing but were no longer represented by attorneys. Apparently, all their attorneys quit after the Roney children refused to listen to them. We did not get our entire verdict collected, but we got basically all the assets remaining in the trust together with the insurance policy. There were several million dollars in the trust. Our clients were happy that there were no funds to distribute to the bad children of Mr. Roney.

Epilogue

The Feketa trial occurred in 2019. In a typical year, while I would handle many cases, only about three would be reached for trial each year. Unfortunately, because of COVID-19, the courthouses here in St. Lucie County and throughout the State of Florida were, essentially, closed for trial purposes for about two years. Thankfully, things are returning to normal, and I am set to start a major trial in a couple of months here in 2022. I have several other trials coming quickly on the horizon.

In the couple of years after the Feketa trial, I received referrals from people that Stewart knew who were injured in accidents. In addition, Stewart's wife was involved in a rear-end collision and received injuries, and that case was referred to me. Thankfully, it was settled amicably fairly early in the process. Stewart himself had a severe auto crash with injuries requiring surgery on his back and his hip. Initially, there was a diagnosis of a fractured leg, but that appeared to be a mistake by the hospital, as when the orthopedic surgeon x-rayed it himself, the fracture was not there. We were thankful we settled Stewart's injury case nicely. That litigation was just wound up as of the writing of this story. I was requested by Stewart Feketa to include the facts and names in the story. I decided to dedicate this book, in part, to Santia Feketa and Britney Poindexter.

About the Author

Roger N. Messer is a civil trial attorney living in Port St. Lucie, Florida. He graduated from Florida State University with a degree in government. Thereafter, he worked as a legislative research assistant in the offices of the Secretary of the Air Force in the Pentagon from 1972 until 1974. Roger attended law school at Stetson University College of Law in St. Petersburg, Florida. He has had over forty-five years of experience, particularly in the area of tort law in the State of Florida, and is a veteran of over one hundred jury trials in both state and federal courts. In 2019, the National Trial Lawyers named Roger one of the top 100 plaintiff civil attorneys in the United States.

www.ingramcontent.com/pod-product-compliance
Lightning Source LLC
LaVergne TN
LVHW090106250926
848814LV00049B/53/J
* 9 7 9 8 8 8 9 6 0 2 7 9 8 *